All Things Considered

Advanced Reader of Modern Chinese

周质平
Chih-p'ing Chou

夏岩
Yan Xia

吴妙慧
Meow Hui Goh

D1344683

All Things Considered

Advanced Reader of Modern Chinese

事事关心

现代汉语高级读本

周质平
Chih-p'ing Chou

夏岩
Yan Xia

吴妙慧
Meow Hui Goh

Princeton University Press
Princeton and Oxford

Copyright © 2001 by Princeton University Press
Published by Princeton University Press, 41 William Street,
Princeton, New Jersey 08540
In the United Kingdom: Princeton University Press,
3 Market Place, Woodstock, Oxfordshire OX20 1SY

Library of Congress Catalog Card Number 2001089189

ISBN 0-691-09048-3 (pbk.)

The publisher would like to acknowledge the authors of this volume for
providing the camera-ready copy from which this book was printed

Printed on acid-free paper. ∞

www.pup.princeton.edu

Printed in the United States of America

5   7   9   10   8   6
ISBN-13: 978-0-691-09048-1 (pbk.)
ISBN-10: 0-691-09048-3 (pbk.)

目录

Table of Contents

（一） 会话篇

（二）　读报篇

序

过去十年来，普林斯顿大学对外汉语教研室的同仁共同编写了一系列的教科书。这些教科书除了供普大及普林斯顿北京汉语培训班使用外，美、加及其他地区也有不少学校用作教材。从多年教学实践中，我们感到：从中级教材到高级教材之间，跨越的幅度过大，在衔接上有一定的困难。这一衔接的"断层"现象也不独普大教材为然，坊间一般的教材在不同的程度上都有这个问题。

初级和中级的教材是特别为学习汉语的学生所写的。在词汇和句型的安排上都做了一定的控制。但三年级以上的材料则是选自现当代作家的作品，在文体上包括：报刊、散文、小说，和短剧等。在时间上则横跨自五四以来的八十年。

美国对外汉语教学界所说的"高级汉语"，其实，是很不"高级"的，是指学过两年以上现代汉语的学生而言。一般来说，在汉字的掌握上，一年级的学生约在五、六百字之间，二年级的学生约在一千二百字左右。但实际的使用能力则远低于此数。如用近年来为许多学校所采用的"口语能力测定标准"，学过两年汉语的学生至多能达到"一级上"到"中级下"之间，也就是勉强能用汉语作些日常生活的会话，谈谈身边琐事，有点购物和问路的能力，如此而已。换句话说，使用"高级"教材的学生其语言能力是很有限的，是连"文字初通"都谈不上的。

但是现有的坊间高级对外汉语教材却不少是选自鲁迅、胡适、巴金、矛盾等现代作家的作品。试问一个仅仅学了两年（实际上是两学年，约60个星期，每星期约四、五小时）汉语的美国学生，如何有能力看鲁迅这样风格特殊的白话文。这些二十年代作家所写的白话文虽是现代汉语的典范作品，但这种书面语和口语的距离是很大的。要在这些作品之中选出一篇真能"上口"的文字真是少之又少。被许多学校选为高级读本的鲁迅小说选，对美国学生来说，哪里是"现代汉语"。在他们日常生活中既听不到，也看不到类似这样的句子：

　　"但心又不竟堕下去而至于断绝，他只是很重很重地堕着、堕着。"（鲁迅《野草·风筝》）

这样的句子，对一个对外汉语教师而言，既不是"现代汉语"，也不是"古代汉语"，它简直就是病句！

　　鲁迅是现代中国文学的宗师巨匠，他可以写这样的"病句"，但我们却不能用这样的"病句"作为"样板"来教外国学生。

　　我看了不少学校用鲁迅的小说来教学了两年汉语的美国学生。可怜！那些学生何尝"读"过鲁迅的小说，他们只是在死记每个故事的"生字表"，透过死记硬背，将故事的情节寻出一个大概来。因为故事的深刻和动人，学生也都一致叫好。但若细细分析他们到底学到了多少现代汉语那真是少得可怜了。

　　我们有鉴于现行高级汉语读本在语言难度上远远超过学生的能力，在经过几次讨论以后，决定另编一本在现有中级和高级读本之间的读物。在内容上仍以讨论与日常生活有关的问题为主，第一部分是对话。有些话题在一本教科书上出现也许有人会觉得不甚得体。但我们觉得只要是日常生活中使用的语言，都不妨教给学生。至於雅俗或格调之高下则见仁见智，不必勉强求同。我们平心静气的想想，在日常生活之中的话题是否都是得体而又高雅的。一定程度的"不得体"正是真实和生动之所自来。我们力求对话生动有趣并富争议性，以便在上课时进行讨论。

除了编写的会话以外，我们从最近两年国内的报纸上选了20篇新闻报导或短评，从日常生活到国家大事，无所不谈，反映了一个在快速变动中的中国社会。有些对话的题材是从新闻中脱胎而来，所用的词汇大同小异，可以收复习强化的功效。

本书课文是由周质平编写的。对报刊原文作了必要的增删，以便教学。对话部分的生词和词语例句是吴妙慧编的。读报部分和全部的练习是夏岩编的。

《事事关心》初稿成於2000年春季。我们在普林斯顿大学暑期北京汉语培训班和普大东亚系试用了一年，极受学生欢迎，有些学校也已将此书作为教材。

本书每课课文采繁简并列方式，课文之后有生词解释和词语例句，并备有配合课文和生词的录音带。

在编写的最后阶段，普大的杨玖老师和王晶玉老师校看书稿，为我们提供了许多宝贵的意见。Mr. David Carini 为我们作了一部分例句的翻译，并校看了生词的英语注释。我们在此向他们深致谢忱。当然，书中如有任何错误，都应该由我们负责。

周质平
夏岩
吴妙慧
2001年2月15日

Preface

All Things Considered is a modern Chinese language textbook designed to bridge the gap between intermediate and advanced Chinese. It is targeted at students who have completed intermediate courses but are not yet prepared for the complexity of advanced Chinese.

The textbook consists of two parts. Part One contains twelve dialogues; Part Two is a selection of Chinese newspaper articles from 1999-2000. The articles offer an introduction to contemporary Chinese society.

A new feature in *All Things Considered* is that several topics appear in both dialogue and essay forms. By covering the same topic twice, students will be able to not only learn the vocabulary and grammatical structures better, but also to see clearly the difference between speaking and writing in Chinese. And by keeping a portion of the textbook in dialogue form we emphasize speaking and reading equally; many advanced books, by contrast, assume that students already speak Chinese well enough and therefore ignore the spoken part of the language altogether. The overall proficiency level required for this textbook is lower than that for the previous advanced textbooks published by the Princeton University Press. We believe such a textbook is badly needed in the field.

The articles that we have selected are all related to contemporary issues in China, and their focus is on everyday life rather than the weighty political and social essays often seen in other advanced textbooks. Some of the topics are controversial; we believe this will evoke students' interest and increase their participation in class discussions. Following the tradition of our earlier textbooks, the text is arranged in both simplified and traditional characters, and vocabulary and sentence patterns accompany the text. Each lesson also contains a series of exercises that teachers will find useful for in-class work or homework assignments.

The draft of *All Things Considered* was written in the spring of 2000 and field-tested over the following year in Princeton Chinese language classes and the Princeton in Beijing summer program. Students consistently gave it high marks in their end-of-year evaluations.

We would like to express our sincere gratitude to Ms. Joanne Chiang and Ms. Jingyu Wang, who have taken pains to proofread the manuscript and have made valuable suggestions for the final version. We are deeply indebted to Mr. David Carini, who has not only translated part of the glossary and sentence patterns into English but also edited all of the English in the book. However, any errors are strictly the responsibility of the authors.

Chih-p'ing Chou
Yan Xia
Meow Hui Goh
February 15, 2001

List of Abbreviations

本书词汇及词语例句部分使用代号如下：

adj. = adjective

adv. = adverb

conj. = conjunction

intj. = interjection

MW = measure word

n. = noun

num. = number

part. = particle

ph = phrase

prep. = preposition

pron. = pronoun

TW = time word

suf. = suffix

v. = verb

v-o. = verb-object

Part One:

Dialogues

（一）会话篇

第一課

剛到中國

甲：你是哪一天到北京的啊？

乙：我是三天以前到的。

甲：你是從紐約直飛北京的嗎？

乙：不是。據我所知，從紐約沒有直飛北京的飛機。我是從紐約直飛東京，在東京轉機再飛北京的。

甲：一路上都很順利吧？

乙：很順利，就是在東京轉機等了三個小時。東京的機場很小，人又多，這三個小時比從紐約到東京還累！

甲：你以前來過中國沒有？

乙：小時候跟父母來過一次。

甲：那是什麼時候的事啊？

乙：那是我上小學的時候，父親到上海去談生意，我跟著他和母親來了一趟中國。都快十年前的事了。

甲：十年前的事還有印象嗎？

乙：雖然快十年了，但是對許多事都還印象深刻呢！

甲：你最難忘的是什麼事啊？

第一课

刚到中国

甲：你是哪一天到北京的啊？

乙：我是三天以前到的。

甲：你是从纽约直飞北京的吗？

乙：不是。据我所知，从纽约没有直飞北京的飞机。我是从纽约直飞东京，在东京转机再飞北京的。

甲：一路上都很顺利吧？

乙：很顺利，就是在东京转机等了三个小时。东京的机场很小，人又多，这三个小时比从纽约到东京还累！

甲：你以前来过中国没有？

乙：小时候跟父母来过一次。

甲：那是什么时候的事啊？

乙：那是我上小学的时候，父亲到上海去谈生意，我跟着他和母亲来了一趟中国。都快十年前的事了。

甲：十年前的事还有印象吗？

乙：虽然快十年了，但是对许多事都还印象深刻呢。

甲：你最难忘的是什么事啊？

乙：我最難忘的是去參觀長城和故宮。

甲：在美國沒見過這麼古老的建築吧？

乙：我對這兩個地方印象特別深倒不是因爲建築古老，而是因爲我不懂爲什麼中國人兩千年來要把自己圍在城牆裏頭。而且一個皇帝竟然住那麼大的房子。在中國當皇帝太舒服了！

甲：那是古代的中國，現代的中國可不一樣了。

乙：噢，是嗎！？

甲：這次你到中國來計劃做些什麼事啊？

乙：我想學習中文，也想體驗一下中國人的生活。上次來中國跟著父母住在大旅館裏，完全沒有機會跟中國人打交道。這種觀光客式的參觀旅游，對一個地方的了解都是很膚淺的。這次來，我想用中文多和中國人談談。吃他們吃的飯，坐他們坐的車，我要把自己的生活盡量"中國化"。

甲：許多美國人都跟我說過同樣的話。他們總把體驗中國人的生活，想成和初中學生"野外求生"差不多，又刺激又好玩。其實你只要在攝氏三十六度的天氣裏乙：我最难忘的是去参观长城和故宫。

甲：在美国没见过这么古老的建筑吧？

乙：我对这两个地方印象特别深倒不是因为建筑古老，而是因为我不懂为什么中国人两千年来要把自己围在城墙里头。而且一个皇帝竟然住那么大的房子。在中国当皇帝太舒服了！

甲：那是古代的中国，现代的中国可不一样了。

乙：噢，是吗！？

甲：这次你到中国来计划做些什么事啊？

乙：我想学习中文，也想体验一下中国人的生活。上次来中国跟着父母住在大旅馆里，完全没有机会跟中国人打交道。这种观光客式的参观旅游，对一个地方的了解都是很肤浅的。这次来，我想用中文多和中国人谈谈。吃他们吃的饭，坐他们坐的车，我要把自己的生活尽量"中国化"。

甲：许多美国人都跟我说过同样的话。他们总把体验中国人的生活，想成和初中学生"野外求生"差不多，又刺激又好玩。其实你只要在摄氏三十六度的天气里過一天沒有空調的生活，你就不想體驗中國人的生活了。

乙：你也未免把我說得太禁不起考驗了。下個周末我就打算坐硬臥去西安呢。

过一天没有空调的生活，你就不想体验中国人的生活了。

乙：你也未免把我说得太禁不起考验了。下个周末我就打算坐硬卧去西安呢。

词汇

刚	剛	gāng	adv. just
北京		Běijīng	Beijing (capital of China)
纽约	紐約	Niǔyuē	New York
直	直	zhí	adj. straight, direct
飞	飛	fēi	v. to fly; (here) to take an airplane 直飞：to fly directly to
东京	東京	Dōngjīng	Tokyo, Japan
转机	轉機	zhuǎnjī	to change flight
再		zài	adv. again
一路上		yílù.shàng	on one's way (to a place)
顺利	順利	shùnlì	adj. smooth, successful, without a hitch
等		děng	v. to wait
机场	機場	jīchǎng	n. airport
还	還	hái	(here = 更) adv. even more
累		lèi	adj. tired; tiring
小时候	小時候	xiǎoshí.hòu	when one was young
上海		Shànghǎi	Shanghai, China
谈	談	tán	v. to talk about
生意		shēng.yì	n. business
跟		gēn	v. to follow
趟		tàng	MW for trips

印象		yìnxiàng	n. impression
深刻		shēnkè	adj. deep
难忘	難忘	nánwàng	adj. memorable (lit. "difficult to forget")
参观	參觀	cān'guān	v. to visit (a place, such as a tourist spot)
长城	長城	Chángchéng	The Great Wall
故宫		Gùgōng	The Forbidden City
古老		gǔlǎo	adj. ancient, old
建筑	建築	jiànzhù	n. building, structure, edifice; architecture
懂		dǒng	v. to understand
千		qiān	num. thousand
围	圍	wéi	v. to surround, to enclose
墙	牆	qiáng	n. wall 城墙：city wall
皇帝		huángdì	n. emperor
竟然		jìngrán	adv. unexpectedly, to one's surprise
住		zhù	v. to live in, to reside
房子		fáng.zǐ	n. house
舒服		shū.fū	adj. comfortable
古代		gǔdài	adj. ancient
现代	現代	xiàndài	adj. modern
一样	一樣	yíyàng	adj. the same, alike
噢		ó	intj. of surprise

次		cì	MW for number of times of occurrence 这次：this time
计划	計劃	jìhuà	v. to plan to
学习	學習	xuéxí	v. to learn
体验	體驗	tǐyàn	v. to personally experience (usu. a kind of life)
生活		shēnghuó	n. life, livelihood
父母		fùmǔ	n. parents 父(=父亲)：father 母(=母亲)：mother
旅馆	旅館	lǚguǎn	n. hotel
完全		wánquán	adv. completely
机会	機會	jīhuì	n. chance, opportunity
打交道		dǎ jiāo.dào	v-o. to make contact with
观光客	觀光客	guān'guāngkè	n. tourist
式		shì	n. type, style
旅游		lǚyóu	n. tour
了解		liǎojiě	v. to understand, to comprehend; (here, used as a noun) understanding
肤浅	膚淺	fūqiǎn	adj. (of one's understanding of a subject or issue) superficial, shallow
尽量	盡量	jìnliàng	adv. to the fullest (amount, degree, etc.)
中国化	中國化	Zhōngguóhuà	v. "sinicize," to become Chinese, to be like Chinese -化：(suffix) -ize, -ify
同样	同樣	tóngyàng	adj. same
总	總	zǒng	adv. always, invariably

初中		chūzhōng	n. junior high school
野外求生		yěwài qiú shēng	n. outdoor education 野外：wilderness 求生：to seek to survive
差不多		chà.bu duō	adj. almost the same
刺激		cìjī	adj. exciting
好玩		hǎowán	adj. fun
其实	其實	qíshí	adv. actually, in fact
只要		zhǐyào	conj. so long as
摄氏		shèshì	n. Celsius 华氏：Fahrenheit
度		dù	MW for degrees
天气	天氣	tiānqì	n. weather
空调	空調	kōngtiáo	n. air conditioning
未免		wèimiǎn	adv. (of something that one finds has gone too far) rather, a bit too
禁不起		jīn.bùqǐ	v. unable to stand (tests, trial, etc.) 禁得起：able to stand
考验	考驗	kǎoyàn	n. test, trial
周末		zhōumò	n. weekend
打算		dǎ.suàn	v. to plan to, intend to
硬卧		yìngwò	n. "hard sleeper" (there are two kinds of seat in the trains in China --- the "hard sleeper" and the "soft sleeper" [ruǎnwò])
西安		Xī'ān	Xi'an, China

词语例句

1. 据我所知，......　　　　　　**According to what I know, ……**

❖ 据我所知，从纽约没有直飞北京的飞机。

According to what I know, there's no direct flight from New York to Beijing.

1) A：他以前来过中国吗？

B：据我所知，这是他第一次来中国。

A: Has he come to China before?

B: According to what I know, this is the first time that he's been in China.

2) 他说中国的火车只有硬卧，但据我所知，还有软卧。

He said that the trains in China only have "hard sleepers," but according to what I know, there are also "soft" ones.

2. 不是......，而是......　　　　　　**it's not ……, but……**

❖ 我对这两个地方印象特别深，倒不是因为建筑古老，而是因为我不懂为什么中国人两千年来要把自己围在城墙里头。

The reason that I remember these two places especially well is not because the buildings there are old, but because I don't understand why the Chinese kept themselves secluded within the Great Wall for two thousand years.

1) 想卖房子的人不是我，而是他。

It is him and not me who wants to buy a house.

2) 我父亲到中国不是去观光的，而是去谈生意的。

My father did not go to China for sight seeing, but to do business.

3) 我不了解中国人不是因为我不想了解他们，而是因为我没有机会跟他们打交道。

The reason I do not understand the Chinese people is not because I do not wish to do so, but because I did not have the chance to make contacts with them.

3. 竟然　　　　　　**unexpectedly, to one's surprise**

❖ 一个皇帝竟然住那么大的房子。

I can't believe that an emperor lived in such a big house!

1) 我没想到东京的机场竟然这么小！

I didn't expect Tokyo's airport to be so small!

2) 那已经是十年前的事了，你竟然还没忘记。

That was something that happened ten years ago, and you still haven't forgotten it?

4. 尽量   to the fullest (amount, degree, etc.)

❖ 我要把自己的生活尽量"中国化"。

I want to make my life as "Chinese" as possible.

1) 今天的菜那么多，你们要尽量吃。

There are so many dishes today; please eat to your heart's content.

2) 我来了中国，一定要尽量多跟中国人打交道。

Now that I'm in China I must do my best to interact more with Chinese people.

5. 只要......就......   so long as ......; as long as ......

❖ 其实你只要在摄氏三十六度的天气里过一天没有空调的生活，你就不想体验中国人的生活了。

In fact, if you live just one day without air-conditioning when the temperature is 36°C, you will not want to experience the Chinese's way of life anymore.

1) A：跟中国人做生意真难！

B：其实只要你能"中国化"一点儿，就能顺利地跟他们做生意了。

A: It's so difficult to do business with the Chinese!

B: Actually, if only you could be a little more "Chinese," you could do business with them smoothly.

2) 只要那个地方是我参观过的，我就会有印象。

As long as I have been to a place, I'll remember it.

6. 未免   (of something that one finds has gone too far) rather; a bit too

❖ 你也未免把我说得太禁不起考验了。

What you have said makes it seem as if I'm incapable of standing up to tests!

1) 转一次飞机要等两天，未免太过分了吧！

Having to wait two days to change a flight is a bit too much!

2) 吃过中国人的饭，坐过中国人的火车，就算是体验过中国人的生活了吗？这种想法未免太肤浅了。

Can you say you have experienced the Chinese way of life just by eating Chinese food and taking a train in China? This is but a rather shallow thought!

练习

I.　Choose the correct answer.

(　　)1. 我没想到这么大的一个旅馆里头_____没有空调！

        a. 虽然　　　b. 竟然　　　c. 当然

(　　)2. A: 你还记得不记得十年以前的事？

      B: _____。

        a. 十年以前的事情对我完全没有印象了

        b. 我对十年以前的事情完全没有印象了

        c. 对我十年以前的事情完全没有印象了

(　　)3. _____你多跟中国人打交道，_____能了解他们的生活。

        a. 只有...就　　b. 只要...才　c. 只要...就

II.　Choose the most appropriate word for each blank and fill in with its Chinese equivalent.

     to the fullest　　smooth　　deep　　rather/a bit too　　superficial

     to make contact with　　memorable　　Americanize

1. 据我所知，他并不是一个_____的人，他对历史、政治都有很_____的看法。

2. 你去哪儿你的父母都要跟着你，他们对你_____太不放心了！

3. 为了让教室里所有的学生都听懂，她_____说得很慢，说得很清楚。

4. 在美国生活了二十年，他的生活已经完全_____了。

5. 他爸爸在日本做生意，常常跟日本人_____。

III. Choose the phrase that is closest in meaning to the underlined phrase in the sentence.

( ) 1. 中国的公共交通非常方便，<u>尤其</u>是北京和上海。
  a. 特别　　　b. 由于　　　c. 有些

( ) 2. 人好看不好看无所谓，<u>最要紧</u>的是性情好。
  a. 严重　　　b. 重要　　　c. 紧张

( ) 3. 她<u>计划</u>周末坐硬卧去上海，不过没有人觉得这是好主意。
  a. 决定　　　b. 打算　　　c. 愿意

IV. Complete the following dialogue between a Chinese person and an American student using the expressions provided.

中国人：你不是中国人吧？这次到中国来计划做些什么事啊？

美国留学生：＿＿＿＿＿＿＿＿＿＿＿＿＿＿＿＿＿＿

＿＿＿＿＿＿＿＿＿＿＿＿＿＿＿＿＿＿＿＿＿＿

＿＿＿＿＿＿＿＿＿＿＿＿＿＿＿＿＿＿＿＿＿＿

（除了…以外，体验，尽量，跟…打交道）

中国人：我很想到纽约去旅游，可是我该怎么去呢？

美国留学生：＿＿＿＿＿＿＿＿＿＿＿＿＿＿＿＿＿＿

＿＿＿＿＿＿＿＿＿＿＿＿＿＿＿＿＿＿＿＿＿＿

＿＿＿＿＿＿＿＿＿＿＿＿＿＿＿＿＿＿＿＿＿＿

（据我所知，转机，直飞，从…到…，累）

V. Composition: 一次难忘的旅行

第二課

租自行車

甲：昨天我想坐公共汽車去天壇，等了幾班車，都上不去。

乙：爲什麼上不去呢？

甲：因爲我排隊，不想跟人搶著上車。

乙：那可不成，別人都搶，你也得搶。

甲：可我從小就習慣排隊。

乙：要是大家都不排隊，你就得搶。要是你怕擠，怕搶，也許坐地鐵好些，地鐵比公共汽車快多了。

甲：地鐵站離學校太遠，走到最近的地鐵站也得二十分鐘。

乙：你既然不想浪費時間，爲什麼不坐出租車呢？

甲：出租車太貴了，坐趟車比吃頓飯還貴呢。

乙：公交車太擠，地鐵太遠，出租車又太貴，我看你只有騎自行車了。

甲：自行車好是好，就是比較危險，北京的交通規則我不熟，萬一出了事儿，可就糟了。

第二课

租自行车

甲：昨天我想坐公共汽车去天坛，等了几班车，都上不去。

乙：为什么上不去呢？

甲：因为我排队，不想跟人抢着上车。

乙：那可不成，别人都抢，你也得抢。

甲：可我从小就习惯排队。

乙：要是大家都不排队，你就得抢。要是你怕挤，怕抢，也许坐地铁好些，地铁比公共汽车快多了。

甲：地铁站离学校太远，走到最近的地铁站也得二十分钟。

乙：你既然不想浪费时间，为什么不坐出租车呢？

甲：出租车太贵了，坐趟车比吃顿饭还贵呢。

乙：公交车太挤，地铁太远，出租车又太贵，我看你只有骑自行车了。

甲：自行车好是好，就是比较危险，北京的交通规则我不熟，万一出了事儿，可就糟了。

乙：北京騎車的人多得很，你跟著大家騎，靠邊儿走，保
　　證安全。

甲：我在北京只待兩個月，買輛新車划不來。

乙：你不想買新車，可以租一輛。

甲：噢，自行車還能租嗎？

乙：當然能啦！新的，舊的，貴的，便宜的，各種式樣
　　的都有，你想租輛什麼樣的車啊？

甲：我想租輛不新不舊的中檔車。每天在街上騎騎，又
　　省錢，又省時間，還可以鍛煉身體。住在宿舍裏什麼
　　運動都沒有，才來了兩個星期就胖了好幾公斤，一定
　　得想個法子運動運動。

乙：北京人大多騎車上班，這不但解決了交通問題，也
　　鍛煉了身體，真是一舉兩得。

甲：這真是個好主意！我明天就去租輛自行車。

—在租車店裏—

甲：師傅，你們租自行車嗎？

乙：我們賣自行車也租自行車。你想租輛什麼樣的車？

乙：北京骑车的人多得很，你跟着大家骑，靠边儿走，保证安全。

甲：我在北京只待两个月，买辆新车划不来。

乙：你不想买新车，可以租一辆。

甲：噢，自行车还能租吗？

乙：当然能啦！新的，旧的，贵的，便宜的，各种式样的都有，你想租辆什么样的车啊？

甲：我想租辆不新不旧的中档车。每天在街上骑骑，又省钱，又省时间，还可以锻炼身体。住在宿舍里什么运动都没有，才来了两个星期就胖了好几公斤，一定得想个法子运动运动。

乙：北京人大多骑车上班，这不但解决了交通问题，也锻炼了身体，真是一举两得。

甲：这真是个好主意！我明天就去租辆自行车。

——在租车店里——

甲：师傅，你们租自行车吗？

乙：我们卖自行车也租自行车。你想租辆什么样的车？

甲：我想租輛不新不舊的中檔車。

乙：這兩天暑期班剛開學，來租車的人特別多，好車都租出去了，只剩下這幾輛了，你看看吧。

甲：我想試試這輛。能騎一下嗎？

乙：行啊，別走遠了，就在店門口騎兩圈ㄦ。

甲：好，好。

——————————————

甲：這車怎麼租啊？一個月多少錢啊？

乙：我們這ㄦ租車不論月，論天數。一天五塊錢。

甲：一天五塊錢，一個月就得一百五十塊錢，兩個月租下來，不是和買輛車差不多了嗎？

乙：三百塊錢可買不到這樣的車。

甲：好吧，好吧，我先租兩個星期試試。

乙：除了租金，你還得付押金，押金一百塊。

甲：我還想買個安全帽，你們有沒有安全帽？

乙：騎自行車戴什麼安全帽？在北京你見過騎車的人戴安全帽嗎？

甲：我想租辆不新不旧的中档车。

乙：这两天暑期班刚开学，来租车的人特别多，好车都租出去了，只剩下这几辆了，你看看吧。

甲：我想试试这辆。能骑一下吗？

乙：行啊，别走远了，就在店门口骑两圈儿。

甲：好，好。

——————————————

甲：这车怎么租啊？一个月多少钱啊？

乙：我们这儿租车不论月，论天数。一天五块钱。

甲：一天五块钱，一个月就得一百五十块钱，两个月租下来，不是和买辆车差不多了吗？

乙：三百块钱可买不到这样的车。

甲：好吧，好吧，我先租两个星期试试。

乙：除了租金，你还得付押金，押金一百块。

甲：我还想买个安全帽，你们有没有安全帽？

乙：骑自行车戴什么安全帽？在北京你见过骑车的人戴安全帽吗？

甲：見倒是沒見過，可是……

乙：放—心—，在北京騎車，沒事儿！

甲：见倒是没见过，可是……

乙：放—心—，在北京骑车，没事儿！

词汇

租		zū	v. to rent
自行车	自行車	zìxíngchē	n. bicycle, bike
昨天		zuótiān	n. yesterday
坐		zuò	v. to sit; (here) to take (a bus, a train, etc.)
公共汽车	公共汽車	gōnggòngqìchē	n. public bus
天坛	天壇	Tiāntán	Temple of Heaven
班		bān	MW for scheduled transport vehicles
排队	排隊	páiduì	v-o. to stand in line, to form a line 排：to line up 队：a row of people, line
抢	搶	qiǎng	v. to scramble for
上车	上車	shàngchē	v-o. to board a bus
不成		bùchéng	Won't do
怕		pà	v. to be afraid of; to fear
挤	擠	jǐ	v. to jostle, to push against; adj. crowded
也许	也許	yěxǔ	adv. perhaps, probably
地铁	地鐵	dìtiě	n. subway
地铁站	地鐵站	dìtiězhàn	n. subway station
离	離	lí	prep. apart from
远	遠	yuǎn	adj. far
近		jìn	adj. near, close

分钟	分鐘	fēnzhōng	MW for time, minutes 二十分钟：twenty minutes
既然		jìrán	conj. since; as; now that
浪费	浪費	làngfèi	v. to waste
时间	時間	shíjiān	n. time
出租车	出租車	chūzūchē	n. cab; taxi 出租：to put out for rental or hiring; to let
贵	貴	guì	adj. expensive
顿	頓	dùn	MW for 吃, 打, 骂 and certain other verbs
公交车	公交車	gōngjiāochē	n. public bus (=公共汽车)
只有		zhǐyǒu	conj. only
骑	騎	qí	v. to ride (a bicycle, a horse, etc.)
比较	比較	bǐjiào	adv. relatively, fairly
危险	危險	wēixiǎn	adj. dangerous
交通		jiāotōng	n. traffic
规则	規則	guīzé	n. rule, regulation
熟		shú	adj. familiar
万一	萬一	wànyī	conj. if by any chance, just in case
出事儿		chūshìr	v-o. to meet with a mishap, to have an accident
糟		zāo	adj. terrible; in a mess
靠		kào	v. to lean (towards /against)
边儿	邊儿	biānr	n. side; edge

保证	保證	bǎozhèng	v. to guarantee
安全		ānquán	adj. safe
待		dāi	v. to stay
辆	輛	liàng	MW for vehicles
新		xīn	adj. new
划不来	划不來	huá.bùlái	not worth it 划得来：worth it
当然	當然	dāngrán	adv. certainly, of course
旧	舊	jiù	adj. old; used; worn
便宜		pián.yí	adj. cheap
各种	各種	gè zhǒng	various kinds
式样	式樣	shì.yàng	n. style; type; model
中档	中檔	zhōngdàng	adj. (of the quality of things) of second rate 中：middle 档：grade of consumer goods
街		jiē	n. street
省		shěng	v. to save
钱	錢	qián	n. money
锻炼	鍛煉	duànliàn	v. to exercise (the body)
身体	身體	shēntǐ	n. body; health
宿舍		sùshè	n. dormitory
运动	運動	yùndòng	n. physical exercise
才		cái	adv. only (here＝只)

胖		pàng	adj. fat
公斤		gōngjīn	measurement for weight: kilograms
法子		fǎ.zǐ	n. means, way
大多		dàduō	adv. mostly
上班		shàngbān	v-o. to go to work
解决	解決	jiějué	v. to resolve
问题	問題	wèntí	n. problem; question; matter
一举两得	一舉兩得	yìjǔliǎngdé	lit."one act two gains," kills two birds with one stone 举：act 得：gain
主意		zhǔ.yì	n. idea
店		diàn	n. shop; store
师傅	師傅	shī.fù	n. a respectful form of address for a service worker
暑期班		shǔqībān	n. summer school 暑期：summer session 班：class
开学	開學	kāixué	v-o. start school, begin a term
特别		tèbié	adv. especially
剩下		shèng.xià	v. to be left (over); to remain
试	試	shì	v. to try
门口	門口	ménkǒu	n. doorway; entrance
圈儿		quānr	MW for rounds; n. circle, round
论	論	lùn	v. to take into account; to regard;

			to determine
天数	天數	tiānshù	n. number of days 天 : day 数 (=数目 [mù]) : number, quantity
租金		zūjīn	n. rental fee; rent
付		fù	v. to pay
押金		yājīn	n. deposit
安全帽		ānquánmào	n. safety helmet
戴		dài	v. to wear (a cap, a watch, etc.)
放心		fàngxīn	v-o. to set one's mind at rest; to feel relieved
没事儿		méishìr	it's nothing; no problem

词语例句

1. 要是……，也许……　　　　　　**If …, perhaps …**

❖ 要是你怕挤、怕抢，也许坐地铁好些。

If you're afraid to squeeze in and to fight (for a seat), perhaps it's better that you take the subway.

[What follows after "也许" is the speaker's suggestion.]

1）要是你觉得直飞太累，也许你可以先到东京住两天。

If you think that flying there directly will make you too tired, maybe you can stop over in Tokyo for two days.

2）要是新车太贵，那我们也许得租辆中档的。

If the new car is too expansive, then we might have to rent a second-rate one.

2. **Adj. 些　　　　　　more adj.**

❖ 坐地铁好些。(see 1. for translation)

1）住在宿舍里虽然挤，可是方便些。

Although the dormitory is crowded, it's more convenient to stay there (than in some other place).

2）坐软卧很贵，但舒服些。

It's very expensive to travel on the "soft sleepers," but it's more comfortable that way.

3. **A 比 B adj. 多了　　　　　A is much more adj. than B**

❖ 地铁比公共汽车快多了。

The subway is much faster than the buses.

1）我们还是坐公车吧！公车站比地铁站近多了。

Let's take a bus! The bus station is much closer than the subway station.

2）他只学了几个月的中文，可是却说得比我好多了。

He has been studying Chinese for only a few months, but he speaks much better than I do.

4. **既然…，为什么不/还…呢？　　　　since (it's the case that) …, why**

29

not/ still …?

❖ 你既然不想浪费时间，为什么不坐出租车呢？

Since you don't want to waste your time, why don't you take a cab?

1）你既然来了北京，为什么不去参观长城和故宫呢？

Since you're here in Beijing, why don't you visit the Great Wall and the Forbidden City?

2）既然他那么怕跟中国人打交道，为什么还要来中国呢？

Since he's so afraid of making contacts with Chinese people, why did he come to China?

5. 只有   **will just have to**

❖ 我看你只有骑自行车了。

I think you'll just have to ride a bicycle.

[In this sentence, as in the following two, "只有" is similar to "只好."]

1）大家都抢着上车，我只有跟着抢了。

Everyone is jostling to get on the bus. I have no choice but to follow suit.

2）你这个菜也不吃，那个菜也不吃，我看你只有吃白饭了。

You won't eat this dish, and you won't eat that one either. I think you'll be left with only white rice to eat.

6. **Adj. 是 Adj.，就是…   is indeed adj., but it's just that ……**

❖ 自行车好是好，就是比较危险。

(Riding) bicycle is good, but it's just more dangerous.

1）坐公共汽车便宜是便宜，就是太浪费时间了。

Taking a bus is indeed cheap, but it's just too time consuming.

2）这么做可以是可以，就是怕会出事儿。

It's fine doing this, but I'm just worried that something might go wrong.

7. **万一   If by any chance; just in case**

❖ 北京的交通规则我不熟，万一出了事儿，可就糟了。

I'm not familiar with the traffic regulations in Beijing. If something goes wrong, it will be terrible.

1) 这辆车那么旧，万一在路上坏了，怎么办呢？

This car is so old, what if it breaks down on the road?

2) 你少做一点儿菜，万一他们不来，也不浪费。

Don't cook so much. If by some chance they do not show up, nothing will be wasted.

8. 保证   **to guarantee**

❖ 北京骑车的人多得很，你跟着大家骑，靠边儿走，保证安全。

There are many bike riders in Beijing, so just follow the crowd and keep to the side. I guarantee you'll be safe.

1) 这种安全帽好得很，戴了保证又舒服又安全又好看！

This kind of safety helmet is just great! I guarantee you'll be comfortable, safe, and good-looking wearing it!

2) 我想的这个主意保证能解决你的问题。

I guarantee that this idea will solve your problems.

9. 划得来\划不来   **worth it \ not worth it**

❖ 我在北京只待两个月，买辆新车划不来。

I'll only be staying in Bejing for two months, so buying a new bicycle is not worth it.

1) 出去吃顿饭得挤公车，到了饭馆还得排队等，真划不来！

You will have to squeeze into a bus to go out for a meal, and when you get to the restaurant you'll still have to wait in line. It's really not worth it!

2) 你想开家店？除了租金，还得先付押金，到底划不划得来？

You're thinking of opening a store? In addition to the rental fee, you'll also have to pay a deposit in advance. Is it really worth it?

10.   **A 的、B 的、C 的**   **A ones, B ones, C ones**

❖ 新的、旧的、贵的、便宜的，各种式样的都有。

We have all different types: new ones, old ones, expensive ones, and cheaper ones.

1) 我这儿的衣服很多，无论是长的、短的，还是大的、小的，我都有。

I have all different types of clothes: long ones, short ones, big ones and small ones — I have everything.

2) 我不喜欢看小说，无论是现代的，还是古代的，无论是讲社会的，还是个人生活的，我都不看。

I do not like to read novels. No matter if they are modern or classical, and no matter if they are about society as a whole or the life of an individual, I simply do not read them.

11.　　不A不B　　　　　　　not A not B; neither A nor B

❖ 我想租辆不新不旧的中档车。

I want to rent a mid-range (price/quality) bicycle that is neither (too) new nor (too) old.

1) 这个房子不大不小，刚好！

This house is neither too big nor too small. It's just right!

2) 这个电影不好不坏，没什么特别的。

This movie is not good, but it's not bad either. There is nothing special about it.

12.　　又…，又…，还…　　　　　　both … and …, in addition, …

❖ 每天在街上骑骑，又省钱，又省时间，还可以锻炼身体。

Ride it on the streets everyday, and you'll save time and money, in addition, you can also get some exercise.

1) 那个地铁站又小，人又多，去那儿还得走二十分钟，我还是坐出租车吧！

That subway station is not only small but also crowded. Moreover, it takes twenty minutes to walk there. I would rather take a cab!

2) 这种东西又好吃，又吃不胖，还很便宜，我得多买一点儿。

This stuff tastes good, and doesn't make you fat. What's more, it's cheap. I have to buy more of it.

13.　　才　　　　　　only

❖ 住在宿舍里什么运动都没有，才来了两个星期就胖了好几公斤。

Staying in the dormitory, I do not get any exercise; as a result I've gained quite a few kilos in just two weeks.

[When 才 appears before a number, it takes the meaning of "only," indicating that the amount is small, or that the duration is short, and the like.]

1) 你才过了一天没有空调的生活就受不了了，还说禁得起考验！

After just one day without air-conditioning, you can't stand it, and yet you claimed you could stand up to the test!

2) 租辆车一个月才一百五十块，便宜得很。

It costs only one hundred and fifty dollars to rent a car for a month. That's very cheap.

14.　　试试　　　　　　to give it a try

❖ 我想试试这辆。

I would like to try this one.

1) 这个电脑我还没有试用过，不知道好不好。

I have not tried using this computer, so I'm not sure if it's good or not.

2) 这儿的安全帽都一样，你不用试了。

The safety helmets here are all the same, you don't need to try one on.

15.　　不论A，论B　　　　　do not go by A, but rather B

❖ 我们这儿租车不论月，论天数。

At our shop, we don't rent out a bicycle by months. We do it by days.

1) 中国人不论磅，论公斤。

Chinese people do not measure weight by pounds; they go by kilograms.

2) 我交朋友不论他有没有钱，只论他人好不好。

When I make friends, I don't care if he's rich; I only care if he's a good person.

练习

I.   Choose the correct answer.

(   )1. 我本来有100块钱，买书用了三十块，买酒用了二十块
          钱，我还_____？
              a. 剩下多少钱   b. 多少钱剩下了   c. 离开多少钱

(   )2. 这条马路有点儿危险，你最好_____。
              a. 向边儿走   b. 靠边儿走   c. 跟边儿靠

(   )3. 中国改革开放_____二十年，_____发生了这么大的
          变化。
              a. 才...就   b. 就...才   c. 已经...竟然

(   )4. 我对这张CD很有兴趣，我可以不可以_____一下？
              a. 听试试   b. 试听   c. 听听试

(   )5. 在这儿租车不_____小时。
              a. 用   b. 论   c. 据

(   )6. _____你要体验中国人的生活，_____还住在这么贵的
          饭店里？
              a. 因为..为什么..   b. 虽然..但是..   c. 既然..为什么..

II.   Choose the most appropriate word for each blank and fill in with its
        Chinese equivalent.

              familiar   to fear   guarantee   to save   follow
              scramble for   to waste   if by any chance

1. 我在这儿住了二十年，对所有的地方都_____得很，只要你
        _____我，我_____你找得到要去的地方。

2. 住在宿舍里，虽然人有点儿多，可是离什么地方都很近，可以_____
        _____很多时间。

3. 中国人在饭馆儿吃饭的时候，常常_____付钱。

4. 虽然校园里很安全，可是你一个女孩子，也不要这么晚一个人走
        路，_____出了什么事，可就麻烦了。

III.   Choose the phrase that is closest in meaning to the underlined phrase in
        the sentence.

(   ) 1. 放心，在北京骑车，<u>没事儿</u>！

         a. 别出事　　b. 没有工作　c. 不会有问题

(   ) 2. 天气这么热，<u>你还戴什么帽子</u>？

         a. 你戴什么式样的帽子

         b. 你戴什么牌子的帽子

         c. 你不必戴帽子

(   ) 3. 昨天我的皮包<u>给</u>一个男人偷了了。

         a. 把　　　　b. 被　　　　c. 要

(   ) 4. 其实去北京学中文真的很<u>划得来</u>，因为又可以在很短的

         时间提高中文水平，又可以比较深刻地了解中国文化。

         a. 省钱　　　b. 值得　　　c. 有用

IV. Composition

1. 你的朋友刚到北京，请你告诉他在北京坐地铁、公共汽车、骑自行车、坐出租车，各有什么好处？坏处？

尽量用以下的生词：抢、挤、离、排队、糟、熟、省、浪费、危险、锻炼、
            解决、尽量、一举两得

尽量用以下的句型：万一、要是…也许…、划不来、A比B adj.多了、adj.些

2. 大学旁边有一家租车店，租自行车也卖自行车，可是生意一直不好，现在请你为这家店写一个广告(guǎnggào: advertisement)来吸引(xīyǐn: to attract)顾客(gùkè: customer)租自行车。

    这个广告的内容(nèiróng: content)应该有：

    a) 租车店的名字、地址(dìzhǐ: address)、电话

    b) 这家店的自行车是什么样的？

    c) 租金、押金的情况

第三課

出了車禍

甲：媽，我昨天出了個車禍。

乙：什麼！出了車禍！受傷了沒有？

甲：受了一點兒小傷，不是太嚴重。我現在是在醫院病房裏給您打電話。

乙：你住院了啊！傷得一定不輕吧？

甲：腿上骨頭給撞折了。

乙：怎麼回事兒啊？

甲：昨天我去學校附近一家飯館兒吃飯，過馬路的時候，我看是綠燈就過街了，沒看到一輛右轉的車，就給撞上了。好在那輛車開得不是太快，要不然大概連命都沒了。

乙：警察來了沒有？

甲：交通警察來得倒挺快，救護車也來了，可是他們都說是我不對，我應該讓汽車先走！

乙：行人讓汽車，汽車不讓行人，這不是太危險了嗎？那個司機有保險嗎？他應該負責醫療費用。

第三课

出了车祸

甲：妈，我昨天出了个车祸。

乙：什么！出了车祸！受伤了没有？

甲：受了一点儿小伤，不是太严重。我现在是在医院病房里给您打电话。

乙：你住院了啊！伤得一定不轻吧？

甲：腿上骨头给撞折了。

乙：怎么回事儿啊？

甲：昨天我去学校附近一家饭馆儿吃饭，过马路的时候，我看是绿灯就过街了，没看到一辆右转的车，就给撞上了。好在那辆车开得不是太快，要不然大概连命都没了。

乙：警察来了没有？

甲：交通警察来得倒挺快，救护车也来了，可是他们都说是我不对，我应该让汽车先走！

乙：行人让汽车，汽车不让行人，这不是太危险了吗？那个司机有保险吗？他应该负责医疗费用。

甲：他是個個體的出租車司機，據他說沒買保險，加
　　上是我不對，醫療費得我自己出。

乙：你在中國出了事儿，不知道美國的保險能不能付錢，
　　明天讓你爸爸給保險公司打個電話問問。

甲：醫生說我得住四、五天院。出院以後還得用輪椅。
　　我擔心功課要被耽誤了。

乙：耽誤功課無所謂，最要緊的是身體，醫院裏設備好
　　不好啊？

甲：我住的是普通病房，一間四、五個人，沒有電視也
　　沒有空調，很不舒服。

乙：你越說我越擔心。要不要我飛去北京照顧你啊？

甲：除了腿受傷，沒什麼其他問題。您放心，不必爲這
　　件事儿飛到北京來。我自己會照顧自己。過兩天再給
　　您打電話吧！

乙：以後走路可千萬得小心啊！

甲：他是个个体的出租车司机，据他说没买保险，加上是我不对，医疗费得我自己出。

乙：你在中国出了事儿，不知道美国的保险能不能付钱，明天让你爸爸给保险公司打个电话问问。

甲：医生说我得住四、五天院。出院以后还得用轮椅。我担心功课要被耽误了。

乙：耽误功课无所谓，最要紧的是身体，医院里设备好不好啊？

甲：我住的是普通病房，一间四、五个人，没有电视也没有空调，很不舒服。

乙：你越说我越担心。要不要我飞去北京照顾你啊？

甲：除了腿受伤，没什么其他问题。您放心，不必为这件事儿飞到北京来。我自己会照顾自己。过两天再给您打电话吧！

乙：以后走路可千万得小心啊！

词汇

车祸	車禍	chēhuò	n. car accident
出车祸	出車禍	chū chēhuò	v-o. to get into a car accident
受伤	受傷	shòushāng	v-o. to become injured
严重	嚴重	yánzhòng	adj. (of a state or problem) serious
医院	醫院	yīyuàn	n. hospital
病房		bìngfáng	n. "sickroom," ward (of a hospital)
住院		zhùyuàn	v-o. to be hospitalized 住：to stay 院：医院
轻	輕	qīng	adj. slight, not serious; light
腿		tuǐ	n. leg
骨头	骨頭	gǔ.tóu	n. bone
给	給	gěi	(here) passive marker, same as 被
撞		zhuàng	v. to hit
折		shé	v. to break, to become broken
绿灯	綠燈	lǜdēng	n. green light
过	過	guò	v. to cross; to pass 过街：to cross the street
右		yòu	n. the right side 左 (zuǒ)：the left side
转	轉	zhuǎn	v. to turn
好在		hǎozài	adv. luckily, fortunately
要不然		yào.bùrán	conj. otherwise, or else

大概		dàgài	adv. probably
命		mìng	n. one's life 没命了：lost one's life, dead
警察		jǐngchá	n. police
挺		tǐng	adv. quite
救护车	救護車	jiùhùchē	n. ambulance
让	讓	ràng	v. to yield to; to allow
行人		xíngrén	n. pedestrian
司机	司機	sījī	n. driver
保险	保險	bǎoxiǎn	n. insurance
负责	負責	fùzé	v. to be responsible for; to be in charge of
医疗	醫療	yīliáo	n. medical treatment
费用	費用	fèi.yòng	n. cost, expense
个体	個體	gètǐ	n. individual
据说	據說	jùshuō	adv. it is said 据 sb. 说：according to sb.
加上		jiā.shàng	conj. moreover, in addition
出		chū	v. to go; to come out; (here) to pay
公司		gōngsī	n. company
出院		chūyuàn	v-o. to be discharged from hospital
轮椅	輪椅	lúnyǐ	n. wheelchair
耽误	耽誤	dān.wù	v. to delay, to hold up
无所谓	無所謂	wúsuǒwèi	adj. doesn't matter (to sb.), (sb.) doesn't care

要紧	要緊	yàojǐn	adj. important, urgent
设备	設備	shèbèi	n. equipment, facilities
普通		pǔtōng	adj. common, ordinary 普通病房：standard ward
间	間	jiān	MW for rooms
其他		qítā	pron. other
不必		búbì	adv. need not
为	爲	wèi	prep. for
千万	千萬	qiānwàn	adv. be sure to, must
小心		xiǎoxīn	adj. to be careful

要紧

设备

词语例句

1. 好在…，要不然…　　　　　**luckily …, otherwise …**

❖ 好在那辆车开得不是太快，要不然大概连命都没了。

Luckily that car wasn't going too fast, otherwise I probably would have lost my life.

1) 好在我来中国以前已经学了一年的中文，要不然连吃顿饭都会有问题。

Luckily I had already learned a year of Chinese before I came to China; if not, I would have problems even with getting a meal.

2) 好在你买了保险，要不然你怎么付得起这么贵的医疗费呢？

Luckily you have insurance; otherwise how can you afford such expensive medical fees?

2. 负责　　　　　**to be responsible for; to be in charge of**

❖ 他应该负责医疗费用。

He should be responsible for the medical charges.

1) 张先生负责外国学生的事儿，你有问题可以找他。

Mr. Zhang is in charge of foreign students' affairs. You can go to see him if you have problems.

2) 生了孩子，就要负责照顾他。

After giving birth to a child, one must be responsible for its care.

3. 据 sb. 说　　　　　**according to sb.**

❖ 据他说没买保险，…

According to him he has no insurance, …

1) 据我的朋友说，在这儿是人让车，不是车让人。

According to my friend, here it's pedestrians who should yield to cars and not vice versa.

2) 据说这儿的出租车司机大多都是个体户。

It is said that most of the taxi drivers here are self-employed individuals.

4. …，加上…　　　　　**…, in addition …**

❖ 据他说没买保险，加上是我不对，医疗费得我自己出。

He said he has no insurance; and in addition, I'm at fault, so I have to pay for the medical charges myself.

1) 我吃得多了，加上没运动，所以胖了好几公斤。

I've been eating more lately and haven't been exercising, so I've gained quite a few kilos.

2) 这家医院有好的医生，再加上有好的设备，所以很有名。

This hospital has good doctors as well as good equipment. That's why it's well known.

5. 耽误   to delay; to hold up

❖ 我担心功课要被耽误了。

I'm worried that my studies will be held up.

1) 你别在这儿耽误我的时间了，快回去吧！

Don't stay here and waste my time — go back, quickly!

2) 我因为出了车祸，所以把整个出国的计划都耽误了。

My whole plan of going abroad was delayed because I got into an accident.

6. ...无所谓，最要紧的是...   It doesn't matter that ..., what's most important is ...

❖ 耽误功课无所谓，最要紧的是身体。

It doesn't matter that your study has been delayed; what's most important is your health.

1) 我来中国学不好中文无所谓，最要紧的是好好地玩儿。

Coming to China but not learning Chinese well doesn't bother me; what's most important is to have a lot of fun.

2) A：你想租辆什么样的自行车？

B：好不好看都无所谓，最要紧的是能骑，又便宜。

A: What kind of bicycle are you looking for (to rent)?

B: It doesn't matter if it looks good; what's most important is that it works and is cheap.

7. 不必   **need not**

❖ 你不必为这件事飞到北京来。

You don't have to fly over to Beijing for this matter.

[You are reminded that "不必" does not have a positive form, therefore never say "必." To say "must," or "need to," use "得" (děi) or "必须" (bìxū).]

1) 我会好好儿地照顾自己，你们不必担心！

I'll take good care of myself. You don't have to worry!

2) 在美国，开车的人一定得卖保险，可是在中国却不必。

In the United States, a person who drives has to buy insurance, but in China, one does not have to do that.

8. 千万   **be sure to; must**

❖ 以后走路可千万得小心啊！

From now on you must be cautious when you walk (on the street)!

1) 你一个人在北京千万要照顾好身体，别让我担心啊！

Now that you're in Beijing by yourself, you must take good care of your health. Don't make me worried!

2) 那家店的自行车你千万别租，都是坏的。

Make sure you don't rent any bikes from that shop; they're all bad.

练习

I.   Complete the following dialogue using expressions provided.

在路上，一辆出租车出了事，交通警察马上赶来⋯⋯

警察：怎么回事儿啊？撞伤了一个孩子，是不是你开得太快了？

司机：不是，是他过街的时候没让车，＿＿＿＿＿＿＿＿＿＿＿＿＿＿

＿＿＿＿＿＿＿＿＿＿＿＿＿＿＿＿＿＿＿＿＿＿＿＿＿＿＿＿＿＿＿＿

＿＿＿＿＿＿＿＿＿＿＿＿＿＿＿＿＿＿＿＿＿＿＿＿＿＿＿＿＿＿＿＿

（好在⋯，要不然⋯）

警察：谁该负责医疗费呢？

司机：＿＿＿＿＿＿＿＿＿＿＿＿＿＿＿＿＿＿＿＿＿＿＿＿＿＿＿＿＿＿

（据⋯说）

警察：你知道那个孩子的腿被撞折了，他父母会跟你要很多钱的。

司机：＿＿＿＿＿＿＿＿＿＿＿＿＿＿＿＿＿＿＿＿＿＿＿＿＿＿＿＿＿＿

（⋯无所谓，最要紧的是⋯）

警察：你为什么那么不小心，你为什么不等一等呢？

司机：我的孩子病了，我要送他去医院。＿＿＿＿＿＿＿＿＿＿＿＿

＿＿＿＿＿＿＿＿＿＿＿＿＿＿＿＿＿＿＿＿＿＿＿＿＿＿＿＿＿＿＿＿

（耽误，怕，要是⋯⋯）

警察：＿＿＿＿＿＿＿＿＿＿＿＿＿＿＿＿＿＿＿＿＿＿＿＿＿＿＿＿＿＿

（千万）

司机：是，是，我记住了，我以后再也不开这么快了。

II.   Answer the question using as many new words that you've learnt as possible.

1. 你认为应该是行人让车，还是车让行人？出了车祸，行人有没有责任(zé rèn: responsibility)呢？在美国，行人是不是被宠坏(chǒnghuài: spoiled)了？

2. 你出过车祸吗？要是你出了车祸应该怎么办？

III. Composition: Rewrite the dialogue of Lesson Three into an essay.

第四課

旗袍和筷子

甲：這件衣服眞漂亮，是在哪儿買的啊？

乙：不是買的，是定做的。現成的也有，可是沒這麼合身。

甲：這是什麼衣服啊？

乙：這是旗袍，據説是清朝女人穿的衣服，可是民國以後穿的人還是很多。

甲：可是我在中國怎麼從來沒見過女人穿旗袍？

乙：因爲穿了旗袍行動工作都不方便，所以大家都不穿了。

甲：印度人一般都穿他們自己的服裝。中國人在穿著上好像不太堅持自己的傳統。

乙：穿衣服是天天都得做的事儿，最要緊的是方便和實用。如果爲了堅持傳統，每天穿著旗袍上課工作，那就太不方便了。這樣的傳統是不值得堅持的。

甲：中國人在穿著上完全接受了西方的影響，但是在飲食上好像就比較保守了。一般來説中國人都用筷子吃

第四课

旗袍和筷子

甲：这件衣服真漂亮，是在哪儿买的啊？

乙：不是买的，是定做的。现成的也有，可是没这么合身。

甲：这是什么衣服啊？

乙：这是旗袍，据说是清朝女人穿的衣服，可是民国以后穿的人还是很多。

甲：可是我在中国怎么从来没见过女人穿旗袍？

乙：因为穿了旗袍行动工作都不方便，所以大家都不穿了。

甲：印度人一般都穿他们自己的服装。中国人在穿着上好像不太坚持自己的传统。

乙：穿衣服是天天都得做的事儿，最要紧的是方便和实用。如果为了坚持传统，每天穿着旗袍上课工作，那就太不方便了。这样的传统是不值得坚持的。

甲：中国人在穿着上完全接受了西方的影响，但是在饮食上好像就比较保守了。一般来说中国人都用筷子吃飯，在中國我還沒見過用刀叉吃飯的中國人。

乙：不用刀叉吃飯，倒不一定是爲了維持傳統。因爲用
筷子又簡單又方便，沒什麼理由把筷子淘汰掉。我認
爲兩種文化交流的時候，用什麼和不用什麼的標準只
是實用，和維持傳統是沒有關係的。

甲：筷子方便是方便，但是我覺得不太衛生。大家一桌
吃飯，都把筷子伸到盤子裏去夾菜。要是有人感冒，
就很容易傳染。

乙：這個我同意，尤其是喝湯的時候，大家都用湯勺儿在
湯碗裏舀來舀去，然後再放進嘴裏喝，還有人用筷子
往湯碗裏夾東西吃，簡直像在湯裏洗筷子，看了讓我
惡心。

甲：現在比較高檔的飯館都有"公筷"和"公勺儿"，大
家已經不用自己的筷子和湯勺儿去夾菜舀湯了。

乙：你指出了一個很有趣的問題。雖然這只是一件小
事儿，但是卻可以說明一個文化交流的現象。中西文
化交流的時候，並不一定是西方的取代中國的，或者
中國的取代西方的。有時中國受了西方的影響，開始
有了變化，用"公筷"，"公勺儿"就是一個最好的

饭，在中国我还没见过用刀叉吃饭的中国人。

乙：不用刀叉吃饭，倒不一定是为了维持传统，因为用筷子又简单又方便，没什么理由把筷子淘汰掉。我认为两种文化交流的时候，用什么和不用什么的标准只是实用，和维持传统是没有关系的。

甲：筷子方便是方便，但是我觉得不太卫生。大家一桌吃饭，都把筷子伸到盘子里去夹菜。要是有人感冒，就很容易传染。

乙：这个我同意，尤其是喝汤的时候，大家都用汤勺儿在汤碗里舀来舀去，然后再放进嘴里喝，还有人用筷子往汤碗里夹东西吃，简直像在汤里洗筷子，看了让我恶心。

甲：现在比较高档的饭馆都有"公筷"和"公勺儿"，大家已经不用自己的筷子和汤勺儿去夹菜舀汤了。

乙：你指出了一个很有趣的问题。虽然这只是一件小事儿，但是却可以说明一个文化交流的现象。中西文化交流的时候，并不一定是西方的取代中国的，或者中国的取代西方的。有时中国受了西方的影响，开始有了变化，用"公筷"，"公勺儿"就是一个最好的例子，這叫 " 改良 " 。有時西方也受中國的影響，就像最近豆腐成了美國超級市場上一種日常食品，這就是中美文化交流的結果。

例子，这叫"改良"。有时西方也受中国的影响，就像最近豆腐成了美国超级市场上一种日常食品，这就是中美文化交流的结果。

词汇

旗袍		qípáo	n. *qipao* ("long gown"), a traditional Chinese costume for women
漂亮		piào.liàng	adj. beautiful
定做		dìngzuò	v. tailored-made (lit. "reserved-made") 定：to subscribe to, to book 做：to make
现成	現成	xiànchéng	adj. ready-made
合身		héshēn	adj. (of clothes) fitting
清朝		Qīngcháo	n. Qing dynasty (1644-1911)
民国	民國	Mín'guó	n. Republic of China (established in 1911)
行动	行動	xíngdòng	v. to move, to get about
印度人		Yìndùrén	n. an Indian (person from India)
一般		yìbān	adj. (here) usually, commonly; general, ordinary, common
服装	服裝	fúzhuāng	n. clothing, costume
穿着	穿著	chuānzhuó	n. dress, attire
好像		hǎoxiàng	v. seem to be
坚持	堅持	jiānchí	v. to persist in, to insist on
传统	傳統	chuántǒng	n. tradition
实用	實用	shíyòng	adj. practical, pragmatic, functional
值得	值得	zhí.dé	adj. to deserve, to be worth

接受		jiēshòu	v. to accept; to receive (honors, etc.)
西方		xīfāng	n. the West
影响	影響	yǐngxiǎng	n. influence
饮食	飲食	yǐnshí	n. food and drink, diet
保守		bǎoshǒu	adj. conservative
一般来说	一般來説	yìbānláishuō	generally speaking
筷子		kuài.zǐ	n. chopsticks
刀叉		dāochā	n. knife and fork
简单	簡單	jiǎndān	adj. simple, uncomplicated
理由		lǐyóu	n. reason, grounds, justification
淘汰		táotài	v. to eliminate through selection or competition
认为	認爲	rènwéi	v. to think that, to believe that
文化		wénhuà	n. culture
交流		jiāoliú	v. to exchange (each other's experiences, views, etc.)
标准	標準	biāozhǔn	n. standard, criterion
卫生	衛生	wèishēng	n. hygiene, sanitation; (here) adj. hygienic
伸		shēn	v. to extend, to stretch
盘子	盤子	pán.zǐ	n. plate; tray
夹		jiā	v. to press from both sides; (here) to pick up (with chopsticks)
感冒		gǎnmào	v. to catch a cold

容易		róng.yì	adj. easy
传染	傳染	chuánrǎn	v. to spread (a disease), to infect
同意		tóngyì	v. to agree
尤其		yóuqí	adv. especially
喝		hē	v. to drink
汤	湯	tāng	n. soup; broth
勺儿	勺儿	sháor	n. spoon
往		wǎng	v. to go toward
碗		wǎn	n. bowl
舀		yǎo	v. to spoon out, to scoop up
嘴		zuǐ	n. mouth
简直	簡直	jiǎnzhí	adv. simply, really
洗		xǐ	v. to wash
恶心	惡心	ě.xīn	adj. disgusting; to feel like vomiting
高档	高檔	gāodàng	adj. (of the quality of things) first rate; high-class
公		gōng	adj. public, common 公筷：a pair of chopsticks that is shared by all for the purpose of picking up food from the main platter; same for 公勺儿
指出		zhǐchū	v. to point out
有趣		yǒuqù	adj. interesting
说明	説明	shuōmíng	v. to show, to illustrate, to explain

现象	現象	xiàn.xiàng	n. phenomenon
取代		qǔdài	v. to replace; to supersede
受(到)		shòu (dào)	v. to be subjected to
开始	開始	kāishǐ	v. to begin, to start
变化	變化	biànhuà	n. change, transformation
例子		lì.zǐ	n. example; case, instance
改良		gǎiliáng	n. reform
豆腐		dòu.fǔ	n. bean curd
超级市场	超級市場	chāojíshìchǎng	n. supermarket
日常		rìcháng	adj. daily, day-to-day
食品		shípǐn	n. foodstuff, food
结果	結果	jiéguǒ	n. result; outcome; consequence

词语例句

1. 从来没 V. 过　　　　　has never V. before

❖ 可是我在中国怎么从来没见过女人穿旗袍？

But how come I've never seen women wearing *qipao* in China?

1) 你坐我的车可以放心。我开了十几年的车，从来没出过车祸。

You can be worry-free when you're riding in my car. I have been driving for more than ten years and have never been in an accident.

2) 你出的主意怎么从来都没解决过一个问题？

How come the ideas that you came up with have never resolved a single problem?

2. 一般　　　　　usually

❖ 印度人一般都穿他们自己的服装。

The Indians usually wear their own (traditional) costumes.

1) 去饭馆吃饭很不方便，所以我们一般都在学校的食堂吃。

It's inconvenient to go to a restaurant, so we usually eat at the school's dinning hall.

2) 北京的老人一般喜欢在公园里锻炼身体。

Old folks in Beijing usually like to exercise in the parks.

[一般 can also appear before a noun to modify it. In such cases it means "the common," "the usual," and is usually translated as "most" or "most of the." For example:]

3) 一般的印度人都穿他们自己的服装。

Most Indians wear their own (traditional) costumes.

[When something is said to be 一般, it means it is ordinary or common. For example:]

4) 对印度人来说，他们的传统服装可能很一般，可是对我们来说，那种服装却很特别。

To Indians, their traditional costumes might seem very ordinary, but to us they are very unique.

3. **好像**　　　　　　　　**seem to be**

❖ 中国人在穿着上好像不太坚持自己的传统。

In terms of clothing, the Chinese do not seem to be too insistent on keeping with their traditions.

1）他今天不说话也不笑，好像不太高兴。

He isn't talking or smiling today. He seems to be unhappy.

2）美国人天天谈的、想的都是美国的事，好像世界上只有美国一个国家。

The things Americans talk and think about everyday consist only of matters related to America, as if it were the only country on earth.

4. **如果/要是…，(那)就…**　　　　　　**If …, then …**

❖ 如果为了坚持传统，每天穿着旗袍上课工作，那就太不方便了。

It would be too inconvenient if, for the sake of keeping with tradition, a woman wore a *qipao* to class or to work everyday.

[The "那" here means "in this/that case," referring to that which is mentioned after "如果/要是." It is optional.]

1）如果你能跟我一块儿去西安，那就太好了。

It will be great if you can go to Xi'an with me.

2）这件旗袍要是试穿以后觉得合身，我就买。

If, after trying it on, I think that this *qipao* fits me, I'll buy it.

5. **值得V.**　　　　　　**deserve to be V.; worth V-ing**

❖ 这样的传统是不值得坚持的。

Such a tradition is not worth keeping (lit. "insisting upon").

1）这是一本少有的好书，很值得看！

This is a good book that is rare to come by. It's really worth reading!

2）像他那样的人，不值得你对他那么好。

A person like him does not deserve such good treatment from you.

6. **接受**　　　　　　**to accept; to receive**

❖ 中国人在穿着上完全接受了西方的影响。

The Chinese completely follow the West's lead (lit. "accept the West's influence") in terms of clothing.

1) 你说的很有道理，我接受你的看法。

What you said makes good sense. I agree with you (lit. "accept your view").

2) 要是我们都能接受别人不同的看法，这个世界就好多了。

If we can all accept the different views of others, this world will be so much better.

7.　一般来说　　　　generally speaking

❖ 一般来说中国人都用筷子吃饭。

Generally speaking, the Chinese use chopsticks to eat.

["一般来说" is sometimes used as "一般说来."]

1) A：中国人从小就用筷子吗？

　 B：一般来说是这样的。

A: Do Chinese use chopsticks from an early age?

B: That's usually the case.

2) 我觉得中国人一般来说比美国人保守些。

I think Chinese are, generally speaking, more conservative than Americans.

3) 一般说来，文化交流的结果不会是一种文化取代另一种。

Generally speaking, culture interaction will not result in the replacement of one culture by another (lit. "the outcome of culture interaction will not be the replacement of one culture by another").

8.　V. 掉　　　　　　V. away

❖ 没什么理由把筷子淘汰掉。

There's no reason to abolish (the use of) chopsticks.

1) 你别再说话了，快把汤喝掉！

Don't talk anymore, finish up the soup fast!

2) A：糟了！汤里有只苍蝇！

　 B：快舀掉！别让人看到！

A: Oh my God! There's a fly in the soup!

B: Scoop it out fast! Don't let anyone see it!

9. ⋯，尤其是⋯　　　　　⋯, especially ...

❖ 这个我同意，尤其是喝汤的时候，大家都用汤勺儿在汤碗里舀来舀去，⋯⋯，看了让我恶心。

I agree with this point, especially when it comes to drinking soup --- everyone takes from the (same) soup bowl with their own spoon, ... it really disgusts me.

1) 从美国飞一趟北京真累，尤其是转机的时候，更是受不了。

Taking a plane from America to Beijing is really tiring, especially when you're changing flights --- it's even more unbearable.

2) 她看起来很像中国人，尤其是穿上了旗袍，简直和中国人完全一样！

She looks very much like a Chinese person, especially when she wears a *qipao* --- she looks exactly like one!

10. V. 来 V. 去　　　　　V. around; V. back and forth

❖ 用汤勺儿在汤碗里舀来舀去

Lit. "use the soup spoons to stir around in the soup bowl"

1) 你为什么一直在这儿走来走去？是不是在等人？

Why do you keep walking back and forth? Are you waiting for someone?

2) 他在书桌上找来找去，找了很久，还是没找到他的笔。

He searched all over the desk, but after searching for a long time, he still could not find his pen.

11. 简直　　　　　simply; at all

❖ 简直像在汤里洗筷子...

This is just like washing one's chopsticks in the soup ...

["简直" is used for exaggeration.]

1) 他怎么可以这样对他的父母？他简直不是人！

How could he treat his parents in this manner? He's simply inhuman!

2) 什么？你到现在还没把功课做完？你简直太糟了！

What? You still haven't finished your homework? You're really terrible!

61

12. 说明　　　to show; to illustrate; to explain

❖ 虽然这只是一件小事儿，但是却可以说明一个文化交流的现象。

Although it's only a trivial matter, it illustrates a phenomenon in (the process of) cultural exchanges.

1）他不接受新的看法说明他这个人比较保守。

His refusal to accept new ideas shows that he's quite conservative.

2）中国人到现在还在用筷子。这说明筷子很方便、很实用。

The Chinese continue to use chopsticks even today. This shows that chopsticks are convenient and useful.

13. 取代　　　to replace; to supersede

❖ 中西文化交流的时候，并不一定是西方的取代中国的，或者中国的取代西方的。

When Eastern and Western cultures interact, the West does not necessarily replace the East; nor does it have to be the other way around.

1）新的取代旧的、好的取代坏的，这是很自然的。

The new replaces the old, and the good replaces the bad. It is only natural.

2）清朝的改良做得不好，所以被民国取代了。

The Qing dynasty did not do well in its reforms, therefore it was replaced by the Republic of China.

14. 结果　　　result; outcome; consequence

❖ ……就像最近豆腐成了美国超级市场上一种日常食品，这就是中美文化交流的结果。

……such as bean curd: it became a daily food in the American supermarkets recently. This is exactly a result of Sino-American cultural exchanges.

1）你吃得多又不运动，发胖是很自然的结果。

You eat more than normal and do not exercise. Gaining weight is but a natural result.

2）A：你为什么要叫他骑自行车呢？他被车撞了，你知道吗？

B：我只是想让他省点钱，没想到会有这样的结果。

A: Why did you advise him to ride a bicycle? He was hit by a car, do you know that?

B: I was only thinking of helping him save a little money. I did not expect such an outcome.

练习

I.　Choose the correct answer.

(　　)1. 我是去北京学习的，所以带一两件_____就够了。
　　　　　　a. 穿着　　　b. 衣服　　　c. 服装

(　　)2. 昨天我请班上最漂亮的女生吃饭，她_____了，我真高兴。
　　　　　　a. 受到　　　b. 收到　　　c. 接受

(　　)3. 他什么事都觉得无所谓，可是_____工作_____却特别认真。
　　　　　　a. 以…来说　b. 在…上　　c. 对…来说

(　　)4. 那个人有点奇怪，总是_____。
　　　　　　a. 一边站，一边写功课
　　　　　　b. 站着写功课
　　　　　　c. 写功课站着

(　　)5. 不上大学也可以成功，也可以赚很多钱，Bill Gates 就是最好
　　　　的_____。
　　　　　　a. 例子　　　b. 结果　　　c. 理由

(　　)6. 你最好用公勺把汤_____到你的碗里，再用自己的勺儿喝，要不
　　　　然别人会觉得恶心。
　　　　　　a. 伸　　　　b. 夹　　　　c. 舀

II.　Choose the most appropriate word for each blank and fill in with its
　　　Chinese equivalent.

　　　　　infect　　quality　　fitting　　to insist on　　practical　　replace

1. 母亲在孩子心中的地位，是任何人都不能_____的。
2. 在医院里面不要走来走去，因为那样的地方比较容易_____病。
3. 他的父母不放心他一个人去中国，可是他_____要去。
4. 这些碗筷看起来是很漂亮，可是一点儿也不_____。

III.　Fill in the blank with the most appropriate word.

　　　行动、印象、合身、订做、坚持、竟然、耽误、

影响、当然、实用、淘汰、认为、如果、确定

我是一件很旧的旗袍，两百年前是为皇帝的太太＿＿＿＿＿＿的。我刚做好的时候既＿＿＿＿＿＿又漂亮，主人常常把我穿在身上，让所有见到她的人留下深刻的＿＿＿＿＿＿。而现在没有人愿意再看我一眼。我知道女人穿上了旗袍，工作、＿＿＿＿＿＿都不方便，容易＿＿＿＿＿＿事情。所以大家＿＿＿＿＿＿旗袍已经不＿＿＿＿＿＿了，可能不久以后，旗袍就会被＿＿＿＿＿掉。我想说的是，现代的中国人太容易受西方的＿＿＿＿＿＿，为了方便和实用可以不＿＿＿＿＿＿传统，＿＿＿＿＿＿有一天中国的传统都没有了，那么，我们要到哪里去找"中国"呢？

IV. Composition

作者批评中国人忘了传统，因为他们不再穿旗袍了。你觉得不穿旗袍能不能说明中国人不坚持传统？在实用和坚持传统有冲突 (chōngtū:conflict) 的时候，你会选择哪一个？为什么？

第五課

一次性產品

甲：北京的飯店旅館用的都是一次性的東西，真是又方便又衛生。

乙：我最討厭一次性的東西，不但質量差，而且也不見得衛生。上次去飯店，桌上的一雙竹筷子黑黑的，黏黏的，看了真惡心。後來服務員給換了一雙，但是一夾菜就斷了。這種一次性的筷子還不如傳統的筷子呢。

甲：我覺得大量使用一次性的產品還是一種進步。盡管目前有些產品質量太差，但是使用一次性產品的這個方向是對的。

乙：我不同意你的話。用一次性的產品其實是一種浪費。像中國這樣人口多、資源少的國家應該盡量回收資源，重復使用，而不是用一次就丟掉，這麼做不但浪費資源而且污染環境。你想全中國十幾億人口，如果每個人吃一頓飯就扔一雙筷子，一年下來得用掉多少竹子？

第五课

一次性产品

甲：北京的饭店旅馆用的都是一次性的东西，真是又方便又卫生。

乙：我最讨厌一次性的东西，不但质量差，而且也不见得卫生。上次去饭店，桌上的一双竹筷子黑黑的，黏黏的，看了真恶心。后来服务员给换了一双，但是一夹菜就断了。这种一次性的筷子还不如传统的筷子呢。

甲：我觉得大量使用一次性的产品还是一种进步，尽管目前有些产品质量太差，但是使用一次性产品的这个方向是对的。

乙：我不同意你的话。用一次性的产品其实是一种浪费。像中国这样人口多、资源少的国家应该尽量回收资源，重复使用，而不是用一次就丢掉，这么做不但浪费资源而且污染环境。你想全中国十几亿人口，如果每个人吃一顿饭就扔一双筷子，一年下来得用掉多少竹子？

甲：每一件事儿總是有好處也有壞處。難道一次性的產品就沒有一點儿好處嗎？

乙：好處當然有，就是方便。但是在我看來，以目前中國的經濟條件來説，大量使用一次性產品會造成許多資源的浪費和環境的污染。美國大概是世界上用一次性產品最多的一個國家。紙杯、紙盤、紙碗、紙巾，甚至於紙内褲，都是用一次就丢。而做紙的原料是樹木，現在已經有人爲了保護森林、保護環境，提倡少用一次性產品，尤其是造成污染最嚴重的塑料產品。

甲：是啊，最近北京電視上已經有勸大家少用塑料袋的廣告了。

乙：這眞是一大進步！但是我覺得在中國垃圾回收的工作做得還不夠，可回收和不可回收的垃圾常常混在一起。

甲：是的，在垃圾回收上，我們分類的工作做得還不夠，但是在中國有些人靠撿垃圾爲生，所以實際上造成的浪費並沒有你想像的那麼大。

乙：是的，我每次去風景區都看到有人在撿易拉罐儿或礦泉水的瓶子。我們應該感謝這些人爲保護環境所做的

甲：每一件事儿总是有好处也有坏处。难道一次性的产品
　　就没有一点儿好处吗？

乙：好处当然有，就是方便。但是在我看来，以目前中
　　国的经济条件来说，大量使用一次性产品会造成许多
　　资源的浪费和环境的污染。美国大概是世界上用一次
　　性产品最多的一个国家。纸杯、纸盘、纸碗、纸巾，
　　甚至于纸内裤，都是用一次就丢。而做纸的原料是树
　　木，现在已经有人为了保护森林、保护环境，提倡少
　　用一次性产品，尤其是造成污染最严重的塑料产品。

甲：是啊，最近北京电视上已经有劝大家少用塑料袋的
　　广告了。

乙：这真是一大进步！但是我觉得在中国垃圾回收的工
　　作做得还不够，可回收和不可回收的垃圾常常混在一
　　起。

甲：是的，在垃圾回收上，我们分类的工作做得还不
　　够，但是在中国有些人靠捡垃圾为生，所以实际上造
　　成的浪费并没有你想像的那么大。

乙：是的，我每次去风景区都看到有人在捡易拉罐儿或矿
　　泉水的瓶子。我们应该感谢这些人为保护环境所做的

工作。保護環境不只是爲了我們自己，也是爲了我們的下一代。

工作。保护环境不只是为了我们自己，也是为了我们的下一代。

词汇

一次性		yícì.xìng	adj. one-time
产品	產品	chǎnpǐn	n. product 一次性产品："one-time product" (disposable product)
饭店	飯店	fàndiàn	n. restaurant; hotel
讨厌	討厭	tǎo.yàn	v. to dislike, to loathe
质量	質量	zhìliàng	n. quality
差		chà	adj. poor, inferior
不见得	不見得	bùjiàn.dé	adv. not necessarily, not likely
双	雙	shuāng	MW: pair
竹		zhú	n. bamboo
黑		hēi	adj. black; dark
黏		nián	adj. sticky
服务员	服務員	fúwùyuán	n. waiter 服务：to serve; service 员：personnel
换	換	huàn	v. to change
断	斷	duàn	v. to break
不如		bùrú	v. to be unequal to, to be inferior to
大量		dàliàng	n. large quantity
使用		shǐyòng	v. to use, to employ
进步	進步	jìnbù	n. improvement, progress; v. (intr.) to advance, improve
尽管	盡管	jǐn'guǎn	conj. even though, despite

目前		mùqián	n. at present, at the moment
方向		fāngxiàng	n. direction
人口		rénkǒu	n. population
资源	資源	zīyuán	n. natural resources
少		shǎo	adj. few; little
回收		huíshōu	v. to reclaim, to retrieve; (here) to collect (used materials) for recycling 回：to return 收：to collect
重复	重復	chóngfù	v. to repeat
丢		diū	v. to discard
污染		wūrǎn	v. to pollute, to contaminate
环境	環境	huánjìng	n. environment
全		quán	adj. whole, entire
亿	億	yì	num. hundred million
扔		rēng	v. to throw away; to throw, to toss
好处	好處	hǎochù	n. advantage
坏处	壞處	huàichù	n. disadvantage
难道	難道	nándào	adv. could it be that … ? (used in a rhetorical question to make it more forceful)
经济	經濟	jīngjì	n. economy
条件	條件	tiáojiàn	n. condition, term; requirement, prerequisite
造成		zàochéng	v. to cause, to bring about (problems, or other undesirable

consequences)

世界		shìjiè	n. world 世界上：in the world
国家	國家	guójiā	n. country, nation
纸	紙	zhǐ	n. paper
杯		bēi	n. cup, glass
纸巾	紙巾	zhǐjīn	n. paper towel, tissue paper
甚至于	甚至於	shènzhìyú	conj. even, even to the point that, so much so that
内裤	內褲	nèikù	n. underpants, panties 内：inside 裤(=裤子)：pants
树木	樹木	shùmù	n. trees; wood
保护	保護	bǎohù	v. to protect
森林		sēnlín	n. forest
提倡		tíchàng	v. to advocate
塑料		sùliào	n. plastics
最近		zuìjìn	adv. recently, lately
电视	電視	diànshì	n. television
劝	勸	quàn	v. to urge, to persuade, to exhort
袋(子)		dài(.zi)	n. bag, sack 塑料袋：plastics bag 口袋：pocket
广告	廣告	guǎnggào	n. advertisement
垃圾		lājī	n. garbage

混		hùn	v. to mix
分类	分類	fēnlèi	v-o. to sort, to classify 分：to divide, to separate 类：kind, type, category
靠		kào	v. to rely on, to depend on
捡	撿	jiǎn	v. to pick up; to collect, to gather
生		shēng	n. livelihood
实际上	實際上	shíjì.shàng	in reality, in actual fact (= 事实上)
想像		xiǎngxiàng	v. to imagine
风景区	風景區	fēngjǐngqū	n. scenic spot 风景：scenery 区：area, region
易拉罐儿		yìlāguànr	n. pop-top, pull-top, flip-top
矿泉水	礦泉水	kuàngquǎnshuǐ	n. mineral water
瓶子		píng.zǐ	n. bottle
感谢	感謝	gǎnxiè	v. to thank, to be grateful
下一代		xià.yídài	n. the next generation 上一代：the previous generation

词语例句

1. 不见得　　　　**not necessarily; not likely**

❖ 我最讨厌一次性的东西，不但质量差，而且也不见得卫生。

I hate disposable things. They not only are of cheap quality, but aren't necessarily hygienic either.

["不见得" does not have a positive form, therefore, do not say "见得." It can be used similarly as "不一定."]

1) A：你不会念这个字，为什么不去问那个中国人呢？

B：他虽然是中国人，可是不见得就会念这个字！

A: Since you don't know how to pronounce this character, why don't you go and ask that Chinese person?

B: Even though he's Chinese, he doesn't necessarily know how to read this character!

2) A：旗袍穿起来那么不方便，谁会买呢？

B：那倒不见得！我就买了三件。

A: Wearing a *qipao* is so inconvenient. Who would buy anything like that?

B: That's not necessarily the case! I, for one, bought three.

2. A 不如 B　　　　**A cannot be compared to B; A is not as good as B**

❖ 这种一次性的筷子还不如传统的筷子呢。

Disposable chopsticks are not as good as traditional ones.

["不如" also does not have a positive form, so it is incorrect to say "A 如 B." To say that two things are equal or comparable, use "A 跟 B 一样."]

1) 这是一辆高档的自行车，可是骑起来还不如我那辆中档的快呢！

This is a top-quality bike, yet (when you ride on it) it doesn't go as fast as my mid-range bike.

2) 这家旅馆的服务不如那家好，我们走吧！

The service at this hotel is not as good as at the other one. Let's leave!

3. 尽管　　　　**even though; despite**

❖ 尽管目前有些产品质量太差，但是使用一次性产品的这个方向是对的。

Despite the bad quality of some current disposable products, the increasing use of these products is a right development.

1) 尽管那家饭馆的桌子、椅子都是黏黏的、黑黑的，我还是喜欢到那儿去吃东西。

Even though the tables and chairs in that restaurant are all dark and sticky, I still enjoy eating there.

2) 他常去看中国电影，尽管他听不懂。

He frequently went to see Chinese movies, even though he couldn't understand Chinese.

4. **Time duration + 下来**   **after + Time duration**

❖ 一年下来得用掉多少竹子？

How much bamboo will be used up in a year's time?

1) 你才来了一个星期就胖了三公斤，两个月下来还得了？

You have been here for only a week, yet you have gained three kilos. What's going to happen in two months?

2) 他说要体验中国人的生活，可是三天下来就受不了了。

He said he wanted to experience the Chinese way of life, but after just three days he couldn't take it anymore.

5. **难道······吗？**   **could it possibly be that … ?**

❖ 难道一次性的产品就没有一点儿好处吗？

Could it be possible that disposable products have no advantages at all?

1) 你每顿饭都用纸杯、纸盘，难道你不觉得浪费吗？

You use paper cups and plates at every meal. Don't you find it wasteful?

2) 汽车和空调都不能开，纸巾和塑料袋也都不能用，难道你要我们回到古代吗？

We shouldn't drive a car nor turn on the air-conditioning, and we shouldn't use paper towels or plastic bags too --- are you suggesting that we should go back to the ancient times?

6. **以······来说**   **based on …; speaking from …**

❖ 以目前中国的经济条件来说，大量使用一次性产品会造成许多资源的浪费和环境的污染。

With its present economic conditions, using disposable products on a large scale in China will cause a great waste of resources and create a lot of pollution.

1) 这种新产品是贵了点儿，但是以质量来说，却比旧的好多了。

This new type of product is indeed a bit too expensive, but its quality is much better than the old one (lit. "but in terms of quality, it's much better than the old one").

2) 以饮食来说，中国人好像很传统，但是以穿着来说，他们却完全接受了西方的影响。

Chinese seem very traditional in terms of food and drink, but when it comes to clothing, they completely follow the West's lead (lit. "they accept the Western influence completely").

7. 甚至(于)　　　even; even to the point that; so much so that

❖ 纸杯、纸盘、纸碗、纸巾，甚至于纸内裤，都是用一次就丢。

Paper cups, paper plates, paper bowls, paper towels, and even paper underpants are all disposed of after only one use.

1) 他什么东西都不扔，甚至空的矿泉水瓶子，他都收着。

He doesn't throw away anything. He will keep even an empty mineral water bottle.

2) 在这儿开车很危险，要是出车祸，不只伤得很重，甚至连命都可能没了！

It's very dangerous to drive here. If you get into an accident, you might not only be injured, but even lose your life!

8. 在……上　　　in terms of ...

❖ 在垃圾回收上，我们分类的工作做得还不够。

In our collection of garbage (lit. "in terms of garbage collection"), we have not done enough work in making classification (of the garbage collected).

1) 我们在纸张的使用上，应该尽量做到不浪费。

When we use paper we should try not to waste any of it.

2) 在环境保护的工作上，我们还得更进一步。

We should go a step further in our work for protection of the environment.

9. 靠……为生   **rely on … for living; do … for living**

❖ 在中国有些人靠捡垃圾为生。

In China there are some people who make a living by collecting garbage.

1) 他是靠开出租车为生的，所以对这儿的交通规则特别熟。

He drives a cab for living, so he knows the traffic regulations here very well.

2) 你天天都在学中文，难道以后想靠中文为生吗？

You study Chinese everyday. Are you thinking of using it to make a living in the future?

10.   实际上   **actually; in reality; in actual fact**

❖ ……所以实际上造成的浪费并没有你想像的那么大。

……so the amount of waste that is actually created is not as much as you have imagined.

1) 这些房子看起来很古老，实际上是去年才建的。

These houses look old, but actually they were only built last year.

2) 你以为大家都在担心环境的问题，实际上很多人都不知道这个问题有多严重。

You assume that everyone is worried about environmental problems, but in fact, many people do not know how serious they are.

练习

I.　Choose the correct answer.

(　　) 1. 我的中国朋友都＿＿＿＿＿我不要骑自行车上街。

　　　　a. 提倡　　　　　　b. 劝　　　　　　c. 同意

(　　) 2. 对不起，今天我＿＿＿＿＿，所以不能去上课了。

　　　　a. 感冒得很利害　　b. 有一个利害的感冒　　c. 有一个坏的感冒

(　　) 3. 塑料产品大多是不可回收的产品，所以污染环境最＿＿＿＿＿。

　　　　a. 严重　　　　　　b. 重要　　　　　　c. 严

(　　) 4. 我想，＿＿＿＿＿他现在的电脑水平＿＿＿＿＿，找到一个工作应该很容易。

　　　　a. 以...来说　　　b. 在...上　　　　c. 据...说

II.　Choose the most appropriate word for each blank and fill in with its Chinese equivalent.

repeat　　classify　　pollute　　advocate

next generation　　protect　　persist in　　mix

1. 很多外国人到了美国后努力地学英文，可是却要他们的＿＿＿＿＿尽量＿＿＿＿＿他们自己国家的传统。

2. 你丢垃圾以前，要记得把垃圾先＿＿＿＿＿，别把纸和易拉罐＿＿＿＿＿在一起。

3. 学一门外语的时候，所有的语言老师都＿＿＿＿＿学生大量练习，大量＿＿＿＿＿，这样才能学好外语。

III.　Choose the phrase that is closest in meaning to the underlined phrase in the sentence.

(　　) 1. 一次性产品就是用了一次就<u>丢</u>的东西。

　　　　a. 捡　　　b. 换　　　c. 扔

(　　) 2. 没有变化并<u>不见得</u>就是坚持传统最好的法子。

a. 不一定　　　b. 不必　　　c. 不得

(　　) 3. 朋友告诉我纽约的地铁<u>实际上</u>并不象他们说得那么危险。

a. 实在　　　b. 真的　　　c. 其实

(　　) 4. <u>在垃圾回收上</u>，中国的工作还做得很不够。

　　　　　　a. 在垃圾回收方面

　　　　　　b. 在垃圾回收方向

　　　　　　c. 在垃圾回收的上面

IV.　　Complete the following dialogue using the grammar structure given.

1. A：明明是他撞了你，为什么他不负责你的医疗费？

　 B：_____

　　　　　（尽管…，但是…）

2. A：_____

　　　　　（…，难道…吗？）

　 B：我不是不知道他住院了，只是没有时间去看他。

3. A：听说他在外国生活得不太好，是不是真的？

　 B：_____

　　　　 _____

　　　　　（靠…为生，甚至于）

V.　　Write a passage in response to the question.

1. 对中国来说，为什么使用一次性产品是一种进步，也是一种浪费？大量使用一次性产品会造成什么结果？（至少100字）

第六課

防盜和防火

甲：師傅，我一早起來想去校園裏跑跑步鍛煉鍛煉，可是大門鎖著，出不去。能不能換個鎖，讓宿舍裏面的人能出去，但是外面的人進不來？

乙：裏面的人出去了，萬一沒把門鎖上，外頭的人不是就能進來了嗎？我們是為了學生的安全才鎖門的。

甲：我覺得這樣鎖門不但不方便而且也不安全。

乙：鎖上門，外頭的人進不來了，怎麼會不安全呢？

甲：你們總以為只要外面的人進不來就安全了，可是你們沒想到裏面的人出不去才更危險。

乙：我們是晚上十二點以後才鎖門的，大家都睡覺了，為什麼還要出去呢？

甲：萬一失火了，門鎖著出不去，大家不是都燒死了嗎？

乙：失火？我在這個單位工作二十幾年了，從來沒失過火，可是偷東西的事兒卻常聽說。你覺得防火比防盜更重要嗎？

第六课

防盗和防火

甲：师傅，我一早起来想去校园里跑跑步锻炼锻炼，可是大门锁着，出不去。能不能换个锁，让宿舍里面的人能出去，但是外面的人进不来？

乙：里面的人出去了，万一没把门锁上，外头的人不是就能进来了吗？我们是为了学生的安全才锁门的。

甲：我觉得这样锁门不但不方便而且也不安全。

乙：锁上门，外头的人进不来了，怎么会不安全呢？

甲：你们总以为只要外面的人进不来就安全了，可是你们没想到里面的人出不去才更危险。

乙：我们是晚上十二点以后才锁门的，大家都睡觉了，为什么还要出去呢？

甲：万一失火了，门锁着出不去，大家不是都烧死了吗？

乙：失火？我在这个单位工作二十几年了，从来没失过火，可是偷东西的事儿却常听说。你觉得防火比防盗更重要吗？

甲：小偷固然應該防範，但是火災造成的傷害比偷竊嚴重得多，小偷頂多不過偷個照相機或偷點ㄦ現金，但是一旦失火，卻可能燒死幾十個甚至幾百個人，財產的損失更是遠遠超過偷竊了。

乙：失火你可能一輩子碰不到一次，可是小偷卻可能就在你的身邊ㄦ。我們鎖大門主要還是從防盜這一點著想。我們從來沒想過鎖門跟火災有什麼關係。不過，聽你這麼一說，好像也很有道理，我明天和領導匯報一下。

甲：小偷固然应该防范，但是火灾造成的伤害比偷窃严重得多，小偷顶多不过偷个照相机或偷点儿现金，但是一旦失火，却可能烧死几十个甚至几百个人，财产的损失更是远远超过偷窃了。

乙：失火你可能一辈子碰不到一次，可是小偷却可能就在你的身边儿。我们锁大门主要还是从防盗这一点着想。我们从来没想过锁门跟火灾有什么关系。不过，听你这么一说，好像也很有道理，我明天和领导汇报一下。

词汇

防盗		fángdào	v-o. to guard against theft
			防(＝防止 zhǐ)：to prevent
			盗(＝盗窃 qiè)：theft, burglary
防火		fánghuǒ	v-o. to prevent fires
			火：fire
校园	校園	xiàoyuán	n. campus
跑步		pǎobù	v-o. to jog (lit. "to run in steps")
			跑：to run
			步：step
大门	大門	dàmén	n. main entrance
			门：door
锁	鎖	suǒ	v. to lock (up); n. lock
让	讓	ràng	v. to allow
里面	裏面	lǐ.miàn	n. inside; interior
外面		wài.miàn	n. outside
外头	外頭	wài.tóu	＝外面
以为	以爲	yǐwéi	v. to think, believe or consider erroneously; to assume incorrectly
晚上		wǎn.shàng	TW: (in the) evening, (at) night
失火		shīhuǒ	v-o. to catch fire, to be on fire
烧	燒	shāo	v. to burn
死		sǐ	v. to die
单位	單位	dānwèi	n. work unit
偷		tōu	v. to steal

听说	聽説	tīngshuō	v. to hear that, heard of
重要		zhòngyào	adj. important
小偷儿		xiǎotōur	n. thief
固然		gùrán	conj. though of course, no doubt, admittedly
防范	防範	fángfàn	v. to be on guard, to keep a lookout
火灾	火災	huǒzāi	n. fire disaster
伤害	傷害	shānghài	v. to harm, to injure; n. harm
偷窃	偷竊	tōuqiè	n. stealing, theft
顶多	頂多	dǐngduō	adv. at (the) most
不过	不過	búguò	adv. merely, only
照相机	照相機	zhàoxiàngjī	n. camera
现金	現金	xiànjīn	n. cash
一旦		yídàn	conj. once, some time or other
甚至		shènzhì	conj. even (to the point of), so much so that
财产	財産	cáichǎn	n. property
损失	損失	sǔnshī	n. loss; v. to lose
超过	超過	chāoguò	v. to exceed, to surpass
一辈子	一輩子	yíbèi.zi	n. all one's life, a lifetime
碰		pèng	v. to encounter, to run into
主要		zhǔyào	adv. mainly
着想	著想	zhuóxiǎng	v. to give consideration to (the interests of sb. or sth.)

明天		míngtiān	n. tomorrow
领导	領導	lǐngdǎo	n. leader, leadership
汇报	匯報	huìbào	v. to report, to give an account of

词语例句

1. 为了⋯，才⋯　　　　　　**It's only for the sake of sb./sth. that one …**

❖ 我们是为了学生的安全才锁门的。

It was only for the sake of the students' safety that we locked the door.

1）他是为了到中国去做生意才开始学中文的。

He began learning Chinese in order to do business in China.

2）我刚到的时候常常坐出租车，后来为了省钱，才租了辆自行车。

I took cabs frequently when I first got here. Later, in order to save some money, I rented a bike.

2. 以为　　　　**to think, believe or consider erroneously; to assume incorrectly**

❖ 你们总以为只要外面的人进不来就安全了，可是你们没想到里面的人出不去才更危险。

You always assume that it will be safe as long as outsiders can't get in, but you overlook the fact that it's even more dangerous when people can't get out.

1）他看我的门锁着，以为我出去了，其实我还在睡大觉呢！

When he saw that my door was locked, he thought that I had gone out, but in fact I was still sleeping like a log!

2）你不要以为一定不会有问题，等真的出了事就太晚了。

Don't assume that nothing will go wrong. If something really does happen, it will be too late to do anything.

3. 听说　　　　　　**to hear that**

❖ 我在这个单位工作二十几年了，从来没失过火，可是偷东西的事儿却常听说。

I have worked in this unit for more than twenty years. There was never a fire, but we often heard that things were stolen.

1）A：我听说老李被车撞了，是真的吗？

B：没这样的事！你是听谁说的？

A：我是听老张说的。

A: I heard that old Li was hit by a car, is it true?

B: No! Who told you this? (lit. "who did you hear it from?")

A: I heard it from old Zhang.

4. 固然···，但是···　　　　it's true that …, but ….

❖ 小偷固然应该防范，但是火灾造成的伤害比偷窃严重得多。

There's no doubt that we should guard against thieves, but the damage caused by a fire is much more serious than that caused by stealing.

1) 传统固然重要，可是我们不应该为了坚持传统而不要进步。

It's true that tradition is very important, but we shouldn't give up progress merely for the sake of keeping with tradition.

2) 你说的固然比他说的有道理，但他是领导，我得听他的。

Undoubtedly what you said makes more sense (than what he said), but he's the supervisor, so I have to listen to him.

5. 顶多　　　　　　at (the) most

❖ 小偷顶多不过偷个照相机或偷点儿现金，但是一旦失火却可能烧死几十个甚至几百个人···。

At most a thief will steal a camera or a little cash, but once a fire breaks out, it might cost tens or even hundreds of lives.

1) 这辆自行车那么旧了，顶多能骑几个月，你还是买辆高档点的吧！

This bike is so worn out that it will last only a few more months at the most. I suggest you buy a better one!

2) 去趟西安顶多耽误一点儿功课，有什么好担心的呢？

Going to Xi'an will only hold up your studies a little bit. So what is there to worry about?

6. 不过　　　　　　merely; only

(see 5. for original sentence in text and trans.)

1) 我不过是指出了他的一个问题，他就受不了了。

I merely pointed out one of his problems, but he couldn't take it.

2) 不过一、两块钱的东西，丢了就丢了吧！

It's only worth a dollar or two. If it gets lost, let it be!

7. 一旦　　　　　　　　**once**

(See 5. for original sentence in text and trans.)

1) 你还是先把这些东西分好吧！一旦混起来了，想再分类，就难了。

It's better that you organize these things properly now. Once they're mixed up, it's hard to sort them again.

2) 人们总是喜欢新的东西而讨厌旧的。他们一旦看到新产品，就想把旧的换掉。

People always like new things and dislike old ones. Once they see a new product, they will want to replace the old one.

练习

I.   Choose the correct answer.

(   )1. 这件事情我不能自己决定，我得跟领导_____，再告诉你结
            果。

                a. 汇报汇报   b. 汇一下报   c. 汇汇报报

(   )2. 请最后一个离开实验室的人关灯，把门_____。

                a. 锁着   b. 锁   c. 锁上

(   )3. 他很聪明，也很努力，他_____有机会，就会成为一个有名
            的人。

                a. 万一   b. 一旦   c. 尽管

(   )4. 他真像个小孩子，我_____跟他开了个玩笑，他就生气了。

                a. 顶多   b. 最多   c. 不过

(   )5. 父母离婚的时候，常常是孩子受到最大的_____。

                a. 伤害   b. 伤   c. 损失

II.   Choose the most appropriate word for each blank and fill in with its
        Chinese equivalent.

            to assume incorrectly   simply   at least
            run into   even (to the extent of)   catch fire

1. 我_____他的英文很好，后来才知道他一点儿都不会说。

2. 他什么坏事都做，_____会伤害自己的朋友。

3. 昨天我在街上_____一个十年没见的朋友，我们谈得很高兴。

4. 你不应该把孩子锁在家里，万一_____，孩子会被烧死的。

III.　　Answer the question using the expressions given.

1. 你觉得防盗跟防火哪一个重要？

　　　　（远远、固然、顶多、甚至、碰到、一旦）

2. 为什么在中国学生的宿舍师傅晚上十二点以后要锁大门？

　　　　（为了…才、以为、只要、从…着想、跟…有关系）

第七課
我不給乞丐錢

甲：今天下午我從西單購物中心出來的時候被一群小乞丐給圍住了。其中一個扯住了我的裙子，你瞧，好好的一條裙子給弄成這樣！我很生氣，一毛錢都沒給他們。

乙：你怎麼一點儿同情心都沒有呢？他們也是別人的孩子啊！他們出來做乞丐也是不得已啊！

甲：我覺得給乞丐錢就是鼓勵他們不勞而獲。不工作的人沒飯吃是公平的，也是應該的。你所謂的"同情心"不但解決不了他們的生活問題，而且還會養成他們懶惰和依靠別人的習慣，所以在我看來，給乞丐錢不但不是幫他們的忙，反而是害了他們。

乙：找不到工作並不一定是他們懶，而是社會制度不合理，貧富不均。有錢的人越來越有錢，窮的人越來越窮。所以有些人成了乞丐，並不是不努力，而是社會的過錯。

第七课
我不给乞丐钱

甲：今天下午我从西单购物中心出来的时候被一群小乞丐给围住了。其中一个扯住了我的裙子，你瞧，好好的一条裙子给弄成这样！我很生气，一毛钱都没给他们。

乙：你怎么一点儿同情心都没有呢？他们也是别人的孩子啊！他们出来做乞丐也是不得已啊！

甲：我觉得给乞丐钱就是鼓励他们不劳而获。不工作的人没饭吃是公平的，也是应该的。你所谓的"同情心"不但解决不了他们的生活问题，而且还会养成他们懒惰和依靠别人的习惯，所以在我看来，给乞丐钱不但不是帮他们的忙，反而是害了他们。

乙：找不到工作并不一定是他们懒，而是社会制度不合理，贫富不均。有钱的人越来越有钱，穷的人越来越穷。所以有些人成了乞丐，并不是不努力，而是社会的过错。

甲：把個人失敗的責任推給社會，這是最不負責任的態度，任何一個社會都免不了有競爭。只要有競爭就免不了有人失敗，我們不能把失敗者的生活變成成功者的負擔。這種表面上看來充滿同情心的作法其實是阻礙社會發展的。

乙：你說的也不是完全沒有道理。

甲：從前在辦公室裏努力工作的人和天天喝茶看報的人都拿一樣的工資。那樣的制度合理嗎？凡是覺得競爭不合理的人都是失敗的人，一個有能力又努力的人是不會害怕競爭的。

乙：如果人人都像你這樣對窮人沒有一點儿同情，這個社會一定會變得非常殘酷。

甲：進步是有代價的，如果因為有了乞丐有了無家可歸的人就懷疑改革開放的方向，那麼我們就只有永遠在大鍋飯的制度下過著喝稀飯吃饅頭的日子。

甲：把个人失败的责任推给社会，这是最不负责任的态度，任何一个社会都免不了有竞争。只要有竞争就免不了有人失败，我们不能把失败者的生活变成成功者的负担。这种表面上看来充满同情心的作法其实是阻碍社会发展的。

乙：你说的也不是完全没有道理。

甲：从前在办公室里努力工作的人和天天喝茶看报的人都拿一样的工资。那样的制度合理吗？凡是觉得竞争不合理的人都是失败的人，一个有能力又努力的人是不会害怕竞争的。

乙：如果人人都像你这样对穷人没有一点儿同情，这个社会一定会变得非常残酷。

甲：进步是有代价的，如果因为有了乞丐有了无家可归的人就怀疑改革开放的方向，那么我们就只有永远在大锅饭的制度下过着喝稀饭吃馒头的日子。

词汇

乞丐		qǐgài	n. beggar
西单购物中心	西單購物中心	Xīdān gòuwù zhōngxīn	n. Xi'dan shopping center
群		qún	MW: group; flock; swarm
围住	圍住	wéizhù	v. to surround; to enclose
扯住	扯住	chězhù	v. to pull
裙子		qún.zi	n. skirt
瞧		qiáo	v. to look at, to see
好好的		hǎohāo.de	adj. good
条	條	tiáo	MW for long, narrow things
弄		nòng	v. to make
毛		máo	MW: a dime; 1/10th yuan
同情心		tóngqíngxīn	n. sympathy, compassion
不得已		bùdéyǐ	v. to have no alternative
鼓励	鼓勵	gǔlì	v. to encourage
不劳而获	不勞而獲	bù láo ér huò	v. to reap without sowing
公平		gōngpíng	adj. fair
所谓	所謂	suǒwèi	adj. so-called
解决	解決	jiějué	v. to solve, to resolve
解决不了	解決不了	jiějuébùliǎo	v. not able to solve
养成	養成	yǎngchéng	v. to form, to cultivate (habit)

懒惰		lǎnduò	adj. lazy, indolent
依靠		yīkào	v. to rely on
习惯	習慣	xíguàn	n. habit
害		hài	v. to harm, to injure
懒		lǎn	adj. lazy
社会制度	社會制度	shèhuìzhìdù	n. social system
合理		hélǐ	adj. reasonable, equitable
贫富不均	貧富不均	pínfùbùjūn	great difference in wealth between the rich and the poor
努力		nǔlì	v./adj. to work hard; to make great effort
过错	過錯	guòcuò	n. fault, mistake
个人	個人	gèrén	n. individual (person)
失败	失敗	shībài	v. to fail, to lose
责任	責任	zérèn	n. responsibility, blame
推		tuī	v. to shift, to defuse
负责任	負責任	fùzérèn	adj. responsible
态度	態度	tài.dù	n. attitude
任何		rènhé	adj. any, whatever
免不了	免不了	miǎn.buliǎo	adj. inevitable, unavoidable
竞争	競爭	jìngzhēng	n./v. competition, to compete
只要		zhǐyào	conj. so long as; provided that
. . . 者		. . . zhě	suf. one who . . .

成功		chénggōng	v./n. to succeed; success
负担	負擔	fùdān	n. burden
表面上		biǎomiàn.shàng	adv. on the surface, in name only
看来		kànlái	adv. it looks, it appears, it looks as if
充满		chóngmǎn	v. to be full of
做法		zuò.fǎ	n. way of doing or making a thing, a method of work, practice
阻碍	阻礙	zǔài	v. to hinder, to impede
有道理		yǒudào.lǐ	v. to make sense
从前	從前	cóngqián	n. in the past, formerly
办公室	辦公室	bàn'gōngshì	n. office
喝茶		hēchá	v-o. to drink tea
看报	看報	kànbào	v-o. to read newspaper
拿		ná	v. to receive
工资	工資	gōngzī	n. wages, pay
凡是		fánshì	conj. all, any
能力		nénglì	n. ability
害怕		hàipà	v. to fear
残酷	殘酷	cánkù	adj. cruel
代价	代價	dàijià	n. price
无家可归	無家可歸	wújiākěguī	v. to be homeless, to wander about without a home to

			go back
怀疑	懷疑	huáiyí	v. to suspect, to doubt
改革开放	改革開放	gǎigékāifàng	n. "the reform and open up" policy that began in 1979
方向		fāngxiàng	n. direction
永远	永遠	yǒngyuǎn	adv. forever
大锅饭	大鍋飯	dàguōfàn	n. "big pot rice" --- a metaphor for life in China before the reform --- everyone ate the same kind and amount of food from the same big pot
稀饭	稀飯	xīfàn	n. rice gruel, congee
馒头	饅頭	mán.tóu	n. steamed bun

词语例句

1. **给**
- 今天下午我从西单购物中心出来的时候被一群小乞丐给围住了。

  This afternoon when I came out from the Xi'dan shopping center, I was surrounded by a group of young beggers.

["给" is used in a passive sentence to introduce either the doer of the action or the action itself if the doer is not mentioned.]

1) 后来我才发现我给小贩骗了。

  It was only until later I found out that I was cheated by the vender.

2) 那个小偷刚要偷东西的时候就给抓住了。

  The thief was caught just as he was about to steal something.

2. **弄**　　　　**to make**
- 你瞧‧好好的一条裙子给弄成这样。

  See, a fine skirt ended up like this (lit. "made to become like this")!

1) 小心别把衣服弄脏了。

  Be careful, don't get your clothes dirty.

2) 他的话真的把我弄糊涂了。

  What he said really confuses me (lit. "makes me confused").

3. **不得已**　　　　**to have no alternative**
- ……他们出来做乞丐也是不得已啊。

  …… they became beggars only because they have no choice.

1) 我不得已才请了几天假。

  I had no choice but to ask for a few days' leave.

2) 请你原谅她吧‧她这么做也是不得已的。

  Please forgive her, she did it because she had no choice.

4. **不是…，而是…**　　　　**it's not ……., but …….**
- 找不到工作不一定是他们懒‧而是社会制度不合理。

It may not be because they are lazy that they can't find a job, but because the social system is unjust.

1) 有些人很成功并不是因为他们很努力，而是因为他们依靠父母。

Some people were very successful not because they worked hard but because they depended on their parents.

2) 对他来说，最大的痛苦不是没有钱、没有朋友，而是没有书看。

To him, the greatest suffering is not to have no money or no friend, but having no book to read.

5. 免不了　　　　inevitable; unavoidable

❖ ……任何一个社会都免不了有竞争。

……. competition is inevitable in every society.

1) 考试考得不好免不了让他很难过。

It is inevitable that he feels sad when he did not do well in the examination (lit. "Not doing well in the examination inevitably makes him sad").

2) 刚到外国，免不了有点儿不习惯。

One will inevitably find it a little difficult to adapt when he first goes abroad.

6. 凡是…都…　　　　all; any

❖ 凡是觉得竞争不合理的人都是失败的人……。

Anyone who finds competition unreasonable is a loser…….

1) 凡是到了十八岁的人，都有选举权。

Everyone who has reached the age of 18 has the right to vote.

2) 你搬家的时候，凡是你不要的东西，都留给我。

Leave anything that you don't want to me when you move.

练习

I.   Make a sentence using the underlined expression(s).

1. 我觉得给乞丐钱<u>就是鼓励</u>他们<u>不劳而获</u>。

2. <u>在我看来</u>，给乞丐钱<u>不但不</u>是帮了他们的忙，<u>反而</u>是害了他们。

3. 有些人成了乞丐，<u>并不是</u>不努力，<u>而是</u>社会的<u>过错</u>。

4. 把个人失败的责任推给社会，<u>这是最不负责任的态度</u>。

5. <u>任何</u>一个社会<u>都免不了</u>有竞争。

6. 这种<u>表面上</u>看来充满了同情心的作法<u>其实</u>是阻碍社会发展的。

7. <u>如果人人都象你这样</u>对穷人没有一点同情，这个社会<u>一定会</u>变得非常残酷。

II.   Choose the most appropriate word or expression for each blank and fill in with its Chinese equivalent.

        to have no alternative   not able to solve   to rely on

        reasonable   to be responsible for   inevitable/unavoidable

        to hinder   to be full of   to doubt

1. 你应该去找工作，不能总是_____父母的钱过日子。

2. 每一种社会制度都_____有不合理的地方。

3. 我们不能为了保持传统而_____社会的进步。

4. 他是_____才偷东西的，你再给他一次机会吧！

5. 大家都知道这件事是_____的，所以没有人愿意_____。

6. 我_____这种新产品质量有问题，因为只用了一次就坏了！

III.   Complete the following dialogues with expressions provided.

1. A: 你不愿意上最好的大学，是不是害怕竞争啊？

    B: _____。

        （不是……，而是……）

2. A: 大锅饭的制度让每个人都有饭吃，这不是很合理吗？

   B: _____ 。

        （表面上......，其实......）

3. A: _____ 。

        （凡是......都......）

   B: 我不同意。一次性的产品也有质量很好的。

IV.   Answer the questions using the words given.

1. 你在街上看到乞丐会不会给他们钱？为什么？你同意不同意给乞丐钱是鼓励他们不劳而获的说法？

（养成、习惯、公平、依靠、懒、过错、同情、残酷）

2. 美国有没有贫富不均的问题？你认为造成这个问题的原因是什么？政府可以用什么方法来解决这个问题？

（竞争、失败、责任、合理、制度、鼓励、工资、发展、改革）

3. 竞争是不是一定是残酷的？你对竞争的态度是什么？在竞争中成功的人有没有责任帮助失败的人？比方说，有钱的人对穷人有没有责任？

（怀疑、永远、有能力、阻碍、方向、变成、负担、代价、推给）

第八課

打官司

甲：美國人眞是世界上最喜歡打官司的人。

乙：這話怎麼説呢？

甲：我昨天在報上看到有個人在麥當勞買了一杯咖啡，因爲咖啡太燙，燙傷了手，於是她就告麥當勞，麥當勞還賠了她好幾十萬美元呢。這在中國是不可思議的。

乙：是啊，在美國什麼事儿都可以告到法院去。從一杯咖啡到人權，從交通事故到國家大事都可以告。政府可以告老百姓，老百姓也可以告政府；單位可以告個人，個人也可以告單位。像那個人告麥當勞，這種事儿是常有的，一點儿也不稀奇。

甲：美國這麼多人打官司，律師的生意一定很好咯？

乙：你説的一點儿都不錯，律師是美國最賺錢的職業之一。出了車禍得找律師，買賣房子得找律師，離婚得找律師，甚至於立遺囑還得找律師，美國人一生之中，從生到死都得跟律師打交道。

第八课

打官司

甲：美国人真是世界上最喜欢打官司的人。

乙：这话怎么说呢？

甲：我昨天在报上看到有个人在麦当劳买了一杯咖啡，因为咖啡太烫，烫伤了手，于是她就告麦当劳，麦当劳还赔了她好几十万美元呢。这在中国是不可思议的。

乙：是啊，在美国什么事儿都可以告到法院去。从一杯咖啡到人权，从交通事故到国家大事都可以告。政府可以告老百姓，老百姓也可以告政府；单位可以告个人，个人也可以告单位。像那个人告麦当劳，这种事儿是常有的，一点儿也不稀奇。

甲：美国这么多人打官司，律师的生意一定很好咯？

乙：你说的一点儿都不错，律师是美国最赚钱的职业之一。出了车祸得找律师，买卖房子得找律师，离婚得找律师，甚至于立遗嘱还得找律师，美国人一生之中，从生到死都得跟律师打交道。

甲：律師在中國還是個比較新的行業，過去兩個人有了
爭執，常常是找單位領導來解決問題，除非不得已是
不打官司的。中國人自古就不提倡打官司。

乙：美國人喜歡打官司，表示美國是個法治的社會，大
家對司法制度有信心，相信打官司可以得到公平合理
的解決。最近幾年因為侵害知識產權的案子大量增
加，律師的生意就更好了。

甲：拿現在跟改革開放以前比較，中國人打官司也在增
加，老百姓漸漸學著由法律制度來解決互相的爭執。
有些人擔心這種打官司的風氣會影響到社會的和諧，
我倒不擔心。

乙：我覺得老百姓開始打官司是件好事兒，中國幾千年來
都是人治，現在也漸漸走上了法治的道路，所以打官
司就成了不可避免的事兒了，而律師也成了一個重要
的行業了。

甲：律师在中国还是个比较新的行业，过去两个人有了争执，常常是找单位领导来解决问题，除非不得已是不打官司的。中国人自古就不提倡打官司。

乙：美国人喜欢打官司，表示美国是个法治的社会，大家对司法制度有信心，相信打官司可以得到公平合理的解决。最近几年因为侵害知识产权的案子大量增加，律师的生意就更好了。

甲：拿现在跟改革开放以前比较，中国人打官司也在增加，老百姓渐渐学着由法律制度来解决互相的争执。有些人担心这种打官司的风气会影响到社会的和谐，我倒不担心。

乙：我觉得老百姓开始打官司是件好事儿，中国几千年来都是人治，现在也渐渐走上了法治的道路，所以打官司就成了不可避免的事儿了，而律师也成了一个重要的行业了。

词汇

打官司		dǎguān.sī	v. to go to court
			官司: n. lawsuit
麦当劳	麥當勞	Màidānglāo	n. McDonald's
咖啡		kāfēi	n. coffee
烫	燙	tàng	v./adj. to burn, to scald; boiling hot
于是	於是	yú.shì	conj. consequently, as a result
告		gào	v. to sue, to go to law against
赔	賠	péi	v. to compensate, to pay for
好几	好幾	hǎojǐ	adj. quite a few
不可思议	不可思議	bù kě sī yì	Idiom: unimaginable, inconceivable
法院		fǎyuàn	n. court
人权	人權	rénquán	n. human rights
交通		jiāotōng	n. traffic
事故		shìgù	n. accident
大事		dàshì	n. a great event, a major important matter
老百姓		lǎobǎixìng	n. common people, civilians
单位	單位	dānwèi	n. work unit
个人	個人	gèrén	n. individual (person)
稀奇		xīqí	adj. rare, strange, unusual and seldom seen
律师		lǜshī	n. lawyer

生意		shēng.yì	n. business
咯		.lo	part. for showing obviousness
职业	職業	zhíyè	n. occupation
...之一		... zhīyī	one of .....
出车祸	出車禍	chūchēhuò	v-o. to get into a car accident
离婚	離婚	líhūn	v-o. to get a divorce
甚至于	甚至於	shènzhìyú	adv. even, so much so that
立		lì	v. to set up, (here) to write up
遗嘱	遺囑	yízhǔ	n. will
一生		yìshēng	n. all one's life
打交道		dǎjiāodào	v. to make contact with, to have dealing with
行业	行業	hángyè	n. profession
争执	爭執	zhēng.zhí	v./n. to dispute, to stick to one's guns; dispute
领导	領導	lǐngdǎo	n. leader
解决	解決	jiějué	n./v. solution, settlement; to solve, to settle (a problem)
除非		chúfēi	conj. only if, unless
不得已		bù.de.yǐ	v. to have no alternative
自古		zìgǔ	n. since ancient time
提倡		tíchàng	v. to advocate, to encourage
表示		biǎoshì	v. to show, to indicate
法治		fǎzhì	n. rule and order; rule of law

司法		sīfǎ	adj. judicial
制度		zhìdù	n. system
有信心		yǒuxìnxīn	adj. to be confident of
得到		dédào	v. to gain, to get
公平		gōngpíng	adj. fair, just, impartial
合理		hélǐ	adj. reasonable
侵害		qīnhài	v. to infringe upon
知识产权	知識產權	zhī.shíchǎnquán	n. intellectual property right
案子	案子	àn.zǐ	n. (law) case
大量		dàliàng	n. large quantity
比较	比較	bǐjiào	adv./v. fairly; to compare
渐渐	漸漸	jiànjiàn	adv. gradually
学着	學著	xué.zhe	v. to learn to
由		yóu	prep. by; through
风气	風氣	fēngqì	n. common practice
和谐	和諧	héxié	adj. harmonious
人治		rénzhì	n. rule of people (in contrast to "法治")
不可避免	不可避免	bùkěbìmiǎn	adj. inevitable, unavoidable

词语例句

1. **打官司**　　　　　**to go to law; to go to court**

❖ 美国人真是世界上最喜欢打官司的人。

Americans like to take matters to court more than anyone else in the world.

1）这位律师去年帮人打赢了六场官司。

This lawyer won six lawsuits for his clients last year.

2）他最近正在跟一家出版社打官司，因为他们没有得到他的同意，就出版了他的一本书。

He has been suing a publishing house recently because they published one of his books without his permission.

2. **告**　　　　**to sue; to take (sb.) to court**

❖ ……于是她就告麦当劳。

…… therefore she sued McDonald's.

1）我的邻居威胁我说，要是我不把狗拴起来，他就去告我。

My neighbor threatened to sue me if I didn't keep my dog tied up.

2）这个老人因为儿子不养他，把儿子告到法院。

Because his son didn't support him, the old man took his son to court.

3. **找**　　　　**to call on (sb.); to seek (the help of sb.)**

❖ 出了车祸得找律师，买卖房子得找律师，离婚得找律师，甚至于立遗嘱还得找律师……。

You have to find a lawyer if you get into a car accident, or if you want to buy or sell a house, or to get a divorce; you'll need a lawyer even to write up a will …..

1）你最好找朋友帮忙。

You'd better call on your friends to help you.

2）过去中国人有了争执，常常找领导来解决问题。

In the past, Chinese people usually sort out their supervisors for resolution when they had conflicts with each other.

4. 除非　　　　　　　**only if; unless**

❖ （中国人）除非不得已是不打官司的。

(Chinese people) would not go to court unless they had no choice.

1）除非她先道歉，否则我不道歉。

I won't apologize unless she apologizes first.

2）他一般不会迟到，除非他没有赶上汽车。

Unless he misses the bus, he's usually not late.

5. 不得已　　　　　　**to have no alternative**

❖ 中国人除非不得已是不打官司的。(see 4. for trans.)

1）我是不得已才骗你的。

It was only because I had no choice that I cheated you.

[see lesson 7 for more examples.]

6. 拿A跟B比较　　　　　　**to compare A with B**

❖ 拿现在跟改革开放以前比较，中国人打官司也在增加……。

Comparing the present with the time before the "reform and opening-up," Chinese people who go to court are increasing ……

1）拿这个跟那个比较，你就知道哪个好了。

Compare this with that, and you will see which one is better.

2）要是你总拿自己的长处跟别人的短处比较，你是永远不会进步的。

You won't make any progress if you are always comparing your strengths with others' weak points.

练习

I.   Choose the most appropriate word for each blank and fill in with its
     Chinese equivalent.

> to sue   to write up   to compensate   rare   a will
>
> to compare   to mimic/to learn to   look down upon

1. 你把我的车撞坏了，要是你不 _____ 我，我就去法院 _____ 你。
2. 他过去不喝咖啡，到了美国以后也开始 _____ 喝咖啡了。
3. 这位老人在死以前，_____ 了一份 _____，把所有的钱都给了一所
   大学。
4. A：你听说了吗？那个女人已经三十岁了，还没有结婚，真 _____ 。
   B：这没什么嘛！在美国一辈子没结婚的人也有的是。
   A：但是，你不能拿中国跟美国 _____ ，在中国要是一个女人不结
   婚，她会面临很多压力的，会被别人 _____ 的。

II.   Choose the correct answer.

1. 由于知识产权的问题，这两家公司一直在【打官司；告】。
2. 我对这个律师没有什么【相信；信心】，因为我听说他输了很多次。
3. 为了停车，他们两个人【发生了争执；有了一个争执】。

III.   Make a sentence using the underlined expression.

1. 麦当劳因为他的咖啡烫伤了顾客的手，而赔顾客钱，这在中国是
   不可思议的。
2. 象那个人告麦当劳，这种事是常有的，一点也不稀奇。
3. 律师是美国最赚钱的职业之一。
4. 中国几千年来都是人治，现在也渐渐走上了法治的道路，所以打
   官司就成了不可避免的事儿了。
5. 中国自古就不提倡打官司，所以除非不得已是不打官司的。

第九課

電子郵件

甲：自從電子郵件廣泛使用以後，人們的交流和信息的傳遞有了很大的改變，現在差不多沒人寫信了。

乙：是啊，以前我一星期至少得給家裏寫一封信，現在發個電子郵件比寫封信容易多了。寫信得買信紙、信封ᵣ、郵票，不但貴而且慢。電子郵件又便宜又快，在學校裏用電腦還是免費的呢。

甲：可是，我覺得電子郵件和信還是有些不同，收到信拿在手上慢慢ᵣ地看，一次一次地看，看完了還可以留起來。收到電子郵件就沒有這麼真實的感覺了。

乙：你真是太落伍了！收到電子郵件一樣可以用打印機把它印出來，這跟信有什麼不同呢？

甲：這個道理我知道，但是那種感覺還是有點ᵣ不同。

乙：這只是一個習慣的問題。二十一世紀的孩子除了電子郵件，根本不知道還有別的寫信的法子。他們收到電子郵件的時候肯定跟你收到信是一樣的感覺。

甲：你說的有道理。

第九课

电子邮件

甲：自从电子邮件广泛使用以后，人们的交流和信息的传递有了很大的改变，现在差不多没人写信了。

乙：是啊，以前我一星期至少得给家里写一封信，现在发个电子邮件比写封信容易多了。写信得买信纸、信封儿、邮票，不但贵而且慢。电子邮件又便宜又快，在学校里用电脑还是免费的呢。

甲：可是，我觉得电子邮件和信还是有些不同，收到信拿在手上慢慢儿地看，一次一次地看，看完了还可以留起来。收到电子邮件就没有这么真实的感觉了。

乙：你真是太落伍了！收到电子邮件一样可以用打印机把它印出来，这跟信有什么不同呢？

甲：这个道理我知道，但是那种感觉还是有点儿不同。

乙：这只是一个习惯的问题。二十一世纪的孩子除了电子邮件，根本不知道还有别的写信的法子。他们收到电子邮件的时候肯定跟你收到信是一样的感觉。

甲：你说的有道理。

乙：過去幾年，對我們日常生活影響最大的除了電子郵件以外，就是互聯網。有了互聯網，你不必出門就能知道天下事了。

甲：從前中國人常拿 " 不出門，知天下事 " 來形容一個最聰明的人，其實現在只要有個電腦，上網一看，任何人都能做到 " 不出門，知天下事 "。

乙：科技的進步使許多以前認爲不可能的事都變得可能了。科技使我們縮短了距離，增加了速度，因此也改進了生活。

乙：電子郵件成了我們生活中不可少的一個東西。我愛 " 伊妹兒 " ！

乙：过去几年，对我们日常生活影响最大的除了电子邮件以外，就是互联网。有了互联网，你不必出门就能知道天下事了。

甲：从前中国人常拿"不出门，知天下事"来形容一个最聪明的人，其实现在只要有个电脑，上网一看，任何人都能做到"不出门，知天下事"。

乙：科技的进步使许多以前认为不可能的事都变得可能了。科技使我们缩短了距离，增加了速度，因此也改进了生活。

乙：电子邮件成了我们生活中不可少的一个东西。我爱"伊妹儿"！

词汇

电子邮件	電子郵件	diàn.zǐyóujiàn	n. electronic mail 电子 : electronic 邮件 : mail, postal items
自从	自從	zìcóng	prep. since, ever since
广泛	廣泛	guǎngfàn	adj. extensive, wide-ranging
信息		xìnxī	n. information, news
传递	傳遞	chuándì	v. to transmit, to deliver, to transfer
改变	改變	gǎibiàn	v. to change, to transform; (here) n. change, transformation
差不多		chà.bùduō	adv. almost
信		xìn	n. letter
至少		zhìshǎo	adv. at least
封		fēng	MW for letters
发	發	fā	v. to send out
信纸	信紙	xìnzhǐ	n. letter paper
邮票	郵票	yóupiào	n. stamp
电脑	電腦	diànnǎo	n. computer
免费	免費	miǎnfèi	adj. free of charge
收		shōu	v. to receive
拿		ná	v. to hold, to take
留		liú	v. to keep, to reserve
真实	眞實	zhēnshí	adj. true, real, authentic

感觉	感覺	gǎnjué	n. feeling
落伍		luòwǔ	adj. out of date, behind the times 落：to drop out 伍：rank
打印机	打印機	dǎyìnjī	n. printer
印		yìn	v. to print
点	點	diǎn	MW: a bit, a little (= 一点儿)
习惯	習慣	xíguàn	n. habit
世纪	世紀	shìjì	n. century
孩子		hái.zǐ	n. child
根本		gēnběn	adv. at all, simply
肯定		kěndìng	adv. definitely, surely
互联网	互聯網	Hùliánwǎng	n. Internet 网：net
出门	出門	chūmén	v-o. to go out 出：to exit 门：door
天下事		tiānxiàshì	n. things in the world 天下：under the heaven 事：matters "不出门，知天下事" is abbreviated from the common saying "秀才不出门，能知天下事." "秀才"[xiùcái]，candidates who passed the lowest level examination in the traditional Chinese civil service system, refers to an educated person here.
形容		xíngróng	v. to describe
上网	上網	shàngwǎng	v-o. to get on or log on to the Internet 网＝互联网
科技		kējì	n. science and technology

使		shǐ	v. to make, enable, to cause
缩短	縮短	suōduǎn	v. to shorten
增加		zēngjiā	v. to increase
速度		sù.dù	n. speed, pace
改进	改進	gǎijìn	v. to improve
成		chéng	v. to become
爱	愛	ài	v. to love
伊妹儿		yīmèir	n. email (transliteration)

词语例句

1. **自从…以后** **since … ; ever since …**

❖ 自从电子邮件广泛使用以后，人们的交流和信息的传递有了很大的改变。

Ever since electronic mail was first extensively used, there has been a great change in the way people communicate and pass information.

1）他自从在车祸中把腿撞断了以后，就很少出门了。

Ever since he broke his leg in an accident, he has seldom gone out.

2）自从有了一次性的筷子以后，一般的饭馆儿都不用传统的筷子了。

Ever since disposable chopsticks came into use, most restaurants have stopped using traditional chopsticks.

2. **至少** **at least**

❖ 以前我一星期至少得给家里写一封信。

In the past I would write at least one letter to my family every week.

1）定做一件旗袍，至少得要三、四百块钱吧！

It should cost you at least three or four dollars to get a tailor-made *qipao*.

2）他住院了，你不去看他，至少也应该给他打个电话啊。

He has been hospitalized, so even if you're not going to visit him, you should at least give him a call.

3. **根本** **at all; simply**

❖ 二十一世纪的孩子除了电子邮件，根本不知道还有别的写信的法子。

Children of the 21st century simply do not know that there are other ways to write letters besides email.

1）他说他是学中国古代建筑的，但他其实根本不懂建筑。

He claimed that he majored in ancient Chinese architecture, but in fact he knows nothing at all about architecture.

2）A：你为什么没问过我就拿了我的信？

B：我根本没去过你的房间，怎么可能拿了你的信呢？

A: Why did you take away my letter without asking me?

B: I didn't even go in your room; how could I have possibly taken your letter?

4. 肯定   **definitely; surely**

❖ 他们收到电子邮件的时候肯定跟你收到信是一样的感觉。

When they receive emails, they definitely feel the same way as you do when you receive letters.

1) 只有他来过我的房间，所以我的信肯定是被他拿走的。

He's the only one who has been into my room, so he must have taken my letter (lit. "my letter must have been taken away by him").

2) 现在什么都电脑化了，不会用电脑的人肯定会被社会淘汰掉。

Nowadays everything is computerized. Those who do not know how to use a computer will surely lag behind others (lit. "be kicked out by the society").

5. 除了…以外，就是…   **other than/besides …, there's …**

❖ 对我们日常生活影响最大的除了电子邮件以外，就是互联网。

Other than email, the Internet has had the greatest influence on our daily lives.

1) 现在的孩子除了看电视以外，就是对着电脑。

Besides watching television, what kids nowadays do is sit in front of the computer.

2) 一次性产品的好处除了卫生一点儿以外，就是方便。

The advantage of disposable products is that, besides being a little more hygienic, they are so convenient.

6. 拿 A 来形容 B   **use A to describe B**

❖ 从前中国人常拿"不出门，知天下事"来形容一个最聪明的人。

In the past, Chinese often used the phrase " he who knows the world under heavens without stepping out of the house" to describe the smartest person.

[The "拿" here can be replaced by "用."]

1) 你怎么可以用电脑来形容人脑呢？一个会想，另一个可不会啊！

How can you use a computer to describe a human brain? One can think, but the other can't!

2）我不知道应该拿什么来形容我现在的感觉。

I do not know how to (lit. "what to use to") describe my feeling right now.

7. **A 使 B 变得…**　　　　　　**A makes B (change to be) …**

❖ 科技的进步使许多以前认为不可能的事变得可能了。

Improvements in science and technology have made possible things that were thought to be impossible in the past.

1）使用电脑可以使一些很困难的事变得简单了。

Using computer can make some difficult tasks easier.

2）穿旗袍不见得会使一个女人变得更好看。

Wearing a *qipao* does not necessarily make a woman look better.

练习

I.   Choose the correct answer.

(   ) 1. _____朋友的信的时候，我常常马上回信，可是如果是父母的信，就等几天再给他们回信。

　　　　a. 接受　　　　　　b. 收到　　　　　　c. 受到

(   ) 2. 政府提倡我们不要把用过的塑料袋扔掉，要留_____，以后再用。

　　　　a. 起来　　　　　　b. 出来　　　　　　c. 进来

(   ) 3. 他以前很努力，上了大学以后_____很懒，做什么事都只想不劳而获。

　　　　a. 变成　　　　　　b. 变了　　　　　　c. 变得

II.   Choose the most appropriate word for each blank and fill in with its Chinese equivalent.

extensive/wide-ranging　　　free　　　describe　　　change

get on to the Internet　　　mainly　　　behind the times　　　transmit

1. 据说，美国的高中学生每天花大量的时间_____，_____是跟朋友聊天或者做一些没有意义的事情。

2. 为了让更多的人用自己的产品，有的电脑公司常常为顾客提供_____的服务。

3. 中国人用"脱了裤子放屁"来_____做了多余的事情。

4. 最近二十年来，尤其是改革开放以后，美国和中国在政治上、经济上、文化上 都有了_____的交流。

5. 认为孩子越多，父母越有福气的想法早就_____了。

III. Answer the question using the expressions given.

1. 科技进步真的缩短人们之间的距离了吗？请以飞机、电视、电子邮件等例子来说明。

（改进、改变、增加、速度、影响、落伍、日常生活、广泛、交流、信息）

2. 要是你有想告诉一个人你心里很喜欢他，你会写信给他，还是发电子邮件给他？为什么？

（封、信纸、信封儿、邮票、感觉、真实、留起来、打印、不必）

IV.　　Composition

1. 我和电子邮件

2. 我们还需要更多新的科技产品吗？

第十課

鮮花插在牛糞上

甲：最近在中國老夫少妻的婚姻越來越普遍了，我們家
　　隔壁的那對夫婦，男的比女的大二十幾歲！

乙：大二十幾歲！這哪ㄦ像夫婦啊！簡直是父女嘛。我真
　　不懂這麼年輕漂亮的小姐為什麼要嫁給一個又老又醜
　　的老頭ㄦ。真是鮮花插在牛糞上！

甲：我看他們生活得很幸福，一點ㄦ問題也沒有。那個男
　　的雖然年紀大一點ㄦ，但是學問好，收入高，對妻子
　　又體貼。在我看來，是很理想的一對ㄦ。

乙：剛結婚的時候往往看不出老夫少妻的問題來，但是
　　十年二十年以後他們的問題就會變得很嚴重了。

甲：怎麼說呢？

乙：十年二十年以後，男的在體力上會顯著地不如女
　　的，而且就常識來說，男人的平均壽命比女人的短，
　　所以年輕妻子守寡的可能就很高。

甲：現在是二十一世紀的新中國，妻子死了，丈夫可以
　　再娶；丈夫死了，妻子也可以再嫁。在我父母那個時

第十课
鲜花插在牛粪上

甲：最近在中国老夫少妻的婚姻越来越普遍了，我们家隔壁的那对夫妇，男的比女的大二十几岁！

乙：大二十几岁！这哪儿像夫妇啊！简直是父女嘛。我真不懂这么年轻漂亮的小姐为什么要嫁给一个又老又丑的老头儿。真是鲜花插在牛粪上！

甲：我看他们生活得很幸福，一点儿问题也没有。那个男的虽然年纪大一点儿，但是学问好，收入高，对妻子又体贴。在我看来，是很理想的一对儿。

乙：刚结婚的时候往往看不出老夫少妻的问题来，但是十年二十年以后他们的问题就会变得很严重了。

甲：怎么说呢？

乙：十年二十年以后，男的在体力上会显著地不如女的，而且就常识来说，男人的平均寿命比女人的短，所以年轻妻子守寡的可能就很高。

甲：现在是二十一世纪的新中国，妻子死了，丈夫可以再娶；丈夫死了，妻子也可以再嫁。在我父母那个时

代，再嫁的女人是讓人看不起的，現在可沒這個問題
了。

乙：對老夫少妻的婚姻我常常懷疑夫妻之間是不是眞的
有愛情。我覺得一個年輕女人嫁給一個老頭儿，往往
是爲了他的地位和財富，女的並不是眞愛男的。

甲：這個我不同意。婚姻完全是一件個人的事儿。要嫁
誰，要娶誰，都只是他們兩個人的事儿。兩人之間有
沒有愛情，只有他們自己知道。

乙：你見過一個漂亮的女人嫁給一個又老又醜又窮又沒
有地位的男人嗎？

甲：這個……這個……我一時想不出一個例子來。

乙：所以我說一個男人年齡大不大不要緊，只要他有錢
有地位，就能娶到年輕漂亮的女人。

甲：你這樣說，對女人是不公平的。即使一個女人爲了
錢爲了地位而嫁給一個比她大十幾二十幾歲的男人，
那也是她自己的選擇。再說男人也有爲了金錢和地位
而跟一個比自己年長的女人結婚的。我希望不但有"
老夫少妻"，也有"老妻少夫"。這樣才能顯出這個

代，再嫁的女人是让人看不起的，现在可没这个问题了。

乙：对老夫少妻的婚姻我常常怀疑夫妻之间是不是真的有爱情。我觉得一个年轻女人嫁给一个老头儿，往往是为了他的地位和财富，女的并不是真爱男的。

甲：这个我不同意。婚姻完全是一件个人的事儿。要嫁谁，要娶谁，都只是他们两个人的事儿。两人之间有没有爱情，只有他们自己知道。

乙：你见过一个漂亮的女人嫁给一个又老又丑又穷又没有地位的男人吗？

甲：这个……这个……我一时想不出一个例子来。

乙：所以我说一个男人年龄大不大不要紧，只要他有钱有地位，就能娶到年轻漂亮的女人。

甲：你这样说，对女人是不公平的。即使一个女人为了钱为了地位而嫁给一个比她大十几二十几岁的男人，那也是她自己的选择。再说男人也有为了金钱和地位而跟一个比自己年长的女人结婚的。我希望不但有"老夫少妻"，也有"老妻少夫"。这样才能显出这个

社會確實開放了，選擇增加了。"老夫少妻"也好，

"老妻少夫"也好，這都是他們自己的事儿，別人是

沒有權利干涉的。

社会确实开放了，选择增加了。"老夫少妻"也好，"老妻少夫"也好，这都是他们自己的事儿，别人是没有权利干涉的。

词汇

鲜花		xiānhuā	n. fresh flower
插		chā	v. to stick in, to insert
牛粪	牛糞	niúfèn	n. cow dung
鲜花插在牛粪上		xiānhuā chā zài niúfèn .shàng	Idiom: "fresh flower sticking in cow dung" --- what a waste!
老夫少妻		lǎofūshàoqī	n. old husband and young wife 夫妻：husband and wife
婚姻		hūnyīn	n. marriage
普遍		pǔbiàn	adj. common; prevalent
隔壁		gébì	n. next door
夫妇	夫婦	fūfù	=夫妻
男		nán	n. man; male
女		nǔ	n. woman; female
父女		fùnǔ	n. father and daughter 父=父亲 女=女儿
嘛		ma	part. Indicates that sth is obvious
年轻	年輕	niánqīng	adj. young
小姐		xiǎo.jiě	n. young (unmarried) lady
嫁		jià	v. (of women) to marry
丑	醜	chǒu	adj. ugly
老头儿	老頭儿	lǎotóur	n. old man; old chap
生活		shēnghuó	v. to live

幸福		xìngfú	adj. happy, fortunate; felicity
年纪	年紀	niánjì	n. age
学问	學問	xuéwèn	n. knowledge
收入		shōurù	n. income, earnings
高		gāo	adj. high
妻子		qī.zǐ	n. wife
体贴	體貼	tǐtiē	v. to show consideration for, to give every care to
理想		lǐxiǎng	adj. ideal
对儿	對儿	duìr	MW: couple; pair
结婚	結婚	jiéhūn	v-o. to get married
往往		wǎngwǎng	adv. more often than not, often, frequently
变	變	biàn	v. to become different, to change
体力	體力	tǐlì	n. physical strength
显著	顯著	xiǎnzhù	adj. notable, obvious
常识	常識	chángshí	n. common knowledge
男人		nánrén	n. men
平均		píngjūn	adj. average
寿命	壽命	shòumìng	n. life span
女人		nǚrén	n. women
短		duǎn	adj. short (in length, duration, height)
守寡		shǒuguǎ	v-o. to remain a widow, to live in

			widowhood
丈夫		zhàng.fū	n. husband
娶		qǔ	v. (of men) to marry, to take (a wife)
父母		fùmǔ	n. parents 父=父亲 母=母亲
时代	時代	shídài	n. times, age, era
看不起		kàn.bùqǐ	v. to look down on 看得起：to think highly of
怀疑	懷疑	huáiyí	v. to suspect, to doubt
爱情	愛情	àiqíng	n. romantic love
地位		dìwèi	n. (social) status
财富	財富	cáifù	n. wealth
件		jiàn	MW for matters in general
个人	個人	gèrén	n. individual
穷	窮	qióng	adj. (financially) poor
一时	一時	yìshí	adv. for the moment
例子		lì.zǐ	n. example, case, instance
年龄	年齡	niánlíng	=年纪
不要紧	不要緊	bú yàojǐn	It doesn't matter, never mind (= 没关系)
公平		gōngpíng	adj. fair; just
即使		jíshǐ	conj. even, even if, even though
选择	選擇	xuǎnzé	n. choice

年长	年長	niánzhǎng	adj. older
显出	顯出	xiǎnchū	v. to show; to reveal
社会	社會	shèhuì	n. society
确实	確實	quèshí	adv. indeed; really
开放	開放	kāifàng	v. to open up (to the outside world)
权利	權利	quánlì	n. right
干涉		gānshè	v. to interfere, to intervene, to meddle

词语例句

1. 在 Sb. 看来   In sb.'s view

❖ 在我看来，是很理想的一对儿。

In my view, it's a perfect match.

1) 在你看来，这件事很简单，可是在他看来，却困难得很。

To you this is a very simple matter, but to him it couldn't be more difficult.

2) 在美国人看来，言论自由是最基本的人权。

The way Americans see it, freedom of speech is the most basic rights of men.

2. 往往   tend to be

❖ 刚结婚的时候往往看不出老夫少妻的问题来。

It's always hard to see the problem of an "old husband and young wife" marriage at the beginning.

["往往" expresses a tendency or likelihood. Another example that appears later in the text is:]

❖ 我觉得一个年轻女人嫁给一个老头儿，往往是为了他的地位和财富，女的并不是真爱男的。

I think that when a young woman marries an old man, more often than not she's only going after his status and wealth. The woman doesn't really love the man.

1) 对一门课没有兴趣，往往就学不好。

If you're not interested in a subject, you tend not to learn it well.

2) 现代化的东西方便是方便，可是往往会造成很大的浪费。

Modern things are convenient, but they usually cause a lot of waste.

3. V. 不出 Obj. 来   unable to V-O

❖ 看不出老夫少妻的问题来 (see 2. for trans.)

1) 我太紧张了，所以想不出答案来。

I'm too nervous, so I can't think of an answer (lit. "can't think out an answer").

2) 他难过得说不出话来。

He feels so bad that he can't even speak (lit. "cannot speak out a word").

4. 在…上　　　　in terms of …

❖ 十年二十年以后，男的在体力上会显著的不如女的。

After ten or twenty years, (since the man will be in his old age by then,) he will obviously be incomparable to his (young) wife in terms of physical strength.

1) 他在学习上比我努力多了。

He works harder in his studies than I do.

2) 他的婚姻生活很幸福，可是在工作上却有许多问题。

His marriage life is wonderful, but he has many problems at work.

[see also lesson 5 for other examples]

5. 就…来说　　　　based solely on …; speaking solely of …

❖ …就常识来说，男人的平均寿命比女人的短。

…by common knowledge we know that a man's average life span is shorter than a woman's.

1) 就交通来说，住在纽约是很方便的。

If you're speaking solely in terms of transportation, living in New York is very convenient.

2) 就收入来说，老李的比老张的高，可是就学问来说，老李却不如老张。

Based solely on his income, you could say that old Li is much wealthier than old Zhang, but in terms of knowledge, old Li cannot be compared with old Zhang.

6. A 和 B 之间　　　　between A and B

❖ 对老夫少妻的婚姻我常常怀疑夫妻之间是不是真的有爱情。

When I see an "old husband and young wife" marriage, I often wonder if there is really love between the couple.

[Another example that appears later in the text is:]

❖ 两人之间有没有爱情，只有他们自己知道。

Only they themselves know if there is love between them.

1）父母和孩子之间有不能说的话吗？

Are there things that cannot be said between parents and their children?

2）中国人和美国人之间的不同不是一个对和错的问题。

The difference between a Chinese person and an American is not a matter of right or wrong.

7. 一时　　　　at the moment

❖ 我一时想不出一个例子来。

I can`t think of an example at the moment.

1）我脑子很乱，一时还不知道怎么办。

My mind is in a mess, so for now I still don't know what to do.

2）他听到坏消息，一时难过，居然哭了起来。

Upon hearing the bad news, he was momentarily overcome by grief and actually began to cry.

8. 即使…，也…　　　　even if …

❖ 即使一个女人为了钱为了地位而嫁给一个比她大十几二十几岁的男人，那也是她自己的选择。

Even if a woman marries a man ten or twenty years older than her for the sake of money and status, it`s still her own choice.

1）他即使变得又老又丑又穷，我也会爱他！

Even if he becomes old, ugly and poor, I'll still love him!

2）即使你跟他结了婚，也不一定会幸福。

Even if you marry him, you (still) might not be happy.

9. 再说　　　　moreover; furthermore

❖ 再说男人也有为了金钱和地位而跟一个比自己年长的女人结婚的。

Moreover there are also men who marry older women for their money and status.

1）你应该结婚了。你有了工作，女朋友又那么好，再说，你年纪也不小了。

It's time you get married. You have a job, and your girlfriend is great, and what's more, you are no longer young.

2）我工作太忙，钱又不多，再说对出国也没兴趣，所以不跟你们去中国了。

I am too busy with my work and do not have much money; furthermore, I'm not interested in going abroad, so I won't go with you to China.

10. 为了…而…   **do sth. for the sake of …**

❖ 为了金钱和地位而跟一个比自己年长的女人结婚。(see 9. for trans.)

1）你会为了爱情而死吗？

Would you die for love?

2）有的父母为了让孩子上好的学校而搬家。

Some parents move (to another place) so that their children can go to a good school.

11. 显出   **to show**

❖ 这样才能显出这个社会确实开放了，选择增加了。

Only by then can we show that our society has really opened up, and we have more choices.

1）你得多体贴你的女朋友才能显出你爱她。

You have to care more for your girlfriend in order to show that you love her.

2）她听了我说的话，显出怀疑的样子。

She had suspicion written on her face after hearing what I said.

练习

I.　　Make a sentence using the underlined expression(s).

1. 这<u>哪儿</u>像夫妇啊，这<u>简直</u>是父女嘛。

2. <u>在</u>我父母的<u>时代</u>，再嫁的女人是<u>让人看不起</u>的。

3. <u>即使</u>一个女人为了钱为了地位而嫁给一个比她大二十几岁的男人，<u>也</u>是自己的选择。

4. 李小姐<u>为了</u>地位<u>而</u>嫁给一个比她大二十几岁的男人。

5. <u>就</u>常识<u>来说</u>，男人的平均寿命比女人短，所以年轻妻子守寡的可能就很高。

II.　　Choose the most appropriate word for each blank and fill in with its Chinese equivalent.

　　　to show/reveal　　　to look down on　　　notable/obvious
　　　to interfere　　　for the moment　　　to give every care to

1. 因为怕被别人_____，他不敢告诉别人他很穷。

2. 这次的考试，他有_____的进步。

3. 她希望她的丈夫能对她_____一点。

4. 我当然认识她，不过_____想不起来她的名字。

5. 那是他们自己的事，你最好不要_____。

III.　　Answer the question using the expressions given.

1. 一般的人对老夫少妻的态度是什么？

(怀疑、地位、往往、公平、财富、真正、年轻、丑、看不起、爱情、

婚姻）

2. 你最好的朋友跟一个又老又丑又没有钱的人认识了一个月，就决定嫁给他。你想劝她再考虑考虑。你会怎么说呢？

(幸福、"鲜花插在牛粪上"、年纪、学问、体贴、理想、严重、体力、寿命、守寡、再嫁、选择)

IV.　Composition:

1. 老夫少妻这样的婚姻可能会有哪些问题？你对这种婚姻的态度是什么？你会不会跟一个比自己年纪大很多或者小很多的人结婚呢？为什么？

2. 为什么"老妻少夫"的婚姻比"老夫少妻"的婚姻少呢？请谈谈你的看法。

第十一課

總統有了女朋友

甲：最近電視上報紙上，天天都報導美國總統有女朋友的事ㄦ。有人覺得美國人真丟臉，怎麼選了一個人品這麼差的總統。

乙：我一點ㄦ也不覺得丟臉，我覺得這是美國人最值得驕傲的地方。這說明美國有非常完備的法律制度，任何人都受到法律的保護，也受到法律的制裁，即使總統也不例外。我想全世界也許只有美國能把這樣的醜聞宣布出來。我們覺得任何貪污腐化都得公布出來。公布出來是制裁貪污腐化最有效的辦法。有些國家的報紙和電視上看不到任何貪污腐化的新聞，那才是最黑暗的。

甲：這個我同意。但是我覺得美國人有點ㄦ小題大作，有沒有女朋友是總統個人的事ㄦ，這跟他是不是一個好總統沒有關係。要是總統夫人不管這件事ㄦ，沒有任何人可以管這件事ㄦ。可是在美國，好像什麼人都可以過問總統個人的事情。有一回我在電視上看到一個

第十一课

总统有了女朋友

甲：最近电视上报纸上，天天都报导美国总统有女朋友
的事儿。有人觉得美国人真丢脸，怎么选了一个人品
这么差的总统。

乙：我一点儿也不觉得丢脸，我觉得这是美国人最值得
骄傲的地方。这说明美国有非常完备的法律制度，任
何人都受到法律的保护，也受到法律的制裁，即使总
统也不例外。我想全世界也许只有美国能把这样的丑
闻宣布出来。我们觉得任何贪污腐化都得公布出来。
公布出来是制裁贪污腐化最有效的办法。有些国家的
报纸和电视上看不到任何贪污腐化的新闻，那才是最
黑暗的。

甲：这个我同意。但是我觉得美国人有点儿小题大作，有
没有女朋友是总统个人的事儿，这跟他是不是一个好
总统没有关系。要是总统夫人不管这件事儿，没有任
何人可以管这件事儿。可是在美国，好像什么人都可
以过问总统个人的事情。有一回我在电视上看到一个

記者，當著許多外國元首的面問總統：" 你到底跟那個女人發生過關係沒有？" 我覺得這未免太讓總統下不了台了。美國人在這件事情上，好像最關心的是總統跟這個女人睡過覺沒有，至於他是不是一個能幹的總統反而不是一個話題。美國人不是最重視個人的隱私權嗎？這件事儿，在我看來，總統的隱私權受到了很大的侵害。

乙：我們一方面強調個人的隱私權，但另一方面更強調政治領袖得誠實。其實大部分美國人也並不在乎總統有沒有女朋友，這是總統個人的事儿，但是他說謊就不對了。我們不能要一個不誠實的總統。

甲：其實，哪個人不說謊啊？我也不覺得美國人對誠實的要求特別高。我看，總統有女朋友的事儿其實還是政治鬥爭。

乙：政治鬥爭肯定是有的，但是新聞單位也起了大作用。美國的新聞單位是監督政府最嚴密的組織，他們恨不得每天都找到政府貪污腐化的地方，這樣他們的銷路和收視率才會提高。但是也正因為他們監督得那麼嚴，所以政府不至於太腐化。

记者，当着许多外国元首的面问总统："你到底跟那个女人发生过关系没有？"我觉得这未免太让总统下不了台了。美国人在这件事情上，好像最关心的是总统跟这个女人睡过觉没有，至于他是不是一个能干的总统反而不是一个话题。美国人不是最重视个人的隐私权吗？这件事儿，在我看来，总统的隐私权受到了很大的侵害。

乙：我们一方面强调个人的隐私权，但另一方面更强调政治领袖得诚实。其实大部分美国人也并不在乎总统有没有女朋友，这是总统个人的事儿，但是他说谎就不对了。我们不能要一个不诚实的总统。

甲：其实，哪个人不说谎啊？我也不觉得美国人对诚实的要求特别高。我看，总统有女朋友的事儿其实还是政治斗争。

乙：政治斗争肯定是有的，但是新闻单位也起了大作用。美国的新闻单位是监督政府最严密的组织，他们恨不得每天都找到政府贪污腐化的地方，这样他们的销路和收视率才会提高。但是也正因为他们监督得那么严，所以政府不至于太腐化。

甲：要是克林頓這一次還能競選總統，你會不會投他的票？

乙：我肯定再投他的票！與其選一個喜歡打仗的總統，不如選一個喜歡談戀愛的總統。

甲：要是克林顿这一次还能竞选总统，你会不会投他的票？

乙：我肯定再投他的票！与其选一个喜欢打仗的总统，不如选一个喜欢谈恋爱的总统。

词汇

总统	總統	zǒngtǒng	n. president
女朋友		nǚpéng.yǒu	n. girlfriend
报纸	報紙	bàozhǐ	n. newspaper
报导	報導	bàodào	v. to report
丢脸	丢臉	diūliǎn	v-o. to lose face, to be disgraced 丢：to lose 脸：face
人品		rén.pǐn	n. moral standing, moral quality, character
骄傲	驕傲	jiāoào	v. to be proud, to take pride in
完备	完備	wánbèi	adj. complete, perfect
法律		fǎlǜ	n. law
制度		zhìdù	n. system
任何		rènhé	adj. any, whatever, whatsoever
制裁		zhìcái	n. sanction, punishment
例外		lìwài	adj. to be an exception
丑闻	醜聞	chǒuwén	n. scandal 丑：ugly; disgraceful, shameful 闻：news, story
宣布		xuānbù	v. to announce; to declare
贪污	貪污	tānwū	v. to embezzle, to practice graft
腐化		fǔhuà	v. to become corrupt
公布		gōngbù	v. to make public, to announce, to promulgate

有效		yǒuxiào	adj. effective
办法	辦法	bànfǎ	n. way, means
新闻	新聞	xīnwén	n. news
黑暗		hēiàn	adj. dark
小题大做	小題大做	xiǎotídàzuò	make a big fuss over a trifle, make a mountain out of a molehill
夫人		fū.rén	n. Lady, Madame, Mrs. 总统夫人：The First Lady
过问	過問	guòwèn	v. to make inquiry about, to concern oneself with, to take an interest in
事情		shì.qíng	n. matter, affair, business
回		huí	MW for occurrences (= 次)
记者	記者	jìzhě	v. reporter, journalist
当面	當面	dāngmiàn	adv. in one's presence, face to face 当着 sb. 的面：in the presence of sb.
元首		yuánshǒu	n. head of state
发生	發生	fāshēng	v. to occur, to happen, to take place
关系	關係	guān.xì	n. relation; (here) sexual relations 发生关系：(here) to have sexual relations (with sb.)
下不了台		xià.bùliǎo tái	to be unable to get out of a predicament or an embarrassing situation 下台：to step down from the platform or stage

睡觉	睡覺	shuìjiào	v-o. to sleep; (here) to have sexual relations (with sb.)
至于	至於	zhìyú	prep. as for
能干	能幹	nénggàn	adj. capable, able, competent
反而		fǎn'ér	adv. on the contrary
话题	話題	huàtí	n. topic of conversation
重视	重視	zhòngshì	v. to take sth. seriously, to value
隐私	隱私	yǐnsī	n. privacy
权	權	quán	n. right 隐私权：the right to keep one's privacy
侵害		qīnhài	v. to encroach upon, to infringe upon
强调	強調	qiángdiào	v. to emphasize, to stress
政治		zhèngzhì	n. politics
领袖	領袖	lǐngxiù	n. leader
诚实	誠實	chéngshí	adj. honest
大部分		dàbù.fèn	adj. most of, a great part of, majority
在乎		zài.hū	v. to care about, to mind
说谎	說謊	shuōhuǎng	v-o. to tell a lie
要求		yāoqiú	n. request, demand, requirement
斗争	鬥爭	dòuzhēng	n. struggle
作用		zuòyòng	n. effect; function
监督	監督	jiāndū	v. to keep watch on and to

			supervise
严密	嚴密	yánmì	adj. closely-knit, tight
组织	組織	zǔzhī	n. organization
恨不得		hèn.bùdé	adv. one wishes one could, one would if one could, be dying to
销路	銷路	xiāolù	n. sales
收视率	收視率	shōushìlǜ	n. (of television programs) the rate of being viewed
提高		tígāo	v. to raise, to increase, to heighten
严	嚴	yán	adj. strict
不至于	不至於	bú zhìyú	adv. cannot or be unlikely to go so far as to
克林顿	克林頓	Kèlíndùn	(Bill) Clinton
竞选	競選	jìngxuǎn	v. to run for (office)
投票		tóupiào	v-o. to cast a vote, to vote
与其	與其	yǔqí	conj. rather than
打仗		dǎzhàng	v-o. to fight a battle, to go to war
不如		bùrú	conj. it would be better to
谈恋爱	談戀愛	tán liànài	v-o. to be in love 谈 : to talk about 恋爱 : romantic love

词语例句

1. 当着sb. 的面　　　　　**in the presence of sb.**

❖ 有一回我在电视上看到一个记者，当着许多外国元首的面问总统…。

Once I saw a journalist on television. He asked the President in front of many foreign political leaders …

1）他当着我的面什么都不说，在别人面前却批评我。

He didn't say anything in front of me, but he criticized me in front of someone else.

2）当着那么多老师的面，我怎么好意思走掉呢？

How can I bring myself to walk away in the presence of so many teachers?

2. 至于　　　　　　　**as for**

❖ 美国人在这件事情上，好像最关心的是总统跟这个女人睡过觉没有，至于他是不是一个能干的总统反而不是一个话题。

It seems that what Americans care most in this matter is whether the President has slept with this woman; as for whether he's a capable president, that is, on the contrary, not an issue.

1）我觉得北京的吃和住都很不错，至于交通，却让我受不了。

I think the food and accommodations in Beijing are both quite good. As for the traffic there, I find it unbearable.

2）只要她很能干、负责就行了，至于人品怎么样，我们不必管。

It's fine as long as she is capable and responsible. As for her personality, we don't need to be concerned about that.

3. 反而　　　　　　**on the contrary**

(see 2. for original sentence in text and trans.)

1）我给他出了个好主意，可是他不但不感谢我，反而说我侵害了他的隐私。

I came up with a good idea for him, but he was not only ungrateful (to me), he even went on to say that, on the contrary, I have infringed upon his privacy.

2) 我们天天都在提倡用电脑，但电脑到底有没有改善我们的生活，我们反而不管。

Everyday we promote the use of computers, but (contradictorily) we do not care if they have really improved our lives.

4. 强调　　　　　　to emphasize; to stress

❖ 我们一方面强调个人的隐私权，但另一方面更强调政治领袖得诚实。

On one hand we emphasize the rights of an individual to his privacy, but on the other hand, we stress even more the honesty of a political leader.

1) 我再强调一次：我跟这件事儿一点儿关系都没有。

Let me stress this again: I have absolutely nothing to do with this matter.

2) 一个社会要是太强调法律也会有坏处。

If a society over-emphasizes the law, it will also cause harm.

5. 在乎　　　　　　to care about; to mind

❖ 其实大部分美国人也并不在乎总统有没有女朋友...。

In fact, most Americans don't care if the President has a girlfriend or not...

1) 你不必太在乎他说的话，他还是个小孩儿。

Don't take what he said too hard; he's just a kid.

2) 她很在乎别人对她的看法，所以活得特别累。

She cares a lot about what people think of her, so she makes life hard for herself (lit. "so living is especially tiring for her").

6. 对…的要求　　　　　what one asks of …

❖ 我也不觉得美国人对诚实的要求特别高。

I don't think Americans set a very high standard for honesty.

1) 我对生活的要求很简单，只要有饭吃、有地方住就可以了。

What I ask of life is very simple. As long as I have food and lodging, that's enough.

2) 对别人不要有太高的要求，对自己却要严些。

Don't ask too much of others, but be more strict to yourself.

7. 起作用/不起作用　　　**have effect/ have no effect**

❖ 政治斗争肯定是有的，但是新闻单位也起了大作用。

Political struggles definitely do exist, but the media has also played a large part (lit. "created great effect").

1）据说这种药（yào: medicine）很有效，但我吃了两个星期，怎么还不起作用呢？

This medicine is said to be very effective, but I've taken it for two weeks — why hasn't it taken effect?

2）无论我跟他说什么都起不了作用，他还是坚持自己的看法。

No matter what I say (to him), I cannot influence him (lit. "have no effect on him); he still insists on his own views.

8. 恨不得　　　**one wishes one could; be dying to**

❖ 他们每天都恨不得找到政府贪污腐化的地方。

Each day, they hope to find evidences of embezzlement and corruption by the government.

1）我真受不了那么冷的天气！我恨不得夏天明天就到！

I can't stand this cold weather! Man, I wish it could be summer tomorrow!

2）他总是小题大做，好像恨不得全世界都知道他的事！

He always makes a big fuss out of small matters, as if he can't wait to have the whole world know about what's going on with him!

9. 不至于　　　**cannot or be unlikely to go so far as to**

❖ 但是正因为他们监督得那么严，所以政府不至于太腐化。

But it's precisely because they have kept such a close watch that the government does not become too corrupt.

1）这么简单的中文课文，他不至于看不懂吧？

This Chinese lesson is very simple. Can't he understand it? (= his Chinese cannot be so bad that he can't understand it, can it?)

2）虽然他不太诚实，但是不至于当着那么多人的面说谎吧？

Even though he's not very honest, he wouldn't go so far as to lie in front of so many people, would he?

10.　　与其…，不如…　　　　　　　　**rather than …, it would be better …**

❖　与其选一个喜欢打仗的总统，不如选一个喜欢谈恋爱的总统。

Instead of electing a president who likes to go to war, it would be better to choose one who likes to fall in love.

1）与其跟一个自己不爱的人结婚，不如一个人生活更好。

It would be better to live alone rather than marrying someone you don't love.

2）付钱坐出租车划得来吗？你与其浪费钱，不如走走路、锻炼锻炼身体呢！

Is it worth it to pay for the taxi fare? Instead of wasting your money, you would be better off walking and getting some exercise!

练习

I.   Choose the correct answer.

(   ) 1. 总统不是一个_____的人，所以他的人品怎么样当然是一件
            很重要的事情。
            a. 普通   b. 普遍   c. 通常

(   ) 2. _____美国人都认为总统有没有女朋友跟他是不是好总统没
            有关系。
            a. 最多   b. 大都   c. 大部分

(   ) 3. 我很喜欢这个地方的环境和建筑，_____天气，我有点不习
            惯。
            a. 至于   b. 关于   c. 对于

(   ) 4. 我觉得他的人品太差，他不但有婚外关系，_____还说谎。
            a. 即使   b. 甚至   c. 连

(   ) 5. 中国人主张"多子多福"是有一定道理的，因为在中国没有
            _____的保险制度，人到了老年就得靠孩子生活。
            a. 完备   b. 完全   c. 全

(   ) 6. 最近十年美国的经济这么好，说明美国总统很_____。
            a. 能力   b. 能干   c. 有能干

(   ) 7. 我要租一辆车，只要能骑就行，我_____好看不好看。
            a. 不在乎   b. 无所谓   c. 不要紧

II.   Choose the most appropriate phrase for each blank and fill in with its
       Chinese equivalent.

        Make a big fuss over a trivial matter   to look down on
        to be effective   to be in love   to value   to announce
        for the moment   be dying to   face to face

1. 一方面我们_____个人的隐私权，另一方面也要把政治领袖的丑闻__
    _____出来。

2. 听说儿子出了车祸，妈妈心里很急，_____马上飞去看他 。

3. 难怪最近他那么高兴，脸上总是带着笑容，原来他在_____。

4. 我只是一次没有上课，你就要给我父母打电话，你未免太_____了。

5. 这件事在电话里说不清楚，我能不能_____跟你谈谈？

6. 中国的人口没有以前增长的那么快了，说明一家一个孩子的政策很___

  ._____。

III.   Answer the question using the words given.

1. 作者为什么说美国的报纸天天报导总统有了女朋友不但不让美国丢脸，反而值得骄傲？

(说明、制裁、例外、即使、只有、公布、黑暗、腐化)

2. 新闻单位的作用是什么？你觉得美国的新闻单位在总统有了女朋友这件事情上做得对不对？

(监督、腐化、不至于、侵害、管、关心、收视率、下不了台)

IV.   Composition

请多用下面的新词：

报导、丢脸、骄傲、制裁、宣布、小题大做、过问、发生、至于、 反而、重视、隐私、侵害、强调、在乎、监督、说谎、提高、不至于、 强调、与其…不如…、恨不得

1. 要是克林顿还可以竞选，你会不会投他的票，为什么？你对一个领导人的要求是什么？

2. 你是一个新闻记者，最近报导了许多关于总统和他女朋友的丑闻，让总统下不了台，而受伤最深的可能是总统的家人。就新闻工作来说，你所做的完全是对的，可是你觉得对不起总统夫人。所以你打算写一封信给总统夫人……

第十二課

保險套與社會道德

甲：真是太不像話了！這樣的東西竟然放在街上賣，給小孩兒看見了多不好啊！

乙：什麼東西啊？

甲：就是你晚上用的那個玩藝兒。

乙：晚上用的？你是説安眠藥啊？

甲：不是！是你最討厭的那個東西。

乙：你在説什麼啊？

甲：就是⋯⋯就是⋯⋯（一邊兒説，一邊兒用手比劃），就是那個嘛。

乙：噢，你是説 "套子" 啊，在哪兒賣啊？

甲：就在隔壁雜貨店門口兒，他們放了一個自動售貨機，只要放一塊錢就自動出一個，比買香煙還方便呢。

乙：中國真是現代化了！連保險套都能在自動售貨機上買到了。這真是改革開放最好的證明啊！

甲：用自動售貨機賣保險套跟改革開放有什麼關係啊？

第十二课

保险套与社会道德

甲：真是太不像话了！这样的东西竟然放在街上卖，给小孩儿看见了多不好啊！

乙：什么东西啊？

甲：就是你晚上用的那个玩艺儿。

乙：晚上用的？你是说安眠药啊？

甲：不是！是你最讨厌的那个东西。

乙：你在说什么啊？

甲：就是……就是……（一边儿说，一边儿用手比划），就是那个嘛。

乙：噢，你是说"套子"啊，在哪儿卖啊？

甲：就在隔壁杂货店门口儿，他们放了一个自动售货机，只要放一块钱就自动出一个，比买香烟还方便呢。

乙：中国真是现代化了！连保险套都能在自动售货机上买到了。这真是改革开放最好的证明啊！

甲：用自动售货机卖保险套跟改革开放有什么关系啊？

該開放的不開放，不該開放的倒開放了。

乙：用自動售貨機賣保險套，表示大家在思想上已經開通了。在先進國家早就這麼做了，這有什麼好大驚小怪的呢？

甲：這樣隨便賣保險套不是鼓勵婚前和婚外的性關係嗎？現在社會已經夠亂了，隨時隨地都能買到保險套，男女關係不知道要亂到什麼地步呢！

乙：讓大家比較容易地買到保險套，不但可以方便避孕，還可以防止性病的傳染，這當然是一大進步咯。你以為買不到保險套就能減少婚前和婚外的關係了嗎？我告訴你，在孔子那個時代，連保險套是什麼都不知道，可是一樣有婚前和婚外的男女關係。

甲：你在胡說什麼啊！保險套跟孔子有什麼關係？今天在自動售貨機上可以買到保險套，明天說不定就能買到"春藥"。這樣下去，社會道德就越來越糟了。

乙：我覺得用不用保險套跟社會道德是沒有關係的，一個買不到保險套的社會是比較不文明不進步的，而不是社會道德水平比較高；同樣的，一個能方便地買到保險套的社會是比較開放比較進步的，並不是社會道该开放的不开放，不该开放的倒开放了。

乙：用自动售货机卖保险套，表示大家在思想上已经开通了。在先进国家早就这么做了，这有什么好大惊小怪的呢？

甲：这样随便卖保险套不是鼓励婚前和婚外的性关系吗？现在社会已经够乱了，随时随地都能买到保险套，男女关系不知道要乱到什么地步呢！

乙：让大家比较容易地买到保险套，不但可以方便避孕，还可以防止性病的传染，这当然是一大进步咯。你以为买不到保险套就能减少婚前和婚外的关系了吗？我告诉你，在孔子那个时代，连保险套是什么都不知道，可是一样有婚前和婚外的男女关系。

甲：你在胡说什么啊！保险套跟孔子有什么关系？今天在自动售货机上可以买到保险套，明天说不定就能买到"春药"。这样下去，社会道德就越来越糟了。

乙：我觉得用不用保险套跟社会道德是没有关系的，一个买不到保险套的社会是比较不文明不进步的，而不是社会道德水平比较高；同样的，一个能方便地买到保险套的社会是比较开放比较进步的，并不是社会道德比較低。方便避孕、防止性病傳染就是改善生活，給大家帶來幸福。我覺得不應該放在自動售貨機上賣的東西不是保險套，而是香煙。

德比较低。方便避孕、防止性病传染就是改善生活，给大家带来幸福。我觉得不应该放在自动售货机上卖的东西不是保险套，而是香烟。

词汇

保险套	保險套	bǎoxiǎntào	n. condom
道德		dàodé	n. morality
不像话		bù xiànghuà	adj. ridiculous
小孩儿		xiǎoháir	n. kid
玩艺儿	玩藝儿	wányìr	n. "plaything," a thing to play with
安眠药	安眠藥	ānmiányào	n. sleeping pill
比划	比劃	bǐ.huà	v. to make hand gestures
套子		tào.zǐ	n. cover, case; (here) condom
杂货店	雜貨店	záhuòdiàn	n. grocery
自动	自動	zìdòng	adj. automatic
售货机	售貨機	shòuhuòjī	n. vending machine
香烟	香煙	xiāngyān	n. cigarette
现代化	现代化	xiàndàihuà	adj. modernized
改革		gǎigé	v. to reform; (here) the economic reform of China that began in 1979
开放	開放	kāifàng	v. to be opened (to the public); (here) the "open policy" of China that was issued in 1979
证明	證明	zhèngmíng	v. to prove; n. proof
该	該	gāi	= 应该
表示		biǎoshì	v. to show; to express
思想		sīxiǎng	n. thought, thinking

开通	開通	kāitōng	adj. open-minded, liberal
先进	先進	xiānjìn	adj. advanced
大惊小怪	大驚小怪	dàjīngxiǎokuài	Idiom: be surprised or alarmed at sth. perfectly normal or trivial, to make a fuss
随便	隨便	suíbiàn	adv. do as one pleases
鼓励	鼓勵	gǔlì	v. to encourage
婚前		hūn qián	before getting married
婚外		hūn wài	out of marriage
性		xìng	n. sex
随时随地	隨時隨地	suíshísuídì	adv. at any time and any place
地步		dìbù	n. extent, stage
避孕		bìyùn	n. contraception 避 : to avoid 孕 : to become pregnant
防止		fángzhǐ	v. to prevent
性病		xìngbìng	n. venereal disease
减少		jiǎnshǎo	v. to reduce, to cut down
孔子		Kǒngzǐ	Confucius
胡说	胡說	húshuō	talk nonsense
说不定	説不定	shuō.búdìng	adv. perhaps, maybe
春药	春藥	chūnyào	n. aphrodisiacs, drugs that induce sexual desire
文明		wénmíng	adj. civilized
水平		shuǐpíng	n. level, standard

改善   gǎishàn   v. to improve

改善   gǎishàn   v. to improve

词语例句

1. 证明   **to prove; proof**

❖ 这真是改革开放最好的证明啊！

This is the best evidence of China's reform and open-up policy!

1）你得证明这件事不是你做的，我们才会相信你。

You'll have to prove you didn't do it before we will believe you.

2）他不说谎，证明他人品不差。

He doesn't tell lies. This proves that he has good character (lit. moral quality).

2. 该 V. 的不 V.，不该 V. 的倒 V.   **those that are supposed to V. do not V., but those that are not supposed to V. do V.**

❖ 该开放的不开放，不该开放的倒开放了。

What should be opened up is not open up; instead, it's what shouldn't be opened up that in fact is.

1）"吃饭"、"睡觉"这些简单的中文你都说不好，骂人的话却说得那么熟。真是该学的不学，不该学的倒学得特别快！

You can't even say simple Chinese words like "chīfàn" and "shuìjiào" well, but you're so fluent in curse words. You didn't learn what you should have learned, but what you shouldn't have learned, you sure learned fast!

2）该学习的时候你在睡觉，不该学习的时候你却拿着书，你这个人真怪！

You slept when it was time to study. When it wasn't time for studying, you would hold a book instead. You're such a weirdo!

3. 有什么好 V. 的呢？   **what is there to V.?**

❖ 这有什么好大惊小怪的呢？

What is all the fuss about? (= There's nothing to fuss about)

1）这儿的风景那么普通，有什么好看的呢？

The scenery here is really ordinary, what is there to see? (= There's nothing worth seeing.)

2）既然你已经决定了，我还有什么好说的呢？

Since you have already decided, what else can I say? (= There's nothing else that I can say.)

4. 随时随地　　　at any time and any where

❖ 随时随地都能买到保险套。

One can buy condoms at any time and at any place.

1) 互联网的好处就是让你随时随地都可以收到国外的消息。

The advantage of the Internet is that it allows you to get news from other countries anytime and anywhere.

2) 人类随时随地都在污染环境。

Man pollutes the environment all the time and everywhere.

5. V./Adj. 到…地步　　　V./Adj. to the extent of …

❖ 男女关系不知道要乱到什么地步呢！

I don't know how much more promiscuous (man-woman) relationships will get.

1) 这儿的垃圾已经多到没办法回收的地步。

There is so much garbage here that we have no way to collect it.

2) 他抽烟抽到不抽就活不下去的地步。

He smokes so heavily that if he didn't smoke, he couldn't go on living.

6. 说不定　　　perhaps; maybe

❖ 今天在自动售货机上可以买到保险套，明天说不定就能买到"春药"。

If one can buy condoms in a vending machine today, it's possible that one could also find aphrodisiacs in it tomorrow!

1) A：已经九点了，美生还没回来，我真担心！

　B：有什么好担心的呢？说不定她去同学的家玩儿了！

　A: It's already nine and Meisheng is still not back yet. I'm really worried!

　B: What's there to worry about? She's probably at her classmate's house having fun!

2) 你的话比总统的还有道理！你去竞选说不定会有很多人投你的票呢。

What you've said makes more sense than what the President said. If you ran (for the presidency), a lot of people might vote for you.

7. **A 给 B 带来…**　　　　　　**A brings … to B**

❖ 方便避孕、防止性病传染就是改善生活，给大家带来幸福。

Making contraception convenient and preventing the spread of venereal diseases makes our lives better, and brings happiness to all.

1) 你戒烟吧！抽烟是不会给你带来任何好处的。

Why don't you quit smoking? It's not going to do you any good.

2) 虽然一次性产品给我们带来了方便，但是也造成了更大的浪费。

Although disposable products bring convenience (to our lives), they also cause more waste.

练习

I. Read the model sentence, and complete the sentences or dialogues that follow based on the same patterns.

A. 他们竟然把保险套放在街上卖，真是太不象话了。

1. 总统竟然…。
2. 这些记者为了提高收视率，竟然…。
3. 买一辆自行车竟然要…。
4. 一个记者竟然当着那麼多人的面…。

B. A：现在社会已经够乱了。

　　B：现在的社会乱到什么地步了呢？

　　A：现在的社会已经乱到没有枪不敢出门的地步。

1. A：这个人很坏。

　　B：…

　　A：…

2. A：那个城市的小偷很多。

　　B：…

　　A：…

3. A：他可真丑。

　　B：

　　A：

4. A：北京的空气污染太利害了。

　　B：…

　　A：…

C. 要是用自动售货机来卖保险套，就能随时随地都能买到保险套。

1. 要是我有大哥大电话，…
2. 要是没有电子邮件，…
3. 要是那些报纸的记者…，…

D. 今天在自动售货机上可以买到保险套，明天也许就能买到"春药"。

　　这样下去，社会道德就越来越糟了。

1. 要是你的孩子今天打人你不批评他，…

2. 要是今天总统有了女朋友，我们不把这件事情公布出来，…

3. 要是今天一个人有了婚外关系我们觉得没有关系，…

4. 要是今天你不上一堂课，老师不批评你，…

II. Choose the most appropriate word for each blank and fill in with its Chinese equivalent.

to make hand gestures   to make a fuss   ridiculous   to encourage   liberal
speak plausibly and at length   crucial   to improve/improvement

1. 她这个人就是喜欢_____，这只是一件小事，根本就没有必要给报纸写信公布出来。

2. 她的父母比较_____，觉得只要她喜欢，嫁给外国人或者老头都没关系。

3. 我说了好几遍她都没听懂，所以我用手_____了一下，她才懂。

4. 他真_____！我不让他跟我女儿谈恋爱，他竟然偷偷地把我女儿带出去了。

5. 自从改革开放以后，人们的生活条件有了很大的_____。

III. Composition

1. 你认为用自动售货机卖保险套是不是鼓励婚前和婚外性行为？让堕胎(duòtāi:abortion)合法化呢？你认为这两种做法是一个健康的问题，还是道德的问题？

2. 你认为美国的社会道德是不是越来越糟了？你担心不担心这个问题？一个社会的道德受什么影响？谁又应该为社会道德的发展负责任呢？

Part Two:

Newspaper Readings

（二）读报篇

1999年7月24日《人民日報》

第十三課

小學生做生意

　　下面是貴州一位市民寫給《人民日報》的一封信，反映了目前中國中小學生的部分生活。

　　前些日子，家中的"隨身聽"不見了，問到讀小學六年級的女兒，才知道她以每天0.5元出租費租給了班上的同學。我很生氣地問她爲甚麼不借給同學聽而去收租金，她卻振振有詞地回答説："爸，班上同學都這樣。"

　　通過女兒出租"隨身聽"的線索，我還驚奇地發現，不僅女兒在班上做生意，就連我妹妹的女兒（正讀初一）也是這樣。兩姐妹經常暗地發生"生意"往來。我還從女兒那裏了解到，她們班上有的同學出租雜誌、書籍、磁帶，春節前夕還有人轉賣明信片儿。

1999年7月24日《人民日报》

第十三课

小学生做生意

　　下面是贵州一位市民写给《人民日报》的一封信，反映了目前中国中小学生的部分生活。

　　前些日子，家中的"随身听"不见了，问到读小学六年级的女儿才知道她以每天0.5元出租费租给了班上的同学。我很生气地问她为什么不借给同学听而去收租金，她却振振有词地回答说："爸，班上同学都这样。"

　　通过女儿出租"随身听"的线索，我还惊奇地发现，不仅女儿在班上做生意，就连我妹妹的女儿（正读初一）也是这样。两姐妹经常暗地发生"生意"往来。我还从女儿那里了解到，她们班上有的同学出租杂志、书籍、磁带，春节前夕还有人转卖明信片儿。

　　青少年上學期間，是培養人生美德的關鍵時期。即使在現在的社會主義市場經濟條件下，小學生做"生意"，我認爲也還是太早了。這種"生意經"不僅會影響孩子的思想品德的培養，也會影響孩子的學習成績。

青少年上学期间，是培养人生美德的关键时期。即使在现在的社会主义市场经济条件下，小学生做"生意"，我认为也还是太早了。这种"生意经"不仅会影响孩子的思想品德的培养，也会影响孩子的学习成绩。

词汇

做生意		zuòshēng.yì	v. to do business
下面		xià.miàn	n. below; following; next
贵州	貴州	Guìzhōu	n. a province in southeastern China
市民		shìmín	n. city resident; townspeople
人民日报	人民日報	Rénmín rìbào	n. The People's Daily
封		fēng	mw for letters
信		xìn	n. letter
反映		fǎn.yìng	v. to reflect
目前		mùqián	n. at the present; at the moment
中小学生	中小學生	zhōng xiǎo xuéshēng	n. short for "中学生和小学生"
部分		bù.fèn	n. part
前些日子		qiánxiē rì.zǐ	n. few days ago
随身听	隨身聽	suíshēntīng	n. walkman
不见	不見	bújiàn	v. to disappear
读	讀	dú	v. to attend (school, class, etc.)
年级	年級	niánjí	n. grade; year (in school, etc.)
以		yǐ	prep. for; by
出租费	出租費	chūzūfèi	n. rental fee
出租		chūzū	v. to rent
租		zū	v. to rent

生气	生氣	shēngqì	adj. angry
借给	借給	jiègěi	v. to lend
而		ér	adv. but; however
收		shōu	v. to collect; to gather
租金		zūjīn	n. rental fee
却	卻	què	adv. but; yet
振振有词	振振有詞	zhènzhènyǒucí	adv. speak plausibly and at length (in self-justification); to assert eloquently
回答		huídá	v. to answer; to reply to; to respond
通过	通過	tōngguò	prep. by means of; through
线索	線索	xiànsuǒ	n. clue; hint
惊奇地	驚奇地	jīngqí.de	adv. with surprise; surprisingly
发现	發現	fāxiàn	v. to find out; to discover
不仅	不僅	bùjǐn	conj. not only
连	連	lián	conj. even
妹妹		mèi.mèi	n. younger sister
初一		chūyī	n. first year in junior high school
姐妹		jiěmèi	n. older sister and younger sister; sisters
暗地		àndì	adv. secretly
经常	經常	jīngcháng	adv. frequently; often
发生	發生	fāshēng	v. to take place; to occur

往来		wǎnglái	n. intercourse; contact
了解	了解	liǎojiě	v. to learn about; to find out
杂志	雜誌	zázhì	n. magazine
书籍	書籍	shūjí	n. books
磁带	磁帶	cídài	n. cassette (lit "magnetic tape")
春节	春節	chūnjié	n. Chines New Year (lit. " Spring Festival")
前夕		qiánxī	n. eve
转卖	轉賣	zhuǎnmài	v. to resell
明信片儿		míngxìnpiànr	n. postcard
青少年		qīngshàonián	n. teenager
期间	期間	qījiān	n. time; period
培养	培養	péiyǎng	v. to develop; to foster
人生		rénshēng	n. life
美德	美德	měidé	n. virtue; moral excellence
关键	關鍵	guānjiàn	adj. crucial; key; very important
时期	時期	shíqī	n. period (of time)
即使		jíshǐ	conj. even if
社会主义	社會主義	shèhuìzhǔyì	n. socialism
市场经济	市場經濟	shìchǎng jīngjì	n. market economy; market-oriented economy
条件	條件	tiáojiàn	n. condition
生意经	生意經	shēngyìjing	n. good business sense; the tricks of the trade

影响	影響	yǐngxiǎng	v. to influence; to affect
思想		sīxiǎng	n. thought; thinking
品德	品德	pǐndé	n. moral character
成绩	成績	chéng.jì	n. results (of work or study); achievements; grade

影响 影響 yǐngxiǎng v. to influence; to affect

思想 sīxiǎng n. thought; thinking

词语例句

1. **下面**   **below; next**

❖ 下面是贵州一位市民写给《人民日报》一封信。

Below is a letter written by a citizen of Guizhou to the People's Daily.

1) 我们学校有五位老师要参加这次会议，下面是他们的资料。

Here in the following is the information about the five teachers in our school who will attend this conference.

2) 这个问题我下面还要谈到。

I'll come back to this point later on.

2. **以**   **by; for**

❖ 她以每天0.5元出租费租给了班上的同学。

She rented it to her classmates for 0.5 *yuan* a day.

1) 这个城市的人口以每年一百万的速度快速增长。

The population of this city is increasing rapidly by about a million people a year.

2) 他以每月300元给儿子请了一位家教。

He hired a tutor for his son for 300 *yuan* a month.

3. **Adj. 地 Verb**

❖ 我还惊奇地发现…

I discovered to my surprise that …

1) 她高兴地去上学了。

She cheerfully went off to school.

2) 他兴奋地告诉父母他已经被大学录取了。

He excitedly told his parents that a university had accepted him.

4. **而**   **but; however**

"而", a conjunction, is usually used in written speech and shows a shift. Here it connects two clauses, indicating two opposite things. It can only be used at the beginning of the second clause.

❖ 我很生气地问她为什么不借给同学听而去收租金。

I angrily asked her why she charged her classmates for the use of her Walkman instead of lending it to them.

1) 我跟妹妹的性格完全不同，她喜欢跟人交往，而我最害怕跟别人说话。

My sister and I have completely different characters; she likes to socialize with people, but what I fear most is talking to people.

2) 为什么你自己不来见我，而让你妹妹来呢？

Why did you let your sister meet me rather than meeting me yourself?

5. 通过　　　　　　　　　　　**through; by means of**

❖ 通过女儿出租"随身听"的线索，我还惊奇地发现，…。

Through the clue that my daughter rented her Walkman to her classmates, I discovered to my surprise that….

1) 通过我妹妹的介绍，我认识了她的老师。

I got to know her teacher through my younger sister.

2) 由于不懂中文，他只能通过翻译跟中国人交谈。

As he didn't know any Chinese, he had to speak through an interpreter.

6. 不仅…也…　　　　　　　　**not only…, but also…**

❖ 不仅女儿在班上做生意，就连我妹妹的女儿也是这样。

My daughter was not the only one who collected rent money in class; my nephew did so as well.

1) 抽烟不仅危害自己的身体，也危害别人的健康。

Smoking is harmful not only to one's health but also to other people's health as well.

2) 这种生意经不仅会影响孩子的思想品德，也会影响孩子的学习成绩。

These "tricks of the trade" will not only affect the children's moral character, but also their academic grades.

7. Verb 到

❖ 我还从女儿那里了解到，她们班上的同学出租杂志。

I also learned from my daughter that her classmates rent magazines to other students.

1) 去了王府井以后，他才认识到中国的人口问题有多么严重。

Only after he had been to Wangfujing, did he realize how severe the problem of Chinese overpopulation was.

2) 他第一次见到她，就注意到她有很重的伦敦口音。

When they first met, he noticed that she spoke with a very strong London accent.

8. 即使…也…　　　　　　　　even though

❖ 即使在现在的市场经济的条件下，小学生做生意也太早了。

Even in a market economy, a primary school student is too young to be involved in business.

1) 即使孩子犯了错误，你也不应该打他。

Even if you child did make a mistake, you shouldn't beat him.

2) 即使他有很多钱，我也不会爱上他。

No matter how rich he is, I will never fall in love with him.

9. 在…（条件\情况）下　　　under (certain condition/situation)

❖ 在现在的市场经济条件下…

In a market economy (lit. "Under the situation in the present economy"), …

1) 这个礼拜我要交三个报告，还有两个考试，在这种情况下，我怎么有时间跟你去逛街呢？

I have three papers due this week and two tests to prepare for, under these circumstances, how could I have time to go window shopping with you?

2) 中国的大学生常常是几个人住在一间屋子里，吃饭、睡觉全在一起，在这种条件下，很难保持个人的隐私。

It is hard for Chinese University students to keep their privacy since they usually eat and sleep with other people together in a room.

练习

I.　　Choose the correct answer.

(　　　) 1. 老师＿＿＿了解到最近两个星期他都病得很利害。

a. 从他的同屋

b. 向他的同屋那里

c. 从他的同屋那里

(　　　) 2. 他发现钱包＿＿＿，怀疑是被旁边的人偷了。

a. 没见了　　　　b. 不看见了　　　c. 不见了

(　　　) 3. 只有＿＿＿，他才会让我用他的电脑。

a. 在他不用下

b. 在他不用的情况下

c. 在他不用的情况上

(　　　) 4. 女儿问我："爸爸，今天晚上我能不能＿＿＿

你的车？"

a. 借给　　　　　b. 借　　　c. 从你借

(　　　) 5. 即使这两个国家关系紧张，他们也还＿＿＿生

意往来。

a. 发生　　　　　b. 出现　　　　c. 做出

II.　　Fill in the blanks with the most appropriate word. Each word should be used only once.

却；地；被；给；到；才；再

今天早晨我发现家里的车撞坏了，问 ① 女儿 ② 知道她昨天晚上开车出去，不小心 ③ 后面的车 ④ 撞了。我生气 ⑤ 问她为什么不先问问我 ⑥ 把车开出去，她 ⑦ 回答说："你已经睡着了。"

①＿＿＿②＿＿＿③＿＿＿④＿＿＿⑤＿＿＿⑥＿＿＿⑦＿＿＿

III.　　Make a sentence using the underlined expression.

1. 要是他不把房子租给你，你可以去告他。

2. 昨天我跟朋友借了一盘非常好听的磁带。

3. 读大学期间，是交朋友的关键时期。

4. 这种生意经不仅会影响孩子的思想品德，也会影响孩子的学习成

绩。

5. 即使在现在的社会主义市场经济条件下，小学生做生意也还是太
早了。

IV.　Answer the following questions.

1. 在你看来，小学生做生意的坏处是什么？

2. 做生意会不会影响人生美德的培养？

3. 美国小学生做不做生意？他们的父母担心不担心他们的思想品德
受到不好的影响？

1999年7月10日《人民日報》

第十四課

寂寞的孩子

　　東北76所學校對一萬多名學生所做的一項心理測試顯示，32%的中小學生不同程度地存在心理異常：討厭上學、想出走等等。分析表明，家庭環境是造成孩子心理障礙的重要原因。許多父母以爲，只要爲孩子投入大量金錢和精力，孩子身體健康，學習成績好就行了，而忽視了不容易察覺的孩子的心理健康問題。家長需要提高自身素質，學習一些關于心理健康教育方面的知識。

　　孩子的身體狀況也令人憂慮。經濟發達了，人民生活水平提高了，青少年的營養狀態反而下降了，肥胖型兒童越來越多。這是因爲孩子學習負擔過重，活動量小。另外也與學生偏食等不良習慣有關。

1999年7月10日《人民日报》

第十四课
寂寞的孩子

　　东北76所学校对一万多名学生所做的一项心理测试显示，32%的中小学生不同程度地存在心理异常：讨厌上学、想出走等等。分析表明，家庭环境是造成孩子心理障碍的重要原因。许多父母以为，只要为孩子投入大量金钱和精力，孩子身体健康，学习成绩好就行了，而忽视了不容易察觉的孩子的心理健康问题。家长需要提高自身素质，学习一些关于心理健康教育方面的知识。

　　孩子的身体状况也令人忧虑。经济发达了，人民生活水平提高了，青少年的营养状态反而下降了，肥胖型儿童越来越多。这是因为孩子学习负担过重，活动量小。另外也与学生偏食等不良习惯有关。

　　另一個不容忽視的問題是孩子們對勞動的認識和態度。近年來，由於升學壓力，家長教師似乎對孩子只有一個要求"學習好就行了"，而忽視了對孩子勞動能力的培養。1997年的一項調查顯示，我國城市孩子平均每日勞動時間只有0.2小時，而美國是1.2小時，韓國是0.7小時，法國是0.6小時，英國是0.6小時。

　　近年來，進入結婚年齡的獨生子女，結婚後雙方不會料理家務，不願幹家務而引起家庭生活不和睦，甚至離婚的事很多。事實說明，熱愛勞動與兒童道德的發展有直接密切的關係，熱愛勞動的孩子獨立性強、責任心強，勞動還有助於培養孩子勤勞簡樸的品德。勞動讓他們懂得珍惜勞動成果，知道父母的血汗錢來得不容易，而更加孝敬父母，同時勞動會給孩子一個健康的身體。

　　現在有些父母只想擠進中產階級，只顧努力地工作，努力地賺錢，而忽視了孩子的教育問題。在今天競爭日益激烈的社會裏，拼命掙錢沒有甚麼可指責的，但別忘了，要盡可能多擠出一點時間給孩另一个不容忽视的问题是孩子们对劳动的认识和态度。近年来，由于升学压力，家长教师似乎对孩子只有一个要求"学习好就行了"，而忽视了对孩子劳动能力的培养。1997年的一项调查显示，我国城市孩子平均每日劳动时间只有0.2小时，而美国是1.2小时，韩国是0.7小时，法国是0.6小时，英国是0.6小时。

近年来，进入结婚年龄的独生子女，结婚后双方不会料理家务，不愿干家务而引起家庭生活不和睦，甚至离婚的事很多。事实说明，热爱劳动与儿童道德的发展有直接密切的关系，热爱劳动的孩子独立性强、责任心强，劳动还有助于培养孩子勤劳简朴的品德。劳动让他们懂得珍惜劳动成果，知道父母的血汗钱来得不容易，而更加孝敬父母，同时劳动会给孩子一个健康的身体。

现在有些父母只想挤进中产阶级，只顾努力地工作，努力地赚钱，而忽视了孩子的教育问题。在今天竞争日益激烈的社会里，拼命挣钱没有什么可指责的，但别忘了，要尽可能多挤出一点时间给孩子，今天花費幾分鐘時間，也許會有益於孩子的一生。

子，今天花费几分钟时间，也许会有益于孩子的一
生。

词汇

寂寞		jìmò	adj. lonely; lonesome
东北	東北	Dōngběi	n. Northeastern China
所	所	suǒ	mw for houses, institutions, etc.
万	萬	wàn	n. ten thousand
项	項	xiàng	mw for items, clauses, etc
心理		xīnlǐ	n. psychology
测试	測試	cèshì	n. survey; test
显示	顯示	xiǎnshì	v. to reveal; to display; to show
程度		chéngdù	n. degree; extent
存在		cúnzài	v. to exist; to be
异常	異常	yìcháng	adj. abnormal; unusual
讨厌	討厭	tǎoyàn	v. to loathe; to dislike; to take an aversion to
出走		chūzǒu	v. to run away from home
分析		fēn.xī	n. analysis
表明		biǎomíng	v. to demonstrate: to make clear
家庭		jiātíng	n. family; household
环境	環境	huánjìng	n. environment
造成		zàochéng	v. to cause; to make; to bring about
障碍	障礙	zhàng'ài	n. obstacle; bar; handicap
心理障碍	心理障礙	xīnlǐ zhàng'ài	n. psychological disorder
原因		yuányīn	n. cause; reason

投入		tóurù	v. to put into; to invest in
大量		dàliàng	adj. a large number; a great quantity; a great deal of
金钱	金錢	jīnqián	n. money
精力		jīnglì	n. energy; vigor
健康		jiànkāng	n./adj. health; healthy
忽视	忽視	hūshì	v. to overlook; to neglect; to ignore
察觉	察覺	chájué	v. to be conscious of; to become aware of; to perceive
家长	家長	jiāzhǎng	n. the parent or guardian of a child
需要		xūyào	v. to need to
提高		tígāo	v. to improve; to enhance;
自身		zìshēn	n. self; oneself
素质	素質	sù.zhì	n. quality
关于	關於	guānyú	prep. about; concerning; regarding
教育	教育	jiàoyù	n. education
方面		fāngmiàn	n. aspect; side; area
知识	知識	zhī.shí	n. knowledge
状况	狀況	zhuàngkuàng	n. condition; state; situation
令人		lìngrén	v. to make people feel
忧虑	憂慮	yōulǜ	adj. worried; anxious; concerned
经济	經濟	jīngjì	n. economy

发达	發達	fādá	v. to prosper; to develop
营养	營養	yíngyǎng	n. nutrition; sustenance
状态	狀態	zhuàngtài	n. state; condition
反而		fǎn'ér	adv. on the contrary; instead; contrarily
下降		xiàjiàng	v. to descend; to drop off; to decrease; to come down
肥胖		féipàng	adj. fat; corpulent; obese
型		xíng	suf. type; shape
儿童	兒童	értóng	n. children
负担	負擔	fùdān	n. load; burden
过	過	guò	adv. excessively; over
重		zhòng	adj. heavy
活动量	活動量	huódòngliàng	n. amount of physical activity
另外		lìngwài	conj. in addition; over and above
与	與	yǔ	prep. with
偏食		piānshí	v. to be partial to a limited variety of food
不良		bùliáng	adj. bad; harmful
不容		bùróng	adv. not allow; to not tolerate
劳动	勞動	láodòng	n. physical labor
认识	認識	rèn.shí	n. understanding
态度	態度	tài.dù	n. attitude; position
近年来		jìnniánlái	n. in recent years

由于	由於	yóuyú	conj. owing to; due to
升学	升學	shēngxué	v. to enter a higher school; to advance to a higher school
压力	壓力	yālì	n. pressure
教师	教師	jiàoshī	n. teacher
似乎		sìhū	adv. it seems that; it appears that; it appears as if
要求		yāoqiú	n. demands; requests; needs
调查	調查	diàochá	n./v. survey; investigation
城市		chéngshì	n. city
平均		píngjūn	adj. average
韩国	韓國	Hán'guó	n. Korea
法国	法國	Fǎguó	n. France
进入	進入	jìnrù	v. to enter into
年龄	年齡	nián.líng	n. age
独生子女	獨生子女	dúshēng zǐnǔ	n. the only child
双方	雙方	shuāngfāng	n. both sides; the two parties
料理		liàolǐ	v. to attend to; to manage; to take care of
家务	家務	jiāwù	n. household chores; housework
干	幹	gàn	v. to do
引起		yǐnqǐ	v. to give rise to; to bring about
和睦		hémù	adj. harmonious
甚至		shènzhì	adv. even (to the point that); so much so that

离婚	離婚	líhūn	v. to divorce
事实	事實	shìshí	n. fact
说明	説明	shuōmíng	v. to illustrate; to explain
热爱	熱愛	rèài	v. to love; to love fervently
道德		dàodé	n. morality; morals
直接	直接	zhíjiē	adj. direct; immediate
密切		mìqiè	adj. close
独立性	獨立性	dúlìxìng	n. the ability to be independent
强	強	qiáng	adj. strong
责任心	責任心	zérènxīn	n. the sense of responsibility
有助于	有助於	yǒuzhùyú	v. to be conducive to; to contribute to; to help to
勤劳	勤勞	qínláo	adj. diligent; hardworking
简朴	簡樸	jiǎnpǔ	adj. simple; unadorned
品德		pǐndé	n. (moral) character; morals
懂得		dǒngdé	v. to understand; to know
珍惜		zhēnxī	v. to treasure; to cherish; to value
成果		chéngguǒ	n. fruits; achievements
血汗钱	血汗錢	xuèhàn qián	n. money earned by hard toil (lit. " blood-sweat money")
更加		gèngjiā	adv. even more
孝敬		xiàojìng	v. to show filial piety and respect for one's parents
挤进	擠進	jǐjìn	v. to squeeze in; to push one's way in; to join eagerly

中产阶级	中產階級	zhōngchǎn jiējí	n. the middle class
只顾	只顧	zhǐgù	v. to be preoccupied solely with
努力		nǔlì	adv. to strive; to endeavor
赚钱	賺錢	zhuànqián	v. to make money; to gain money
竞争	競爭	jìngzhēng	n. competition; contention
日益		rìyì	adv. increasingly; day by day
激烈		jīliè	adj. intense; fierce
拼命		pīnmìng	v. to do sth. desperately; with all one's might
挣钱	掙錢	zhèngqián	v. to earn money
指责	指責	zhǐzé	v. to censure; to criticize; to find fault with
尽可能	盡可能	jìnkě'néng	adv. as far as possible; to the best of one's ability
挤出	擠出	jǐchū	v. to squeeze
花费	花費	huāfèi	v. to spend
有益于	有益於	yǒuyìyú	v. to be good for; to do good to; to benefit
一生		yìshēng	n. all one's life; throughout one's life

词语例句

1. 不同程度地　　　　　　　　　to varying degrees

❖ 32%的中小学生不同程度地存在心理异常。

32% of elementary and middle school students have abnormal psychological problems of varying degrees.

1) 在北京住了一个夏天，所有学生的中文水平都不同程度地提高了。

All the students improved their Chinese to varying degrees after living in Beijing for a summer.

2) 环境、毒品等问题是全球性的，每个国家都不同程度地存在这类问题。

Environmental pollution and drugs are global issues that more or less exist in every country.

2. 反而　　　　　　　　　　　instead; on the contrary

❖ 经济发达了，人民的生活水平提高了，青少年的营养状态反而下降了。

With the development of the economy and the rise in living standards, the nutrition of Chinese teenagers has not improved; on the contrary, it is getting worse.

1) 我帮了他不少忙，他不但不感谢我，反而常常说我的坏话。

I helped him a lot, but he is not grateful to me; on the contrary he often speaks ill of me.

2) 这个坏消息不但没有让她不安，反而对她产生了一种奇怪的镇定效果。

Instead of disturbing her, the bad news had a strangely calming effect on her.

3. 只要⋯就⋯　　　　　　　　as long as; if only ⋯then ⋯

❖ 只要为孩子投入大量金钱和精力，⋯孩子学习好就行。

As long as they put in a great amount of money and energy, ··· and their children have good grades, everything will be O.K.

1) 学语言不难，只要多花时间就行。

Studying a language is not a tough job. You will learn it as long as you spend enough time on it.

2) 两个人只要相爱就可以住在一起，结婚不结婚有什么关系呢？

As long as two people love each other they should be able to live together, what does it matter if they are married or not?

4. 关于　　　　　　　　　　　　**about; on**

❖ 家长需要提高自身素质，学习一些关于心理健康教育方面的知识。

Parents need to improve themselves by studying psychological health.

1) 每天中国日报都有关于新电影、新书、新饭馆的报道。

There are reports on new movies, books, and new restaurants in the *China Daily* every day.

2) 中国日报也有较长的文章，介绍关于商业或者中国各地的情况。

There are also longer articles about business or about different areas of China in *China Daily*.

5. 令 (sb.) adj.　　　　　　　　**make sb. (feel)···**

❖ 孩子的身体状况也令人忧虑。

Children's health is also worrisome.

1) 孩子被有名的大学录取令父母非常高兴。

The parents were very happy that their children were admitted to a famous university.

2) 这家饭馆的服务真令人不满意。

The service of this restaurant is really not satisfactory.

6. —型　　　　　　　　　　　**-type; -shape**

❖ 肥胖型儿童越来越多。

Fat children ("fat –shaped children") are becoming more and more numerous.

1) 他生日的那天，朋友们送给他一个心型蛋糕。

His friends gave him a hear-shaped cake for his birthday.

2) 在传统的社会里，"事业型"的女性不受欢迎。

In traditional society, working women (" career-type") are not welcome.

7. 更加   **even more; more**

❖ 劳动让孩子知道父母的血汗钱来得不容易，而更加孝敬父母。

Taking a laborious job will make children know it is not easy for their parents
to earn money and they will therefore show more respect to their parents.

1) 听说不仅女儿出租随身听，连我妹妹的女儿也做生意，我更加生
气了。

I got angrier when I heard that not only did my daughter rent her walkman,
but my sister's daughter also did business.

2) 上大学以后，他更加努力了。

He worked even harder after he went to university.

8. 日益   **day by day; increasingly**

❖ 在今天竞争日益激烈的社会里，拼命挣钱没有什么可指责的。

In an increasingly competitive society, there is no reason to criticize earning
money desperately.

1) 随着经济的发展，人民的生活日益改善。

With the development of the economy, people's living condition improved
increasingly.

2) 现代社会有心理问题的人数日益增加。

The number of people who have psychological problems is increasing with
each passing day in modern society.

9. 可   **worth; worthy of**

❖ 在今天竞争日益激烈的社会里，拼命赚钱没有什么可指责的。

(see 8. for translation)

1) 这么无聊的电影，有什么可看的呢？

Why would you want to see such a boring movie?

2) 请问，这附近有没有什么可看的地方？

Excuse me, is there any place nearby worth visiting?

10. 引起   **lead up to; give rise to**

❖ 进入结婚年龄的独生子女，…不愿干家务引起家庭生活不和睦。

Those "only-child" who reach the age of marriage, … are not willing to do domestic work, which makes family life unharmonious.

1) 这个有争议的问题，引起了学生的热烈讨论。

This controversial issue evokes a heated discussion in class.

2) 在机场，他的神情太紧张，引起了警察的怀疑。

His overly nervous look aroused the suspicion of the police at the airport.

11. 有助于   **to help to; to contribute to**

❖ 劳动还有助于培养孩子勤劳简朴的品德。

Doing housework is also good for nurturing moral character that values hard working and simplicity in a child.

1) 两国总统的互相访问有助于增加两国的互相了解。

The mutual visits of the two countries' presidents have contributed to a better understanding between the two countries.

2) 《中国日报》上刊登大量的广告，这样有助于降低报纸的成本。

China Daily has plenty of advertisements, which helps to cut the costs of making the newspaper.

12. 尽可能   **as far as possible**

❖ （父母）要尽可能多挤出一点时间给孩子。

(Parents) should try to squeeze in as much time with your children as possible.

1) 你可以参考原文，可是要尽可能用你自己的话。

You may refer to the original text if necessary; but try to use your own words as much as possible.

2) 我尽可能每天都运动。

I try to work out every day.

13. 有益于 **to do good to; to benefit**

❖ （父母多花一点时间跟孩子在一起）也许会有益于孩子的一生。

(If the parents spent a little more time with them,) it might be beneficial throughout the life of the children.

1) 社会的稳定有益于经济的发展。

The stability of society is good for the development of economy.

2) 保持愉快的心情有益于健康。

Keeping a good mood is good for one's health.

练习

I.　Choose the phrase that is closest in meaning to the underlined phrase in the sentence.

（　）1. 孩子的身体状况也令人忧虑。

　　a. 担心　　　　　b. 放心　　　　　c. 小心

（　）2. 由于升学的压力，老师和家长似乎对孩子只有一个要求就是"学习好就行了"。

　　a. 可能　　　　　b. 也许　　　　　c. 好象

（　）3. 为了保护环境，每个国家都要尽可能少用塑料产品。

　　a. 绝对　　　　　b. 尽量　　　　　c. 肯定

（　）4. 另一个不容忽视的问题是中国孩子对待劳动的态度。

　　a. 不容易　　　　b. 不可能　　　　c. 不应该

（　）5. 每天报纸电视上都有很多<u>关于</u>他婚姻的新闻。
　　　　　a. 有关于　　　　　b. 有关　　　　　c. 有关系

（　）6. 八十年代以来，中国学生考大学的竞争<u>日益</u>激烈。
　　　　　a. 每天　　　　　b. 一天比一天　　　　　c. 天天

II.　　Complete the following sentences using the underlined expression.

1. 家庭环境是<u>造成</u>孩子心理障碍的<u>主要原因</u>。
　　这个司机喝酒以后开车是……。
　　父母关系不和睦，常常吵架……。

2. 一些父母<u>只顾</u>赚钱，而<u>忽视</u>了孩子的心理问题。
　　小学生做生意的坏处是……。
　　他们离婚的主要原因是……。

3. 劳动还<u>有助于</u>培养孩子勤劳俭朴的品德。
　　用自动售货机卖保险套……。
　　多读中文报纸，多看中文电影……。

4. 父母应该<u>尽可能</u>多挤出一点时间给孩子。
　　资源少人口多的国家……。
　　在中国住的时候……。

5. 肥胖型儿童越来越多，是因为孩子学习负担太重，活动量小
　　，<u>另外</u>也跟孩子偏食有关。
　　这次我来中国，学了中文……。
　　我反对你跟那个外国人结婚是因为……。

III.　　Make a sentence using the underlined expression.

1. 32%的学生<u>不同程度地</u>存在心理异常的情况。
2. 事实说明，热爱劳动<u>跟</u>儿童道德的发展<u>有直接密切的关系</u>。
3. 在今天竞争日益激烈的社会里，拼命赚钱<u>没有什么可指责的</u>。
4. 经济发达了，人民生活水平提高了，可是青少年的营养状态
　　<u>反而</u>下降了。

1998年7月16日《光明日报》

第十五課

金錢是交往的通行證嗎？

（一）給錢才幫忙

學期剛結束，杭州勝利小學校長見到記者，談到學生的道德教育工作時，講起學期結束前發生的一場大討論。

事情非常簡單。有個男學生有三道數學題不會做，想請同學幫忙，可是從第一排問到最後一排，竟沒有一個同學願意教他。馬上就交作業了，情急之下，這位失望的男學生掏出五毛錢，說："誰教我，我就給誰五毛錢！"金錢馬上起了作用，一個女生走過來，難題很快解開了。那個女生理所當然得到了五毛錢。拿到了報酬，這位女學生得意地對同學說："今後教同學都該這樣收錢。"這件事很快就傳到了班主任的耳朵裏。"起先我很生氣，"

1998年7月16日《光明日报》

第十五课

金钱是交往的通行证吗？

（一）给钱才帮忙

学期刚结束，杭州胜利小学校长见到记者，谈到学生的道德教育工作时，讲起学期结束前发生的一场大讨论。

事情非常简单。有个男学生有三道数学题不会做，想请同学帮忙，可是从第一排问到最后一排，竟没有一个同学愿意教他。马上就交作业了，情急之下，这位失望的男学生掏出五毛钱，说："谁教我，我就给谁五毛钱！"金钱马上起了作用，一个女生走过来，难题很快解开了。那个女生理所当然得到了五毛钱。拿到了报酬，这位女学生得意地对同学说："今后教同学都该这样收钱。"这件事很快就传到了班主任的耳朵里。"起先我很生气，"

她説，"沒想到這個表現不錯的學生竟這麼自私。但事後一想，這件事不能簡單地以對或錯來判斷。"她找這兩位學生談話。第二天，那位女學生勉強把錢還給了那個男生。

事情到此似乎也就結束了，然而…

（二）該不該收錢？

幾天以後，班主任在家長會上講了這件事，希望家長配合學校，注意學生道德上的培養。出人意料的是，家長的反應竟截然不同：有對孩子行為表示贊成，稱贊孩子聰明，長大了不會吃虧的；有擔心孩子小小年紀就學會金錢交易，長大了會唯利是圖的；有家長説，孩子的心靈潔白如紙，過早的金錢意識會污染他們的天真；也有家長認為錢該收，社會美德也該發揚，不必對這件事大驚小怪。一位家長説："老師搞家教可以收錢，學生為什麼就不可以？讓學生從小學會通過勞動獲得報酬，這對他今後走入社會很有好處。"也有家長認為，五毛錢風波實際上是社會現象的反映，某些單位或機關給錢就辦事，不給錢就不辦事，這種現象很容易使孩她说，"没想到这个表现不错的学生竟这么自私。但事后一想，这件事不能简单地以对或错来判断。"她找这两位学生谈话。第二天，那位女学生勉强把钱还给了那个男生。

事情到此似乎也就结束了，然而…

（二）该不该收钱？

几天以后，班主任在家长会上讲了这件事，希望家长配合学校，注意学生道德上的培养。出人意料的是，家长的反应竟截然不同：有对孩子行为表示赞成，称赞孩子聪明，长大了不会吃亏的；有担心孩子小小年纪就学会金钱交易，长大了会唯利是图的；有家长说，孩子的心灵洁白如纸，过早的金钱意识会污染他们的天真；也有家长认为钱该收，社会美德也该发扬，不必对这件事大惊小怪。一位家长说："老师搞家教可以收钱，学生为什么就不可以？让学生从小学会通过劳动获得报酬，这对他今后走入社会很有好处。"也有家长认为，五毛钱风波实际上是社会现象的反映，某些单位或机关给钱就办事，不给钱就不办事，这种现象很容易使孩子接受金錢萬能的觀念，總之，孩子的行爲是社會思想的反映，不能怪孩子。

會議結束了以後，班主任組織同學展開討論。誰知討論變成了辯論，同學們有兩種截然相反的意見。一方認爲，這個世界有比金錢更寶貴的東西。英雄救人的時候，如果想到錢，還肯去救嗎？要是同學之間互相幫助都要付錢，那麼這個世界除了金錢還有什麼？互相幫助是一種美德，不能讓金錢取代！另一方則認爲，"幫助別人就應該得到報酬，街上、電視上的尋物啓事不都說'當面重謝,嗎？沒有重謝，又有多少失物能找回呢？這五角錢該收！錢是生活中的通行證！"

這場風波的主角怎麼看這件事呢？那位男生說："我沒出錢時，同學都愛理不理，我一出錢，就有同學來幫助了，這不是說明錢很有用嗎？今後我還會這樣做的。"而那位女學生卻不明白自己錯在哪裏，她說："老師教學生是老師的義務，學生卻沒有義務教同學。現在辦甚麼事都要錢，我既然付出勞動，就應該得到錢。我沒有錯！"

子接受金钱万能的观念，总之，孩子的行为是社会思想的反映，不能怪孩子。

会议结束了以后，班主任组织同学展开讨论。谁知讨论变成了辩论，同学们有两种截然相反的意见。一方认为，这个世界有比金钱更宝贵的东西。英雄救人的时候，如果想到钱，还肯去救吗？要是同学之间互相帮助都要付钱，那么这个世界除了金钱还有什么？互相帮助是一种美德，不能让金钱取代！另一方则认为，"帮助别人就应该得到报酬，街上、电视上的寻物启事不都说'当面重谢'吗？没有重谢，又有多少失物能找回呢？这五角钱该收！钱是生活中的通行证！"

这场风波的主角怎么看这件事呢？那位男生说："我没出钱时，同学都爱理不理，我一出钱，就有同学来帮助了，这不是说明钱很有用吗？今后我还会这样做的。"而那位女学生却不明白自己错在哪里，她说："老师教学生是老师的义务，学生却没有义务教同学。现在办什么事都要钱，我既然付出劳动，就应该得到钱。我没有错！"

词汇

交往		jiāowǎng	n. association; relationship; contact
通行证	通行證	tōngxíngzhèng	n. pass; permit
帮忙	幫忙	bāngmáng	v. to help; to do a favor
学期	學期	xuéqī	n. semester
结束	結束	jiéshù	v. to end
杭州		Hángzhōu	n. capital city of Zhejiang province
胜利	勝利	shènglì	n. victory; success, here: name of a school
校长	校長	xiàozhǎng	n. (of a primary or secondary school) principal; headmaster (of a college or university) president
记者	記者	jìzhě	n. journalist; reporter
谈到	談到	tán.dào	v. to speak about or of; to mention; to talk about
讲起	講起	jiǎng.qǐ	v. to talk about
发生	發生	fāshēng	v. to happen; to take place; to occur
场	場	chǎng	mw for games, performance. etc.
讨论	討論	tǎolùn	n. discussion; debate
简单	簡單	jiǎndān	adj. simple
道		dào	mw for a question in a test

数学	數學	shùxué	n. mathematics
题	題	tí	n. question in a test or assignment
排		pái	n. row
竟		jìng	adv. unexpectedly
愿意	願意	yuànyì	adv. be willing; be ready
马上	馬上	mǎshàng	adv. at once; right away
交		jiāo	v. to hand over
作业	作業	zuòyè	n. assignment
情急之下		qíngjízhīxià	ph. in a moment of desperation
失望	失望	shīwàng	adj. disappointed
掏出		tāochū	v. to pull out
毛		máo	mw for money
起作用		qǐ zuò.yòng	v. to take effect; to be effective
女生		nǚshēng	n. girl student; schoolgirl
解开	解開	jiěkāi	v. to solve (a mathematical problem, etc.)
理所当然	理所當然	lǐsuǒdāngrán	ph. deservedly; as a matter of fact; to be natural and right
报酬	報酬	bàochóu	n. reward; pay
得意		déyì	adj. to pride oneself on sth. (or doing sth.)
今后	今後	jīnhòu	n. from now on

收钱	收錢	shōuqián	v. to charge
传到	傳到	chuándào	v. to spread to
班主任		bānzhǔrèn	n. the head-teacher of the class
耳朵		ěr.duō	n. ear
起先		qǐxiān	adv. at first; in the beginning; originally
表现	表現	biǎoxiàn	n. performance
自私		zìsī	adj. selfish
事后一想	事後一想	shìhòu yìxiǎng	ph. to think back after the event
或		huò	conj. or
判断	判斷	pànduàn	v. to judge
勉强	勉強	miǎnqiǎng	adv. reluctantly; unwillingly
还	還	huán	v. to return; to give back
到此		dàocǐ	adv. to this point
然而		rán'ér	conj. however
家长会	家長會	jiāzhǎnghuì	n. parents' meeting
配合		pèihé	v. to work with; to cooperate
注意		zhùyì	v. to pay attention to; to keep an eye on; to take notice of
出人意料		chūrényìliào	ph. to come as a surprise; contrary to one's expectations; beyond all expectations
反应	反應	fǎn.yìng	n. response

截然		jiérán	adv. markedly; completely
行为	行爲	xíngwéi	n. behavior
表示		biǎoshì	v. to express
赞成	贊成	zànchéng	v. to approve of; to be in favor of
称赞	稱贊	chēngzàn	v. to praise; to acclaim
聪明	聰明	cōng.míng	adj. smart
长大	長大	zhǎngdà	v. to grow up
吃亏	吃虧	chīkuī	v. to suffer losses; in an unfavorable situation
小小年纪	小小年紀	xiǎoxiǎonián.jì	ph. at a very young age
交易		jiāoyì	n. trade; deals; business transactions
唯利是图	唯利是圖	wéilìshìtú	ph. to be intent on nothing but money; seek only profit
心灵	心靈	xīnlíng	n. heart; soul; spirit
洁白	潔白	jiébái	adj. spotlessly white
如		rú	prep. like; similar to
意识	意識	yì.shí	n. sense; awareness
污染		wūrǎn	v. to contaminate; to pollute;
天真	天眞	tiānzhēn	adj. innocent
美德		měidé	n. virtue; moral goodness or excellence
发扬	發揚	fāyáng	v. to carry on
不必		búbì	adv. need not

大惊小怪	大驚小怪	dàjīngxiǎoguài	ph. to make a fuss about nothing
搞		gǎo	v. to do; to be engaged in
家教	家教	jiājiào	n. tutoring
从小	從小	cóngxiǎo	adv. since one was very young; from one's childhood
获得	獲得	huòdé	v. to obtain; to gain
有好处	有好處	yǒuhǎochù	v. to be good for; to be of benefit
风波	風波	fēngbō	n. disturbance(lit. "wind and wave")
实际上	實際上	shíjì.shàng	adv. in fact; in reality
现象	現象	xiànxiàng	n. phenomenon
单位	單位	dānwèi	n. work unit
机关	機關	jīguān	n. government work unit
办事	辦事	bànshì	v. to handle affairs; to perform work
接受		jiēshòu	v. to accept
金钱万能	金錢萬能	jīnqiánwànnéng	" money is omnipotent"
总之	總之	zǒngzhī	conj. in a word; in short
怪		guài	v. to blame
会议	會議	huìyì	n. meeting; conference
组织	組織	zǔ.zhī	v. to organize; to arrange
展开	展開	zhǎnkāi	v. to launch; to carry out
变成	變成	biànchéng	v. to become; to turn into

辩论	辩論	biànlùn	n. debate; argument
相反		xiāngfǎn	adj. opposite; contrary
宝贵	寶貴	bǎoguì	adj. valuable; precious
英雄		yīngxióng	n. hero
救人		jiùrén	v. to save life
肯		kěn	adv. be willing to
互相		hùxiāng	adv. mutually; each other; one another
取代		qǔdài	v. to replace; to substitute
则	則	zé	adv. however
寻物启事	尋物啓事	xúnwùqǐshì	n. lost and found notice
当面	當面	dāngmiàn	adv. to sb's face; in sb's presence
重谢	重謝	zhòngxiè	v. to present a grand reward
失物		shīwù	n. lost items
主角	主角	zhǔjué	n. main character; leading role
看		kàn	v. to look upon; to view
爱理不理	愛理不理	àilǐbùlǐ	ph. to look cold and indifferent
说明	説明	shuōmíng	v. to indicate; to show
明白		míng.bái	v. to understand; to catch on
义务	義務	yì.wù	n. duty; obligation
付出		fùchū	v. to pay

词语例句

1. ···QW··· ，··· QW···

❖ 谁教我，我就给谁五毛钱。

Whoever will teach me, I'll pay him five *mao.*

1) 谁对我好，我就对谁好。

I will be nice to whoever is nice to me.

2) 你什么时候方便，就什么时候来。

Come whenever is convenient for you.

2. 情急之下　　　　　　　　　　**in a moment of desperation**

❖ ···，情急之下，这位失望的男生掏出五毛钱，说："···。"

···，in a moment of desperation, the disappointed boy pulled out five *mao,* and said, "···."

1) 他在饭馆吃完饭以后，却找不到钱包，情急之下，他把手表交给了服务员。

He couldn't find his purse after having eaten in a restaurant, therefore, in a moment of desperation, he gave his wristwatch to the waiter instead.

2) 他要吃鸡肉，可是服务员听不懂他的话，情急之下，他在纸上画了一只鸡。

He wanted to eat chicken, but the waiter couldn't understand what he said, therefore, in a moment of desperation, he drew a chicken on a piece of paper.

3. 起···作用　　　　　　　　　　**take effect**

❖ 金钱马上起了作用。

The money took effect immediately.

1) 吃了这么多药，我还不好，看来这种药不起作用。

It seems that this medicine doesn't work since I'm not feeling better after having had so much of it.

2) 中国人口增长的速度明显慢下来，显然人口政策起了作用。

The rate of increase of China's population has slowed noticeably, obviously the population policy has been effective.

4. **以…来…**   **use … to …**

❖ 这件事不能简单地以对或者错来判断。

This issue can not be judged just by a simple standard of "right" or " wrong."

1) 你一般以什么标准来判断一个电影好不好？

Normally what standard do you use to judge whether a movie is good or not?

2) 不能以一次考试的成绩来决定学生的成绩。

You can't decide students' grade just by one quiz.

5. **勉强**   **reluctantly**

❖ 那位女学生勉强把钱还给那个男生。

That schoolgirl reluctantly returned the money to that boy.

1) 他勉强同意了。

He reluctantly agreed.

2) 他接受了我们的建议，但是很勉强。

He accepted our suggestion, but rather grudgingly.

6. **出人意料**   **to one's surprise**

❖ 出人意料的是家长的反应竟然截然相反。

To his surprise, the parents are completely slit (on this issue) 〔lit. "the reactions of the parents are completely split"〕.

1) 他的回答出人意料。

His answer surprised people.

2) 很多人觉得他们很快会离婚，出人意料的是，三年以后，他们还很幸福地生活在一起。

Many people thought their marriage wouldn't last long. However, to much surprise, they still lived happily together three years later.

7. **有…的；有…的**   **some… ; some…**

❖ 有对孩子行为表示赞成的；有担心孩子小小年纪就学会金钱交易，长大了会唯利是图的；有认为不必大惊小怪的。

Some parents expressed approval of the children's behaviors; some worried that if children from a very young age learn about money, they will care about nothing but making money when they grow up; some say there is no need to fuss about little things.

1) 毕业以前，所有的学生都很忙；有忙着找工作的，有忙着写论文的，有忙着申请研究所的。

Before graduation, all students are very busy. Some are busy with finding work; some are busy with writing their theses; some are busy with applying for graduate school.

2) 在夜市上有各种各样的小贩。有卖小吃的，有卖服装的，有卖日用品的。

At the night market there are all kinds of vendors. Some vendors sell snacks; some sell clothes; some sell everyday items.

8.　…，总之，…　　　　　　　　　　**in short**

❖　总之，孩子的行为是社会思想的反映，不能怪孩子。

In a word, it is not the children's fault since their behaviors reflect the value of the society.

1) 那个地方没有自来水也没有电，总之，非常落后。

That place has neither electricity nor tap water, in short, it is very backward there.

2) 学生家长、老师、民间组织，总之，很多人反对广告进入校园。

Parents , teachers, non governmental organizations, in short, a lot of people opposed advertisement entering school.

9.　既然…就…　　　　　　　　　　**since …then…**

❖　我既然付出劳动，就应该得到报酬。

Now that I worked for someone, I should get a reward.

1) 既然你没有空，我就自己去了。

As you are busy, I will go without you.

2) 既然你已经决定了，我就不勉强你了。

Now that you have already decided, I won't pressure you anymore.

10.　　…是…的反映　　　　　　　　　**…is the reflection of…**

❖ 孩子的行为是社会思想的反映。

(see 8. for translation.)

1) 有时候，孩子的道德水平就是家长的道德水平的反映。

Sometimes children's moral level can be a reflection of their parents' moral level.

2) 在一定程度上，一个人的言行就是他所受教育的反映。

To certain degree, a person's behavior is a reflection of his education.

练习

I.　Choose the phrase that is closest in meaning to the underlined phrase in the sentence.

1. 老师没有想到家长们的态度竟然截然不同。
   a. 有些　　　　b. 有点儿　　　　c. 完全

2. 老师说："起先我很生气，后来我想不能全怪他们。"
   a. 开始　　　　b. 首先　　　　c. 第一

3. 那个男生请求同学帮忙，可是没有一个人愿意帮他。
   a. 能　　　　b. 肯　　　　c. 会

4. 老师组织学生展开讨论，谁知讨论变成辩论。
   a. 想知道　　　　b. 不知道　　　　c. 没想到

II.   Choose the correct answer.

(   )1. 我以后再也不去这家商店了，那儿的服务员觉得我没有钱，就对我_____。

   a.唯利是图   b.爱理不理   c.大惊小怪

(   )2. 在这次讨论中，男生的看法_____。

   a.相反女生的看法

   b.反对女生的看法

   c.跟女生的看法相反

(   )3. 结婚以前，两个人一定要_____。

   a.了解互相   b.知道互相   c.互相了解

(   )4. 为了事业成功，他拼命工作，结果身体出了问题，_____健康的代价。

   a.付钱   b.付出   c.付了

(   )5. 儿童的心灵洁白如纸，容易受到不良文化的影响，_____加强对儿童思想道德教育非常重要。

   a.因此   b.总之   c.而

(   )6. 在火灾中，因为他不顾危险，救了邻居的孩子，受到了大家的_____。

   a.赞成   b.称赞   c.同意

III.   Choose the most appropriate word for each blank and fill in with its Chinese equivalent.

pride oneself on sth.   reluctantly   beyond all expectations

make a fuss about nothing   replace   to sb's face

1. 要是你对他有意见，应该_____跟他说，别在背后说。

2. 我觉得那个父亲根本就是_____，他的女儿只是把自己不用的随身听租给别人，又不是什么坏事。

3. 很多人认为北京的城墙和四合院完全被现代化的高楼_____是在破坏中国的历史和文化。

4. 他一再请求老板给他一个工作的机会，老板_____答应了。

5. 大家都以为电影的男主角是一个英雄，结果却_____，他才是真正的凶手(xiōngshǒu : killer)。

6. 听到别人称赞他的儿子聪明，他虽然很_____，还是客气地说：

"哪里，哪里。"

IV.　　Complete the following dialogues with patterns given.

1.　A：什么样的人是你的朋友？

　　B：＿＿＿＿＿＿＿＿＿＿＿＿＿＿＿＿＿＿＿＿＿＿。

　　（谁…，谁…）

2.　A：我的同屋又懒又笨，我真讨厌他，不过，别告诉别人。

　　B：为什么？

　　A：＿＿＿＿＿＿＿＿＿＿＿＿＿＿＿＿＿＿＿＿＿＿。

　　（传到…耳朵里；非…不可）

3.　A：美国人是不是都赞成政府送这个非法移民回国呢？

　　B：＿＿＿＿＿＿＿＿＿＿＿＿＿＿＿＿＿＿＿＿＿＿。

　　（截然；有…的；有…的；有…的）

4.　A：那个老师那么年轻，一定教得不太好！

　　B：＿＿＿＿＿＿＿＿＿＿＿＿＿＿＿＿＿＿＿＿＿＿。

　　（以…来判断）

V.　　Find three rhetorical questions in the text, and change them according to the following instruction.

　　例：

　　英雄救人的时候，如果想到钱，还肯去救吗？→英雄救人的时候如果想到钱，就不会去救人了。

　　反问句1.

　　反问句2.

　　反问句3.

VI.　　Composition

　　你的随身听不见了，所以你要写一个"寻物启事"。这个"寻物启事"要包括：在哪儿不见的，是什么样子的，是什么牌子的，为什么它对你很重要，报酬等等。

2000年2月15日《人民日報》（海外版）

第十六課

浙江"好學生殺母事件"引起

社會各界反思

　　一名十七歲中學生因無法忍受學習的沉重壓力殺死親生母親，這個悲劇在浙江省引起社會各界對教育問題的深刻反思。

　　今年十七歲的徐力是浙江省金華市第四中學高二學生。他出生在一個普通的工人家庭。母親吳鳳仙是金華食品公司職工。由於徐父長期在外地火車站工作，徐力從小到大基本上是在母親的照顧下長大的。母親吳鳳仙工資不高，就幫別人織毛衣賺點兒錢供兒子讀書。初中升高中時，徐力考進學校的重點班，但高一上半學期排名全班倒數第二名。通過努力，高一下半學期，徐力進步到了第十名。吳鳳仙喜出望外，要兒子以後每次期中、期末考試都

2000年2月15日《人民日报》（海外版）

第十六课

浙江"好学生杀母事件"引起
社会各界反思

一名十七岁中学生因无法忍受学习的沉重压力杀死亲生母亲，这个悲剧在浙江省引起社会各界对教育问题的深刻反思。

今年十七岁的徐力是浙江省金华市第四中学高二学生。他出生在一个普通的工人家庭。母亲吴凤仙是金华食品公司职工。由于徐父长期在外地火车站工作，徐力从小到大基本上是在母亲的照顾下长大的。母亲吴凤仙工资不高，就帮别人织毛衣赚点儿钱供儿子读书。初中升高中时，徐力考进学校的重点班，但高一上半学期排名全班倒数第二名。通过努力，高一下半学期，徐力进步到了第十名。吴凤仙喜出望外，要儿子以后每次期中、期末考试都排在班級前十名。然而悲劇也就從這時候埋下了種子。

去年十月底，吳鳳仙參加家長會得知，徐力這學期期中考試的成績排在班級第十八名。回家後，吳鳳仙很生氣，狠狠打了兒子一頓。徐力喜歡踢足球，吳鳳仙就說："以後你再去踢足球，我就把你的腿打斷。"重壓之下的徐力感到母親對自己管得太嚴，而且爲無法實現母親提出的目標而深深感到委屈和壓抑。

今年一月十七日，徐力從學校回家，吃完中飯後，想看會儿電視。吳鳳仙提醒兒子期末考試要考前十名。徐力說："很難考，不可能。"母子之間再次爲學習發生衝突。絕望中，徐力從門口拿起一把木柄榔頭朝正在繡花的母親後腦砸去，把母親活活砸死。

徐力殺母震驚了社會。在徐力就讀的金華四中，同學和老師反映，徐力平時一向刻苦和節儉，是個品學兼優的好學生，性格文靜，初中時期一直是三好學生，初二就入了團；進入高中之後，也一直排在班级前十名。然而悲剧也就从这时候埋下了种子。

去年十月底，吴凤仙参加家长会得知，徐力这学期期中考试的成绩排在班级第十八名。回家后，吴凤仙很生气，狠狠打了儿子一顿。徐力喜欢踢足球，吴凤仙就说："以后你再去踢足球，我就把你的腿打断。"重压之下的徐力感到母亲对自己管得太严，而且为无法实现母亲提出的目标而深深感到委屈和压抑。

今年一月十七日，徐力从学校回家，吃完中饭后，想看会儿电视。吴凤仙提醒儿子期末考试要考前十名。徐力说："很难考，不可能。"母子之间再次为学习发生冲突。绝望中，徐力从门口拿起一把木柄榔头朝正在绣花的母亲后脑砸去，把母亲活活砸死。

徐力杀母震惊了社会。在徐力就读的金华四中，同学和老师反映，徐力平时一向刻苦和节俭，是个品学兼优的好学生，性格文静，初中时期一直是三好学生，初二就入了团；进入高中之后，也一直努力學習，對集體活動很熱心，也樂於助人。他們不懂；為什麼這樣的學生會幹出這樣的暴行？

當地有關專家認為，家長望子成龍心切，子女心理脆弱和缺乏法制觀念，是導致這齣悲劇的主要原因。從徐力身上可以看到一個矛盾：他一方面似乎 "訓練有素"，殺死母親後移尸滅跡，還寫字條欺騙父親說媽媽去杭州 "看病" 了，並居然照常參加了考試；但另一方面他又十分脆弱，僅僅因為母親對他學業上的壓力，就殺了母親。這說明他的心理並不健康，而且法制觀念淡薄。

現在的青少年基本上是獨生子女，從小就承受了很大的壓力，家長對子女往往是期望過高。子女考試不理想，就有一種對不起父母的感覺，結果，必然導致心理問題。而現在社會上的凶殺、色情等讀物泛濫，許多青少年受到不良文化的影響。因此，加強對青少年思想道德教育和人格培養是非常重要的。

努力学习，对集体活动很热心，也乐于助人。他们不懂：为什么这样的学生会干出这样的暴行？

当地有关专家认为，家长望子成龙心切，子女心理脆弱和缺乏法制观念，是导致这出悲剧的主要原因。从徐力身上可以看到一个矛盾：他一方面似乎“训练有素”，杀死母亲后移尸灭迹，还写字条欺骗父亲说妈妈去杭州“看病”了，并居然照常参加了考试；但另一方面他又十分脆弱，仅仅因为母亲对他学业上的压力，就杀了母亲。这说明他的心理并不健康，并且法制观念淡薄。

现在的青少年基本上是独生子女，从小就承受了很大的压力，家长对子女往往是期望过高。子女考试不理想，就有一种对不起父母的感觉，结果，必然导致心理问题。而现在社会上的凶杀、色情等读物泛滥，许多青少年受到不良文化的影响。因此，加强对青少年思想道德教育和人格培养是非常重要的。

附錄：

故意殺母案作出一審判決

　　新華社杭州5月1日電，浙江金華市中級人民法院昨天對震驚社會的"徐力殺母"案作出一審判決，以故意殺人罪判處徐力有期徒刑15年。

　　17歲的徐力是浙江省金華市第四中學高二學生，母親吳鳳仙是金華縣食品公司職工。由於徐父長期在外地工作，徐力從小到大基本上是在母親的照料下長大的，母親吳鳳仙工資不高，就幫別人織毛衣賺點錢供兒子讀書。初中升高中時，徐力考進了學校的重點班，吳鳳仙要求兒子以後每次期中、期末考試成績都要排在班級前10名。重壓之下的徐力感到母親對自己管得太嚴，而且爲母親提出的目標無法實現而深感委屈和壓抑。

　　今年1月17日中午，徐力放學回家吃過中飯後，因對母親吳鳳仙管教不滿，便拿了一把鐵榔頭將母親殺害。

附录：

故意杀母案作出一审判决

新华社杭州5月1日电，浙江金华市中级人民法院昨天对震惊社会的"徐力杀母"案作出一审判决，以故意杀人罪判处徐力有期徒刑15年。

17岁的徐力是浙江省金华市第四中学高二学生，母亲吴凤仙是金华县食品公司职工。由于徐父长期在外地工作，徐力从小到大基本上是在母亲的照料下长大的，母亲吴凤仙工资不高，就帮别人织毛衣赚点钱供儿子读书。初中升高中时，徐力考进了学校的重点班，吴凤仙要求儿子以后每次期中、期末考试成绩都要排在班级前10名。重压之下的徐力感到母亲对自己管得太严，而且为母亲提出的目标无法实现而深感委屈和压抑。

今年1月17日中午，徐力放学回家吃过中饭后，因对母亲吴凤仙管教不满，便拿了一把铁榔头将母亲杀害。

　　法院認爲，被告人徐力因對其母學習上的管束不滿而使用鐵榔頭砸其母頭部致死，非法剝奪了其母吳鳳仙的生命，其行爲依照《中華人民共和國刑法》第二百三十二條，已構成故意殺人罪。被告人徐力犯罪時未滿18周歲，依照《中華人民共和國刑法》第十七條第三款，應當從輕處罰，鑒於本案具體情況可依法酌情從輕處罰。爲保護公民的人身權利不受非法侵犯，維護社會治安秩序，貫徹懲罰與敎育相結合的刑事政策，依照法律規定，以殺人罪判處被告人徐力有期徒刑15年。

　　法院认为，被告人徐力因对其母学习上的管束不满而使用铁榔头砸其母头部致死，非法剥夺了其母吴凤仙的生命，其行为依照《中华人民共和国刑法》第二百三十二条，已构成故意杀人罪。被告人徐力犯罪时未满18周岁，依照《中华人民共和国刑法》第十七条第三款，应当从轻处罚，鉴于本案具体情况可依法酌情从轻处罚。为保护公民的人身权利不受非法侵犯，维护社会治安秩序，贯彻惩罚与教育相结合的刑事政策，依照法律规定，以杀人罪判处被告人徐力有期徒刑15年。

词汇

浙江		Zhèjiāng	n. a province in southeast China
杀	殺	shā	v. to kill
母（亲）	母（親）	mǔ(.qīn)	n. mother
事件		shìjiàn	n. incident; event
引起		yǐnqǐ	v. to give rise to; to lead to
各界		gèjiè	n. all walks of life; all circles
反思		fǎnsī	n. introspection; self-examination
因（为）	因（爲）	yīn(wéi)	conj. because; on account of
无法	無法	wúfǎ	adv. unable; incapable
忍受		rěnshòu	v. to endure; to bear
沉重		chénzhòng	adj. heavy; weighty
压力	壓力	yālì	n. pressure
亲生	親生	qīnshēng	adj. one's own (children, parents)
悲剧	悲劇	bēijù	n. tragedy
省		shěng	n. province
深刻		shēnkè	adj. profound; deep
徐力		XúLì	n. a person's name
金华	金華	Jīnhuá	n. name of a city in Zhejiang province
市		shì	n. city; municipality

高二		gāoèr	n. second year in high school
出生		chūshēng	v. to be born
普通		pǔtōng	adj. ordinary; common
工人		gōngrén	n. worker
吴凤仙	吳鳳仙	Wú Fèngxiān	n. a person's name (the mother)
食品		shípǐn	n. food
公司		gōngsī	n. company
职工	職工	zhígōng	n. workers and staff members
父（亲）	父（親）	fù(.qīn)	n. father
长期	長期	chángqī	adv. long-term; over a long period of time
外地		wàidì	n. place other than where one is; other places
火车站	火車站	huǒchēzhàn	n. train station
从小到大	從小到大	cóngxiǎo dàodà	ph. since one's childhood (lit. "from one's childhood to after one has grown up.")
基本上		jīběn.shàng	adv. mainly; on the whole
照顾	照顧	zhàogù	v. to look after; to care for
长大	長大	zhǎngdà	v. to grow; to grow up
工资	工資	gōngzī	n. wages; pay; earnings
织	織	zhī	v. to knit
毛衣		máoyī	n. sweater
供		gōng	v. to support (financially); to supply

初中		chūzhōng	n. junior middle school
升		shēng	v. to go up to a higher level in school
高中		gāozhōng	n. senior high school
考进	考進	kǎojìn	v. to enter a school by passing the entrance examination
重点班	重點班	zhòngdiǎnbān	n. honors class; advanced class
排名	排名	páimíng	v. to rank as; to be ranked as
倒数	倒數	dàoshǔ	v. to count from the end; to count backwards
努力		nǔlì	n. efforts; hard work
进步	進步	jìnbù	v. to progress
喜出望外	喜出望外	xǐchūwàngwài	ph. to be overjoyed (at an unexpected gain or good news)
期中		qīzhōng	n. midterm
期末		qīmò	n. end of semester (here, final examination)
班级	班級	bānjí	n. a class or a level in school
埋下		mái.xià	v. to bury (here, to plant)
种子	種子	zhǒng.zǐ	n. seed (here, "the cause")
月底		yuèdǐ	n. the end of a month
参加	參加	cānjiā	v. to attend
得知		dézhī	v. to have learned of
狠狠		hěnhěn	adv. ferociously

顿	頓	dùn	mw for meals, occurrence, etc.
踢		tī	v. to play; to kick
足球		zúqiú	n. football
打断	打斷	dǎduàn	v. to break
重压	重壓	zhòngyā	n. heavy pressure
之下		zhīxià	n. under
感到		gǎndào	v. to feel
管		guǎn	v. to control
严	嚴	yán	adj. strict; stern
实现	實現	shíxiàn	v. to achieve; to accomplish
提出		tíchū	v. to put forward; to pose
目标	目標	mùbiāo	n. objective; target
深深		shēnshēn	adv. profoundly
委屈		wěi.qū	adj. feel wronged
压抑	壓抑	yāyì	adj. repressive; depressive
提醒		tíxǐng	v. to remind
之间	之間	zhījiān	n. among; between
再次		zàicì	adv. once again; for the second time
冲突	衝突	chōngtū	n. conflict
绝望	絕望	juéwàng	n. hopelessness; despair
把		bǎ	mw for things with handles

木柄榔头	木柄榔頭	mùbǐng láng.tóu	n. a hammer with a wood shaft
朝		cháo	prep. towards
正在		zhèngzài	adv. in the process of; in the middle of
绣花	繡花	xiùhuā	v. to do embroidery
后脑	後腦	hòunǎo	n. the back of the head
砸		zá	v. to smash
活活		huóhuó	adv. while still alive
震惊	震驚	zhènjīng	v. to astonish; to shock
就读	就讀	jiùdú	v. to attend school
反映		fǎnyìng	v. to report; to make known
平时	平時	píngshí	n. ordinarily; in normal times
一向		yíxiàng	adv. always; all the time
刻苦		kèkǔ	adj. painstaking; hardworking
节俭	節儉	jiéjiǎn	adj. frugal
品学兼优	品學兼優	pǐnxuéjiānyōu	ph. (of a student) of good character and scholarship
性格		xìnggé	n. nature; character; disposition
文静	文靜	wénjìng	adj. quiet and gentle
一直	一直	yìzhí	adv. all the time; always
三好学生	三好學生	sānhǎo xuéshēng	n. "three good" student (学习好；体育好；思想好): good in learning; good in sports; good in thinking

入团	入團	rùtuán	v. to be admitted to the Communist Youth League
集体	集體	jítǐ	n. collective; group
热心	熱心	rèxīn	adj. enthusiastic; zealous
乐于助人	樂於助人	lè yú zhù rén	ph. to be glad to help others
干	幹	gàn	v. to do
暴行		bàoxíng	n. violent conduct; atrocities
当地	當地	dāngdì	n. local
专家	專家	zhuānjiā	n. expert
望子成龙	望子成龍	wàngzǐ chénglóng	ph. wish for one's children to be successful (lit. " hope son becomes a dragon")
心切		xīnqiè	adj. eager; anxious
脆弱		cuìruò	adj. fragile
缺乏		quēfá	v. to lack; to be scanty of
法制		fǎzhì	n. legality
导致	導致	dǎozhì	v. to bring about; to result in
出	齣	chū	mw for dramatic pieces
矛盾		máodùn	n. contradiction
训练有素	訓練有素	xùnliàn yǒusù	ph. to be well trained
移尸灭迹	移尸滅跡	yíshī mièjì	ph. to remove the corpse and erase the trace
字条	字條	zìtiáo	n. brief note
欺骗	欺騙	qīpiàn	v. to cheap; to dupe

看病		kànbìng	v. to see a doctor
居然		jūrán	adv. unexpectedly
照常		zhàocháng	adv. (to do sth.) as usual
十分		shífēn	adv. extremely; very
仅仅	僅僅	jǐnjǐn	adv. only; alone
淡薄		dànbó	adj. to be indifferent to
承受		chéngshòu	v. to bear; to sustain
期望	期望	qīwàng	v. to hope; to expect; to anticipate
理想	理想	lǐxiǎng	adj. perfect; desirable; ideal
必然		bìrán	adv. be bound to; inevitable
凶杀	凶殺	xiōngshā	n. homicide; murder; manslaughter
色情		sèqíng	n. pornography
读物	讀物	dúwù	n. reading matter; reading
泛滥	泛濫	fànlàn	v. to spread far and wide; to inundate
不良		bùliáng	adj. harmful; unwholesome
加强	加強	jiāqiáng	v. to enhance; to reinforce
人格		rén'gé	n. moral integrity

附录词汇

故意		gùyì	adv. deliberately; intentionally
一审	一審	yīshěn	n. first trial
判决	判決	pànjué	n. court decision; judgement
新华社	新華社	Xīnhuáshè	n. The China News Agency
电	電	diàn	n. telex
中级	中級	zhōngjí	adj. intermediate
杀人罪	殺人罪	shārénzuì	n. manslaughter; murder
判处	判處	pànchǔ	v. to sentence; to condemn
有期徒刑	有期徒刑	yǒuqī túxíng	n. set term of imprisonment
照料		zhàoliào	v. to take care of; to care for
放学	放學	fàngxué	v. to come home from school; to close school
管教	管教	guǎnjiào	v. to subject sb. to discipline
不满	不滿	bùmǎn	adj. resentful; dissatisfied
便		biàn	=就
铁	鐵	tiě	n. iron
杀害	殺害	shāhài	v. to kill
被告人		bèigàorén	n. defendant; the accused
其		qí	pron. his; her; its; such

管束		guǎnshù	v. to restrain; to control
头部	頭部	tóubù	n. head
致死		zhìsǐ	v. to cause death; to result in death
非法		fēifǎ	adj. illegal
剥夺	剝奪	bōduó	v. to deprive of
生命		shēngmìng	n. life
依照		yīzhào	prep. according to
中华人民共和国	中華人民共和國	Zhōnghuá rénmín gònghéguó	n. the People's Republic of China
刑法		xíngfǎ	n. criminal law
条	條	tiáo	mw for clauses
构成	構成	gòuchéng	v. to constitute; to compose
犯罪		fànzuì	n./v. crime; to commit a crime
未		wèi	adv. not; not yet
满	滿	mǎn	v. to reach
周岁	周歲	zhōusuì	n. one full year of life
款	款	kuǎn	mw for clauses
应当	應當	yīngdāng	adv. should
从	從	cóng	prep. in a certain manner; according to a certain principle
处罚	處罰	chǔfá	v. to punish

鉴于	鑒於	jiànyú	prep. in view of; seeing that; in consideration of
本		běn	pron. this
具体	具體	jùtǐ	adj. specific; concrete
可（以）		kě(.yǐ)	v. to permit
依法		yīfǎ	adv. according to law
酌情	酌情	zhuóqíng	adv. to take into consideration the circumstances
公民		gōngmín	n. citizen
人身		rénshēn	adj. personal
侵犯		qīnfàn	v. to infringe
维护	維護	wéihù	v. to defend; to safeguard
治安		zhìān	n. public security; public order
秩序		zhì.xù	n. law and order
贯彻	貫徹	guànchè	v. to carry through; to implement
惩罚	懲罰	chéngfá	v. to punish
相结合	相結合	xiāngjiēhé	v. to combine; to integrate
刑事		xíngshì	adj. criminal; penal
政策	政策	zhèngcè	n. policy
法律		fǎlǜ	n. law

词语例句

1. 在···下　　　　　　　　　　**under**
❖ 徐力从小到大基本上是在母亲的照顾下长大的。
Xu Li grew up under his mother's care.

1) 在朋友的帮助下，我找到了工作。
I found a job with the help of my friends.

2) 在她的领导和组织下，这个语言培训班很成功。
This language program has been very successful under her leadership and organization.

2. 排名　　　　　　　　　　**rank as**
❖ ...，但高一上半学期排名全班倒数第二名。
..., but he ranked the second from the bottom of the class in the first semester of his first year of high school.

1) 这个学校的电脑系很有名，大概在美国排名第一（大概在美国排第一名）。
This college has a very famous computer department, it probably ranks first in the United States.

2) 这次期中考，我在全班排第一名。
I ranked the first in class in this mid-term exam.

3. 狠狠　　　　　　　　　　**ferociously**
❖ 她很生气，狠狠打了儿子一顿。
She was very angry and gave her son a good beating.

1) 她因为逃学，被父母狠狠骂了一顿。
She was given a good scolding by her parents for cutting class.

2) 中国政府采取各种措施，狠狠打击盗版行为。
China's government took all kinds of vigorous measures to counter the piracy.

4. 震惊　　　　　　　　　　**shock; astonish**
❖ 徐力杀母震惊了社会。

The whole society was astonished by the news that Xu Li killed his mother.

1) 徐力杀母亲，老师跟同学都很震惊。

Xu Li's teachers and schoolmates were shocked by Xu Li's killing his mother.

2) 他去世的消息令人震惊。

The news of his death was a shock to us.

5. **一向**   **all along; consistently**

❖ 徐力在学校一向刻苦。

Xu Li has been always hard working in school.

1) 他对学生一向严格。

He has always been very strict with his students.

2) 他父母一向反对他学中文。

His parents have consistently opposed his studying Chinese.

6. **导致**   **give rise to; lead to**

❖ 家长望子成龙心切，子女心理脆弱和缺乏法制观念，是导致这出悲剧的主要原因。

The fact that children could not live up to the high expectation of parents who eagerly want them to be successful, as well as their lack of the concept of law and order led up to this tragedy.

1) 这些事件导致了第二次世界大战。

The events led up to World War II.

2) 她的粗心导致了这次试验的失败。

His carelessness resulted in the failure of this experiment.

7. **照常**   **as usual; as before**

❖ ..., 并居然照常参加了考试。

…, and he actually took the exam as usual.

1) 即使下雨，比赛也照常进行。

The match will be played as scheduled even in the event of rain.

2) 这家商店节日也照常营业。

This store is open even on holidays.

附录词语例句

1. 以…罪判处…　　　　　　　to sentence sb. to …for …

❖ 浙江省金华市中级人民法院以杀人罪判处徐力有期徒刑15年。

The Intermediate People's Court of Jinhua of Zhejiang Province sentenced Xu Li to fifteen years' imprisonment for murder.

1) 他因为杀人被判了死刑。

He was sentenced to death for murder.

2) 法院以贩毒(fàndú)罪判处他无期徒刑。

The court sentenced him to life imprisonment for selling drugs.

2. 从　　　　　　　　　　in a certain manner; according to

a certain principle

❖ 被告人徐力犯罪时未满18岁，依照《中国刑法》应当从轻处罚。

Xu Li, who committed the offense before he turned 18 years old, should be punished leniently, according to China's criminal law.

1) 他说，对领导的亲戚和子女犯罪，应当从严处理。

He said that the children and relatives of government officials who have committed a crime should be penalized harshly.

2) 因为你以后要当职业的网球运动员，所以对你的训练从严，从难，而他只是为了好玩儿，所以对他的要求不必那么严格。

Since you are going to be a professional tennis player, your training should be hard and strict; on the other hand he plays tennis just for fun, so there is no need to be so demanding with him.

3. 鉴于　　　　　　　　　　seeing that; in view of

❖ 鉴于本案的具体情况，可依法从轻处罚。

In view of the particular circumstances of this case, (Xu Li) could be punished leniently according to law.

1) 虽然你这次的考试成绩不太好，但是鉴于你平时的表现很好，所以我们还是给你一个比较好的成绩。

Although you did poorly on this test, we'll still give you a good grade, seeing that your performance is normally good.

2) 他说话的时候，出了几个错，但是鉴于他只学了三个星期的中文，他的错误都是可以接受的。

He made several mistakes in his speech, but considering that he has studied Chinese for only three weeks, all his mistakes are acceptable.

4. A跟B相 Verb

❖ ···贯彻惩罚与教育相结合的刑事政策···

··· to implement the criminal policy that combines punishment and education ···

1) 这个节目既有意义，又有意思，可以说把娱乐和教育相结合得非常好。

This TV program is both interesting and meaningful; it can be called the perfect combination of entertainment and education.

2) 中国跟发达国家相比，还有很大差距。

Compared with developed countries, China has a long way to go to catch up.

练习

I. Choose the correct answer.

(　　)1. 高中学生杀死同学的事件＿＿＿＿美国全社会对青少年心理问题的讨论。

　　　　a. 造成　　　　　　b. 引起　　　　　　c. 导致

(　　)2. 因为他＿＿＿＿，拼命工作，结果身体出了问题。

　　　　a. 成功心切　　　　b. 心切成功　　　　c 成功得心切.

(　　)3. 这个作家＿＿＿＿，所以写出了许多关于纽约的作品。

　　　　a. 生活在纽约长期

　　　　b. 生活长期在纽约

c. 长期生活在纽约

( )4. 在十四五世纪的欧洲，要是一个人不相信上帝，他会被 _____ 烧死的。

a. 狠狠   b. 活活   c. 深深

II.   Choose the most appropriate word for each blank and fill in with its
       Chinese equivalent.

cheat   one's own(children)   as usual   put forward

feel wronged   wish for one's children to be successful   stand

1. 大部分的中国父母都有_____的观念，他们常常给孩子_____很高
   的目标，比如考进最好的大学，考试第一等等。
2. 虽然今天下雨了，他还是_____去跑步。
3. 他长大以后才知道自己原来并不是父母的_____孩子。
4. 她跟弟弟吵架，两个人都有错，可是父母只怪她，让她很_____。
5. 据说是因为无法_____丈夫常常_____她，她才离婚的。

III.   Choose the phrase that is closest in meaning to the underlined phrase in
       the sentence.

( )1. 子女考试不理想，就觉得对不起父母，结果<u>必然</u>会导致
       心理问题。

a. 一定   b. 必须   c. 必要

( )2. 徐力杀了母亲以后，还<u>居然</u>参加了考试。

a. 自然   b. 当然   c. 竟然

( )3. 徐力的老师都说他是一个<u>品学兼优</u>的好学生。

a. 性格和道德都好
b. 人品和成绩都好
c. 学习和运动都好

( )4. 因为她<u>减肥心切</u>，所以每天只喝点水，吃点儿青菜，
       别的什么都不吃。

a. 很希望减肥   b. 很喜欢减肥   c. 忙着减肥

( )5. 三年以后，他<u>再次</u>来到金华，发现那里有了很大变化。

a. 两次   b. 第二次   c. 下次

( )6. 一般来说，女人不大<u>乐于</u>回答关于她们年龄的问题。

a. 愿意   b. 幸福   c. 反对

IV.   Make a sentence using the underlined expression.

1. 她参加家长会时<u>得知</u>，徐力期中考试的成绩<u>排在</u>班级第十八<u>名</u>。

2. 她说："<u>以后</u>你<u>再</u>去踢球，我<u>就</u>把你的腿打断。"

3. 他太脆弱，<u>仅仅因为</u>母亲对她学习上的压力，<u>就</u>杀了母亲。

4. 他<u>对</u>女儿的<u>期望</u>很高，因此花很多钱让她学弹琴、跳舞、画画等各种技能。

5. 法院<u>对</u>"徐力杀母"案<u>作出判决</u>，<u>以</u>故意杀人罪<u>判处</u>徐力有期徒刑15年。

6. 虽然徐力已经构成杀人罪，<u>但鉴于</u>他未满18岁，应当从轻处罚。

V.   Composition

1. 徐力的同学和老师都很同情徐力。在他们的眼里，徐力是个品学兼优的好学生，他们要给报纸写一封信，为徐力辩护。

    你是徐力的同学， 请你用下面的生字，为他写一封辩护的信。

> 升学压力、忍受、过问、寂寞、忽视、过分、提醒、排名、重视、导致、心理障碍、脆弱、期望、情急之中、大惊小怪、培养、请求、提高、从小、承受、压抑、同情、值得

2. 为什么徐力杀死了亲生母亲？请从下面几方面分析：

    a. 中国的升学考试制度以及中国的社会情况

    b. 父母和子女的关系

    c. 受到不良文化的影响

VI.   Answer the following questions.

1. 看了这个新闻以后，你同情谁？为什么？

2. 什么是"望子成龙"？你的父母有没有望子成龙的态度？"望子成龙"的态度跟社会和文化有没有关系？

3. 近年来，在美国也发生过中学生开枪杀人的事件，他们杀人的原因跟中国学生杀人的原因一样不一样？这反映了什么？

1999年8月15日《中國青年報》

第十七課

中國大學生對性的態度

最近，北京醫科大學公共衛生學院對北京市五所高校1310名在校本科大學生進行了性觀念的調查，其中，男生佔63%，平均年齡20歲。

在對大學生婚前性行爲的態度的調查中，半數以上的被調查的學生（54%）認爲在大學生中婚前性行爲應該絕對禁止。同時，半數以上的學生同意在雙方相愛、關係穩定、雙方正準備結婚的情況下，婚前性行爲是可以接受的。

研究者認爲，這一結果表明受當今西方性自由思潮的影響，大學生對性的態度已經比過去開放多了。

在對大學生性行爲調查中，27.7%的男生和

1999年8月15日《中国青年报》

第十七课

中国大学生对性的态度

最近，北京医科大学公共卫生学院对北京市五所高校1310名在校本科大学生进行了性观念的调查，其中，男生占63%，平均年龄20岁。

在对大学生婚前性行为的态度的调查中，半数以上的被调查的学生（54%）认为在大学生中婚前性行为应该绝对禁止。同时，半数以上的学生同意在双方相爱、关系稳定、双方正准备结婚的情况下，婚前性行为是可以接受的。

研究者认为，这一结果表明受当今西方性自由思潮的影响，大学生对性的态度已经比过去开放多了。

在对大学生性行为调查中，27.7%的男生和

34.4％的女生表示目前他們有穩定的戀人。有過婚前性行爲的，男生15％，女生13％。首次發生性關係的平均年齡：男生爲18.7歲，女生爲19歲左右。女生更傾向於和比她們年齡大的男生發生性關係。

另外，青少年的自我保護意識較差，當首次發生性關係時，只有42.2％的人使用了保險套。

研究人員分析認爲，當今大學生對婚前性行爲的態度正處於混亂和危險的階段。一方面，受我國傳統文化、道德、價值觀的影響，他們表現出傳統的一面：認爲婚前性行爲應該絕對禁止，貞節對男女青年來説還是十分重要的。另一方面，受西方的性自由生活方式的影響，某些大學生的性觀念和性態度已越來越自由化，如調查中已有相當一部分學生對婚前性行爲持寬容和認可的態度。

從發生婚前性行爲的大學生日益增多的現狀來看，出現這一現象的主要原因是因爲缺少性健康敎育，對婚前性行爲後果的嚴重性缺少認識。這種現狀實際上已經使部分大學生面臨未婚先孕、人工流

34.4%的女生表示目前他们有稳定的恋人。有过婚前性行为的，男生15%，女生13%。首次发生性关系的平均年龄：男生为18.7岁，女生为19岁左右。女生更倾向于和比她们年龄大的男生发生性关系。

另外，青少年的自我保护意识较差，当首次发生性关系时，只有42.2%的人使用了保险套。

研究人员分析认为，当今大学生对婚前性行为的态度正处于混乱和危险的阶段。一方面，受我国传统文化、道德、价值观的影响，他们表现出传统的一面：认为婚前性行为应该绝对禁止，贞节对男女青年来说还是十分重要的。另一方面，受西方的性自由生活方式的影响，某些大学生的性观念和性态度已越来越自由化，如调查中已有相当一部分学生对婚前性行为持宽容和认可的态度。

从发生婚前性行为的大学生日益增多的现状来看，出现这一现象的主要原因是因为缺少性健康教育，对婚前性行为后果的严重性缺少认识。这种现状实际上已经使部分大学生面临未婚先孕、人工流

產和性病等問題的威脅。這説明性教育在學校還需
要加強。

产和性病等问题的威胁。这说明性教育在学校还需要加强。

词汇

性		xìng	n. sex; sexual
态度	態度	tài.dù	n. attitude
最近		zuìjìn	n. recently
北京医科大学	北京醫科大學	Běijīng Yīkē Dàxué	n. Beijing Medical University
公共卫生学院	公共衛生學院	Gōnggòng Wèishēng Xuéyuàn	n. School of Public Health
高校		gāoxiào	n. universities and colleges
在校		zàixiào	n. be at school
本科		běnkē	n. undergraduate
进行	進行	jìnxíng	v. to carry out; to conduct
观念	觀念	guānniàn	n. concept
调查	調查	diàochá	n. survey; investigation
其中		qízhōng	n. among (them, which, ect.)
占	佔	zhàn	v. to make up; to account for
平均		píngjūn	adj. average
年龄	年齡	niánlíng	n. age
婚前		hūnqián	adj. premarital
性行为	性行爲	xìng xíngwéi	n. sexual intercourse; sexual behavior
半数	半數	bànshù	n. half (the number)

以上		yǐshàng	n. over and above
认为	認爲	rènwéi	v. to think that; to believe that
绝对	絕對	juéduì	adv. absolutely
禁止		jìnzhǐ	v. to forbid; to prohibit from
双方	雙方	shuāngfāng	n. both parties; both sides
相爱	相愛	xiāng'ài	v. to be in love with each other
稳定	穩定	wěndìng	adj. steady; stable
可以接受的	可以接受的	kě.yǐ jiēshòu.de	adj. acceptable
研究者	研究者	yánjiūzhě	n. researcher
结果	結果	jiéguǒ	n. result; outcome
表明		biǎomíng	v. to demonstrate
当今	當今	dāngjīn	n. at present time; today
西方		xīfāng	n. West; Western
自由		zìyóu	n. freedom
思潮		sīcháo	n. trend of thought
开放	開放	kāifàng	adj. open; liberal
目前		mùqián	n. at present; for the time being
恋人	戀人	liànrén	n. lover; sweetheart
首次		shǒucì	adv. first time
发生	發生	fāshēng	v. to happen; to have

左右		zuǒyòu	prep. about; or so
倾向于	傾向於	qīngxiàngyú	v. to be inclined to; to tend to
自我保护	自我保護	zìwǒ bǎohù	n. self-protection
意识	意識	yì.shí	n. awareness
较	較	jiào	adv. relatively
差		chà	adj. bad
当…时	當…時	dāng …shí	conj. when
保险套	保險套	bǎoxiǎntào	n. condom
人员	人員	rényuán	n. personnel; staff
分析		fēn.xī	v. to analyze
处于	處於	chǔyú	v. to be in
混乱	混亂	hùnluàn	adj. disorderly; chaotic
危险	危險	wēixiǎn	adj. dangerous
阶段	階段	jiēduàn	n. phase; stage
传统	傳統	chuántǒng	n. tradition; convention
价值观	價值觀	jiàzhíguān	n. value system
贞节	貞節	zhēnjié	n. chastity or virginity
青年		qīngnián	n. young people; a youth
方式		fāngshì	n. fashion; way; manner
某些		mǒuxiē	adj. some; certain
自由化		zìyóuhuà	v. to liberalize

如	如	rú	prep. for example; such as
相当	相當	xiāngdāng	adj. quite; considerable
持		chí	v. to hold (an opinion or an attitude)
宽容	寬容	kuānróng	adj. tolerant
认可	認可	rènkě	v. to accept; to approve
增多		zēngduō	v. to grow in number; to increase
现状	現狀	xiànzhuàng	n. the present situation
现象	現象	xiàn.xiàng	n. phenomenon
缺少		quēshǎo	v. to lack; to be deficient in
教育	教育	jiàoyù	n. education
后果	後果	hòuguǒ	n. consequence
严重性	嚴重性	yánzhòngxìng	n. seriousness; gravity
认识	認識	rèn.shí	n. understanding
实际上	實際上	shíjìshàng	adv. in reality
面临	面臨	miànlín	v. to face; to confront
未婚先孕	未婚先孕	wèihūn xiānyùn	v. to get pregnant before marriage
人工流产	人工流產	réngōng liúchǎn	v./n. induced abortion
性病		xìngbìng	n. venereal disease
威胁	威脅	wēixié	v./n. to threaten; threat
加强	加強	jiāqiáng	v. to strengthen; to reinforce

词语例句

1. 对…进行+Verb (two-syllables)

❖ 最近北京医科大学对北京市五所高校1310名在校学生进行了性观念的调查。

Recently Beijing Medical School conducted a survey of thirteen hundred and ten university students from five universities in Beijing on their attitudes toward sex.

1) 最近政府对服务业进行了调查，发现有些饭馆雇佣非法移民和童工。

Recently the government investigated some restaurants and found that they had illegally hired immigrants and children workers.

2) 校园枪杀案发生后，美国人开始对应该不应该保留持枪的自由进行激烈的讨论。

After the shooting at that school, Americans are actively discussing whether they should have the right to carry guns.

2. …，其中，…　　　　among them

❖ 最近北京医科大学对北京五所高校1310在校学生进行了性观念的调查，其中，男生占百分之六十三，平均年龄二十岁。

Recently Beijing Medical University conducted a survey of thirteen hundred and ten university students from five universities on their attitudes toward sex, among the surveyed students, there are 63% of males, with the average age of 20.

1) 据报道，1990年美国的凶杀、强奸抢劫案件达到180,000万起，其中凶杀案件为23,000起。

According to a report in 1990, the number of murder, rape and robbery cases in America reached 180,000, with 23,000 murders.

2) 那一年，卓别林演了35部电影，其中大部分是他自己写自己导演的。

During that year, Chaplin acted in 35 films, many of which he wrote and directed himself.

3. 以上   **over; more than**

❖ 半数以上被调查的学生认为，在大学生中婚前性行为应该绝对禁止。

More than half of the surveyed students are of the opinion that university students should absolutely be prohibited from sexual relations before they get married.

1) 同时，半数以上的学生同意在双方相爱、关系稳定、双方正准备结婚的情况下，婚前性关系是可以接受的。

At the same time, more than half of the students agreed that if the two persons are in love, their relationship is stable, and are ready to get married, premarital sexual relations are acceptable.

2) 在美国，21岁以上的人才可以买酒。

In America people only over 21 years old are allowed to buy alcohol.

4. 认为   **think that; believe that**

❖ 研究人员认为，中国大学生性态度比以前开放，是受了西方的影响。

The researchers thought that it is due to the western influence that Chinese students are more open toward sex.

1) 我们都认为他的建议很可行。

We all think his proposal feasible.

2) 我不认为受教育越多，道德水平越高。

I do not believe that the more education a person has, the higher his or her morality is.

5. 倾向于   **to be inclined to; prefer to**

❖ 女生更倾向于与比她们年龄大的男生发生性关系。

The girl students are more inclined to have sexual relations with older male students.

1) 在这两个方法中，我倾向于第一种。

Of the two plans, I prefer the first.

2) 对于解决这个问题，我倾向于不使用暴力。

I prefer not to use violence in the resolution of this problem.

6. 当…时   when

❖ 当首次发生性关系时，只有百分之42.2%的人使用了保险套。

Only 42.2% of them used condoms when they first had sex.

1) 当我们听说你不能来的时候，我们都很失望。

We were very disappointed at the news that you couldn't come.

2) 每当我看见儿童乞丐的时候，心里就觉得很不舒服。

I feel upset every time when I see a child beggar.

7. 处于   to be in the state of

❖ 研究人员认为，当今大学生对婚前性行为的态度正处于混乱和危险的阶段。

The researchers believed that the college students' attitudes toward sex are in a state of chaos and danger.

1) 由于长期的战争，这个国家的经济一直处于较低的水平。

The economy of this country had been at a comparatively low level owing to the long period of war.

2) 当我们去看他的时候，他还处于昏迷的状态。

He was still in a coma when we visited him in the hospital.

8. 持…态度   hold a …attitude

❖ 如调查中已经有相当一部分学生对婚前性行为持宽容和认可的态度。

For example, in the survey there have been a considerable number of students who have held a tolerant and approving attitude towards the premarital sexual behaviors.

1) 他对别人的好意总是持怀疑的态度。

He is always suspicious of others' good intention. (lit. "holding a suspicious attitude toward others' good intention").

2) 一个世纪以前，中国人对外来的文化持抵抗的态度。

A century ago, Chinese people resisted (lit. "held a resisting attitude toward") foreign culture.

9. …的主要原因是 …   the main reason of… is …

❖ 出现这一现象的主要原因是缺少性教育。

The main reason of this phenomenon is lack of sex education.

1) 他辞职的主要原因是他跟老板合不来。

The main reason that he resigned is that he could not get along with his boss.

2) 把语言培训班设在北京的主要原因是大部分北京人说标准的普通话。

The main reason that this language program is located in Beijing is that most Beijing people speak standard Mandarin Chinese.

练习

I.   Choose the correct answer.

(   )1. 上个星期我读了十本书，＿＿＿＿七本是关于中国历史的。

          a.中间   b.之中   c.其中

(   )2. 这所大学半数＿＿＿＿的学生都是州内的学生。

          a.上面   b.多   c.以上

(   )3. 他们结婚十年了，＿＿＿＿。

          a.他一直相爱她

          b.他们一直相爱

          c.他们一直相爱双方

(   )4. A：一个人很能干，一个人很诚实，你会选谁当总统？

          B：我比较＿＿＿＿选能干的人当总统。

          a.倾向于   b.宁可   c.与其

(   )5. 有些中国人的环境保护意识较差，换句话说，他们＿＿＿＿。

          a.他们没有钱保护环境

          b.他们没有精力保护环境

          c.他们不知道要保护环境。

(   )6. 他开车的时候一直想着别的事，＿＿＿＿出了车祸。

          a.后果   b.结果   c.好在

II.   Choose the most appropriate word for each blank and fill in with its Chinese equivalent.

        prohibit   be in a state of   to be faced with   gravity

1. 上个星期美国总统竞选正＿＿＿＿最紧张的阶段。

2. 七十年代后期中国政府才认识到人口过多的＿＿＿＿。

3. 电影院里＿＿＿＿吸烟。

4. 四年级学生＿＿＿＿的最大压力是找工作和完成毕业论文。

III.   Translation

Survey — Sexual behavior before marriage

Young Chinese are adopting a more tolerant attitude towards pre-marital sex, love and marriage, an urban study found recently.

Only 35.1 percent of respondents voiced agreement with the traditional notion that " pre-marital sex is immoral and should not be permitted under any circumstance." according to results of the study conducted by Beijing Medical University.

The survey also found men and women held different opinions, with 43.9 percent of female respondents, or 18.5 percent more than male counterparts, pointing to the immorality of pre-marital sex.

Respondents with higher education levels voiced a great tolerance towards premarital sex and individuals living in economically developed regions voiced greater tolerance than those in less-developed regions, it says.

The respondents attributed the increasing tolerance of young Chinese towards premarital sex to two main reasons. Firstly, Western culture had prompted young generation to reflect on traditional culture. Secondly, greater tolerance towards premarital sex by the general public reduces the costs which young people must pay for more liberal behavior, they said.

IV.　　Make a sentence using the underlined expression.

1. 家长会以后，老师组织学生对帮助别人应不应该要钱进行讨论。
2. 很多人认为在准备结婚的情况下，婚前性行为是可以接受的。
3. 据调查，相当一部分美国人对政府控制枪持反对态度。
4. 在对婚前性关系的问题上，大多数中国人倾向于反对。
5. 全球环境的变化，使很多动物面临死亡的威胁。
6. 火灾后，整个大楼处于混乱状态。

V.　　Answer the following questions.

1. 在你看来，婚前性关系是不是不道德的行为？为什么？
2. 性观念的开放对整个社会来说是件好事还是坏事？
3. 中国大学生性观念的开放是受西方的影响还是社会发展的必然结果？

2000年7月26日《光明日報》

第十八課

暑假大學生在做什麼？

　　七月的北京，各大高校放了暑假。大學生們是怎樣過這個假期呢？帶著這些疑問，我們採訪了一些大學生。

　　一些大學生選擇了回家"避暑"，大一的學生絕大多數屬於這種情況。一名對外經濟貿易大學讀大一的同學說："北京那麼熱，不回家幹嘛？"

　　許多高校自己組織了一些社會實踐活動，用這種特殊的形式來使同學們與社會多接觸，更重要的是加強對同學們思想上的教育，使同學們在科學文化和思想教育上有些收穫。有的學校組織了一部分學生去陝西延安、河北省平山縣進行參觀考察；還有的學校組織了一部分同學去毛主席紀念堂站崗值勤，維護秩序。

　　在留校的學生中，大部分人還是把學習放在第一位。大一和大二的學生忙著參加各種英語的輔

2000年7月26日《光明日报》

第十八课

暑假大学生在做什么？

七月的北京，各大高校放了暑假。大学生们是怎样过这个假期呢？带着这些疑问，我们采访了一些大学生。

一些大学生选择了回家"避暑"，大一的学生绝大多数属于这种情况。一名对外经济贸易大学读大一的同学说："北京那么热，不回家干嘛？"

许多高校自己组织了一些社会实践活动，用这种特殊的形式来使同学们与社会多接触，更重要的是加强对同学们思想上的教育，使同学们在科学文化和思想教育上有些收获。有的学校组织了一部分学生去陕西延安、河北省平山县进行参观考察；还有的学校组织了一部分同学去毛主席纪念堂站岗值勤，维护秩序。

在留校的学生中，大部分人还是把学习放在第一位。大一和大二的学生忙着参加各种英语的辅導班；而在大三和大四的學生中，考研和考TOEFL和GRE的則佔了相當大的比例。這類輔導班雖然收費都不低，但仍吸引了大批的學生。像北京新東方學校，聚集了全國各大高校的學生。有許多在新疆、青海、雲南、貴州、廣東等地上大學的同學，都不遠千里趕到新東方的TOEFL和GRE的輔導班。據一些大學生介紹，新東方學校的TOEFL和GRE的暑期班早在幾個月之前就報滿了。看來，求學仍是許多當代大學生追求的主要目標。

許多高校自己成立了勤工儉學中心，幫助學生解決了許多後顧之憂。這些打工的同學在做些什麼工作呢？家教、翻譯、市場調查、網頁制作，或者是給一些公司幫忙，報酬為每小時20至100元不等。許多大學生充分發揮自己的專業特長。如學計算機的就給中關村的一些電腦公司做網頁；學外國語專業的就給一些大公司翻譯各種文稿、手冊；而學師範專業的就熱衷於當家教。這些同學每個月都能拿到2000元到3000元，報酬相當可觀。

导班；而在大三和大四的学生中，考研和考TOEFL和GRE的则占了相当大的比例。这类辅导班虽然收费都不低，但仍吸引了大批的学生。像北京新东方学校，聚集了全国各大高校的学生。有许多在新疆、青海、云南、贵州、广东等地上大学的同学，都不远千里赶到新东方的TOEFL和GRE的辅导班。据一些大学生介绍，新东方学校的TOEFL和GRE的暑期班早在几个月之前就报满了。看来，求学仍是许多当代大学生追求的主要目标。

许多高校自己成立了勤工俭学中心，帮助学生解决了许多后顾之忧。这些打工的同学在做些什么工作呢？家教、翻译、市场调查、网页制作，或者是给一些公司帮忙，报酬为每小时20至100元不等。许多大学生充分发挥自己的专业特长。如学计算机的就给中关村的一些电脑公司做网页；学外国语专业的就给一些大公司翻译各种文稿、手册；而学师范专业的就热衷于当家教。这些同学每个月都能拿到2000元到3000元，报酬相当可观。

　　但相比之下，勤工儉學似乎不是太熱。一名中國人民大學的學生認爲，雖然外出打工可以豐富自己的社會經驗，提高自己的能力，並且可以掙一些零花錢和生活費，但是就目前來説，考研和考 TOEFL、GRE大於一切，否則，畢業後很難有機會出國進修或者找到一份好的工作。

　　但相比之下，勤工俭学似乎不是太热。一名中国人民大学的学生认为，虽然外出打工可以丰富自己的社会经验，提高自己的能力，并且可以挣一些零花钱和生活费，但是就目前来说，考研和考TOEFL、GRE大于一切，否则，毕业后很难有机会出国进修或者找到一份好的工作。

词汇

暑假		shǔjià	n. summer vacation
高校		gāoxiào	n. colleges and universities
放（假）		fàng(jià)	v. to have or to be on (holidays or vacations)
过	過	guò	v. to go through; to undergo (a process)
假期	假期	jiàqī	n. vacation; holiday
疑问	疑問	yíwèn	n. question; doubt
采访	採訪	cǎifǎng	v. (of a journalist) to cover (some event); to interview
选择	選擇	xuǎnzé	v/n. to select; to choose; choice; option
避暑		bìshǔ	v. to go away for summer; to stay at a summer resort
大一		dàyī	n. (college) freshman
绝大多数	絕大多數	juédà duōshù	n. vast majority; the overwhelming majority
属于	屬於	shǔyú	v. to belong to; to be part of
对外经济贸易大学	對外經濟貿易大學	Duìwài Jíngjì Màoyì Dàxué	n. University of International Trade and Economics
干嘛	幹嘛	gànmá	ph. do what
组织	組織	zǔzhī	v. to organize; to arrange
特殊		tèshū	adj. special; particular
形式		xíngshì	n. form
接触	接觸	jiēchù	v. to come into contact with

加强	加強	jiāqiáng	v. to reinforce; to strengthen
思想		sīxiǎng	n. ideology; thoughts
教育	教育	jiào.yù	n. education
科学	科學	kēxué	n. scientific knowledge
文化		wénhuà	n. culture
收获	收獲	shōuhuò	n. gains; harvests
陕西		Shǎnxī	n. a province in northwestern China
延安		Yán'ān	n. a place in Shanxi province
河北	河北	Héběi	n. a province in north China
平山		Píngshān	n. a place in Hebei province
县	縣	xiàn	n. county
参观	參觀	cān'guān	v. to visit; to tour
考察		kǎochá	v. to make an on-the-spot investigation; to observe and study
毛主席纪念堂	毛主席紀念堂	Máozhǔxí Jì'niàntáng	n. Chairmen Mao's Memorial
站岗	站崗	zhàn'gǎng	v. to stand guard; to be on sentry
值勤	值勤	zhíqín	v. to be on duty (of police or military)
维护	維護	wéihù	v. to defend; to safeguard
秩序		zhì.xù	n. order; law and order
留校		liúxiào	v. to stay at school
大二		dàèr	n. (college) sophomore

参加	參加	cānjiā	v. to attend
辅导班	輔導班	fǔdǎobān	n. prep course
大三		dàsān	n. (college) junior
大四		dàsì	n. (college) senior
考研		kǎoyán	v. to take an graduate school entrance exam
比例		bǐlì	n. proportion
收费	收費	shōufèi	n./v. charges; fees; to charge
仍		réng	adv. still
大批		dàpī	adj. a large number of ; great deal of
新东方	新東方	Xīndōngfāng	n. New Oriental (name of a school)
聚集		jùjí	v. to gather; to assemble
新疆	新疆	Xīnjiāng	n. a province in northwest China
青海		Qīnghǎi	n. a province in northwest China
云南	雲南	Yúnnán	n. a province in southwest China
贵州	貴州	Guìzhōu	n. a province in southwest China
广东	廣東	Guǎngdōng	n. a province in southern China
地		dì	n. place
不远千里	不遠千里	bù yuǎn qiānlǐ	ph. to go to the trouble of travelling a long distance
赶到	趕到	gǎndào	v. to rush for
介绍	介紹	jièshào	v./n. introduce; introduction

暑期班		shǔqībān	n. summer school
报	報	bào	v. to sign up
满	滿	mǎn	v. to full
看来	看來	kànlái	ph. it seems; it looks as if
求学	求學	qiúxué	v. to attend school
当代	當代	dāngdài	n. of this generation; present-day
追求		zhuīqiú	v. to seek; to pursue
主要		zhǔyào	adj. main
目标	目標	mùbiāo	n. goal; aim
成立		chénglì	v. to establish; to found
勤工俭学	勤工儉學	qín' gōngjiǎn xué	n. part-work and part-study program
中心		zhōngxīn	n. center
解决	解決	jiějué	v. to solve; to resolve
后顾之忧	後顧之憂	hòu gù zhīyōu	n. fear of disturbance in the rear
家教	家教	jiājiào	n. tutor
翻译	翻譯	fānyì	n. interpreter; translator
市场	市場	shìchǎng	n. market
网页	網頁	wǎngyè	n. web page
制作		zhìzuò	v. to make
报酬	報酬	bàochóu	n. rewards; remuneration
不等		bùděng	adj. different

充分		chōngfèn	adv. fully
发挥	發揮	fāhuī	v. to bring (skill, talent, etc.) into full play
专业	專業	zhuānyè	n. major; specialize field or subjects
特长	特長	tècháng	n. a strong point; what one is specially good at; a specialty
中关村	中關村	Zhōngguāncūn	n. a district in Beijing
电脑	電腦	diànnǎo	n. computer
外国语	外國語	wàiguóyǔ	n. foreign language
文稿		wéngǎo	n. manuscript; draft
手册		shǒucè	n. handbook; manual
师范	師範	shīfàn	n. (study of) teaching; "normal"
热衷于	熱衷於	rèzhōngyú	v. to be fond of
可观	可觀	kěguān	adj. considerable (sum of money, losses, etc.); impressive
相比之下		xiāngbǐ zhīxià	ph. by comparison; by contrast
热	熱	rè	adj. popular
人民大学	人民大學	Rénmín Dàxué	n. People's University
外出		wàichū	v. to go out
打工		dǎgōng	v. to do part time job
丰富	豐富	fēngfù	v. to enrich
经验	經驗	jīngyàn	n. experience
提高		tígāo	v. to increase; to improve

能力		nénglì	n. ability
挣	掙	zhèng	v. to earn
零花钱	零花錢	línghuāqián	n. pocket money; incidental expenses
生活费	生活費	shēnghuófèi	n. living expenses
大于	大於	dàyú	v. to be more/bigger than
一切		yíqiè	n. all; everything; every
否则	否則	fǒuzé	conj. otherwise; if not
出国	出國	chūguó	v. to go abroad
进修	進修	jìnxiū	v. to engage in advanced studies
份		fèn	mw for job

词语例句

1. 属于   **belong to; to be part of**

❖ 一些大学生选择了回家"避暑"，大一的学生绝大多数属于这种情况。

Some college students choose going home to "avoid the heat." The vast majority of freshmen belong to this category.

1) 有些学生因为忍受不了学习的压力而杀人，徐力杀死母亲就属于这种情况。

Some students kill people because they can't bear the pressure of their studies; such is the case of Xu Li killing his mother.

2) 喝醉以后，有的人唱歌，有的人不停地说话，他属于哪种类型？

Having gotten drunk, some people sing, some people keep talking; which type is he?

2. 用…来…   **use … to …**

❖ 许多高校自己组织了一些社会活动，用这种特殊的形式来使同学们与社会多接触。

Many universities organized social events. They use this particular form to let students have more contact with society.

1) 古代的人用陶器来做饭，装食物，以及运送东西。

Ancient people used clay pottery for cooking, storing food and carrying things from one place to another.

2) 作者用这个例子来说明，在地位和金钱之间，人们往往更重视地位。

The author used this example to illustrate that people often care more about status than money.

3. 把…放在第一位   **put … first**

❖ 大部分人还是把学习放在第一位。

Most people still put studying first.

1) 目前中国政府把发展经济放在第一位。

At this point, China's government is putting economic development first.

2) 在回答谁是美国最伟大的总统时，很多人把林肯放在第一位。

When answering the question of who is America's greatest president, a lot of people rank Abraham Lincoln first.

4. 占   **to make up**

❖ 而在大三大四的学生中，考研和考TOEFL和GRE的则占了相当大的比例。

There is a considerable proportion of seniors and juniors who will take the graduate entrance exam, the GRE and the TOEFL.

1) Affirmative Action规定，在跟政府有关系的公司中，妇女和少数民族的人数必须占一定的比例。

Affirmative Action provides that in companies related to the government, the number of women and minorities must reach a certain quota.

2) 据报载，中国人花在食物上的钱占总收入的一半（比例）。

It is reported that Chinese people spend half of their salaries on food.

5. 早在…就…   **as early as**

❖ 据一些大学生介绍，新东方的TOEFL和GRE的暑期班早在几个月之前就报满了。

According to what some college students said, the New Oriental School's GRE and TOEFL courses had been full for several months already.

1) 早在卓别林的第二部电影，他就形成了自己的风格，就是戴着小黑帽，穿一条非常肥大的裤子，留着小胡子。

As early as in his second film, Chaplin had developed his own style of acting in which he wore a small black hat and very wide trousers and grow a moustache.

2) 早在二十年前，中国政府就开始控制吸烟的工作。

As early as twenty years ago, the Chinese government had launched an effort to control smoking.

6. 热衷于   **be fond of**

❖ …，而学师范专业就热衷于当家教。

  …, and those majoring in teacher training are very fond of being a tutor.

1) 目前大城市里的青少年很热衷于跳迪斯科。

  Nowadays teenagers in big cities are crazy about disco dancing.

2) 最近几年，中国的中产阶级非常热衷于去欧洲旅游。

  During the past few years, China's middle class have been very fond of going traveling in Europe.

7. 相比之下   **by comparison**

❖ 但相比之下，勤工俭学似乎不是太热。

  By comparison, having a part-time job seemed not very popular (among Chinese college students).

1) …，相比之下，农村人更喜欢便宜、耐用，容易使用的商品。

  Unlike their urban counterparts, farmers prefer cheap, durable and easy-to handle goods.

2) 上课的时候，美国学生常常积极提问，而相比之下，中国学生就显得安静多了。

  American students tend to ask questions actively in class, while Chinese students seem much quieter by comparison.

8. **adj. + 于**   **adj. + than**

❖ 但是就目前来说，考研和考TOEFL和GRE大于一切。

  But for the time being, taking the graduate school exam, the TOEFL and the GRE are more important than anything else.

1) 这种鱼存活有一定的条件，水温不能低于20度。

  This kind of fish needs certain conditions in order to live: the water temperature must not fall below 20 °C.

2) 对他来说，家庭重于事业。

  For him, family is more important than a career.

练习

I. Choose the most appropriate word for each blank and fill in with its
    Chinese equivalent.

    come into contact with   popular   gains(n.)

    fear of disturbance in the rear   fond of

1. 孩子有人照顾，父母工作的时候就没有_____了。

2. 他是一个记者，每天会_____到各种各样的人。

3. 我参加这个辅导班以后，觉得没有什么_____。

4. 他喜欢看书，而他的太太却_____参加各种晚会。

5. 目前最_____的专业就是电脑和网络。

II. Complete the following dialogues with the expressions provided.

     A：你对大学生打工有什么看法？

     B：我觉得大学生打工有好处，也有坏处。

     A：有什么好处呢？

     B：……（首先；赚；其次；丰富；提高；有助于），但是我不打
     工。

     A：既然好处这么多，为什么你不打工呢？

     B：……（相比之下；）。我不打工有两个原因，第一，大部分的
     工作跟我的专业没有关系，虽然……（可观；报酬；充分；特长
     ；发挥）；第二，现在的社会，没有研究生的文凭很难有机会
     找到好工作，所以……（第一位；就目前来说；用…来；忙着；
     否则）

     A：有你这样想法的人多不多？

     B：……（占；早就；满；主要目标）

III. Answer the following questions.

1. 比较中美大学生暑假生活，有什么相同之处？有什么不同之处？

2. 暑期打工，美国大学生比较热衷于做什么工作？中国大学生呢？

3. 中美大学生参加的社会实践活动有什么不同？

IV. Composition

     一个难忘的暑假

2000年7月19日《光明日報》

第十九課

考試的 " 槍手 " 問題

在北京大學的研究生樓前，我看到了這樣的啓事：" 誠聘（急）八月托福（TOEFL）男代考！（價格面議）。" 大概因爲心虛，啓事下面還專門用英文注明：" 對不起，只能用E-mail (XX@yahoo.com)聯繫。" 同時，這類 " 誠聘 " 在北京其他著名大學也常能看到。

代考者又稱 " 槍手 "，意思是專替他人達成目標的人。高額的酬勞無疑是窮學生願意當這個角色的主要原因。

同樣毫無疑問的是，學生們對這類事情的違規性質十分清楚。

教務處的老師並不否認這類事情的存在，他們還舉出了去年發生的幾起代考案。教務處表示，學校對代考的處理是非常嚴厲的。去年學校化學系一個女生爲人代考托福，學校發現後毫不留情地把

2000年7月19日《光明日报》

第十九课

考试的"枪手"问题

在北京大学的研究生楼前，我看到了这样的启事："诚聘（急）八月托福（TOEFL）男代考！（价格面议）。"大概因为心虚，启事下面还专门用英文注明："对不起，只能用E-mail (XX@yahoo.com)联系。"同时，这类"诚聘"在北京其他著名大学也常能看到。

代考者又称"枪手"，意思是专替他人达成目标的人。高额的酬劳无疑是穷学生愿意当这个角色的主要原因。

同样毫无疑问的是，学生们对这类事情的违规性质十分清楚。

教务处的老师并不否认这类事情的存在，他们还举出了去年发生的几起代考案。教务处表示，学校对代考的处理是非常严厉的。去年学校化学系一个女生为人代考托福，学校发现后毫不留情地把她開除了。只要發現這種違規情形，不僅將學生的情況上網，而且在全校發布通告。

但當問起學校是否有其他辦法防止這類事件發生時，幾位老師都認為，想在學校考試範圍之外管住學生這種行為比較困難：首先是考試不一定是在校內進行，難以查找；其次，即使在學校內進行，也只是一部分，而且人數眾多，10多個考場，每個考場少則30-40人，多則60人，沒有那麼多時間和精力去逐一查看；第三，現在假證件四處泛濫，曾經有過一人帶有好幾個身分證的事情出現，而且足以以假亂真，老師們又怎麼能一一識別？再說，張貼廣告的人什麼時候出現，廣告貼在什麼地方，學校不可能時時監督，而且學生在學習之外、校園之外做什麼事情又不是學校可以管得了的。所以，事先採取有效措施制止這一行為幾乎無法做到，只能在發現後給予嚴厲制裁。同時，北大教務處還表示，解決這一問題不能光靠懲罰，還需要考試機制的改革。

這些高等院校的學生是國家最值得驕傲的精英

她开除了。只要发现这种违规情形，不仅将学生的情况上网，而且在全校发布通告。

但当问起学校是否有其他办法防止这类事件发生时，几位老师都认为，想在学校考试范围之外管住学生这种行为比较困难：首先是考试不一定是在校内进行，难以查找；其次，即使在学校内进行，也只是一部分，而且人数众多，10多个考场，每个考场少则30-40人，多则60人，没有那么多时间和精力去逐一查看；第三，现在假证件四处泛滥，曾经有过一人带有好几个身分证的事情出现，而且足以以假乱真，老师们又怎么能一一识别？再说，张贴广告的人什么时候出现，广告贴在什么地方，学校不可能时时监督，而且学生在学习之外、校园之外做什么事情又不是学校可以管得了的。所以，事先采取有效措施制止这一行为几乎无法做到，只能在发现后给予严厉制裁。同时，北大教务处还表示，解决这一问题不能光靠惩罚，还需要考试机制的改革。

这些高等院校的学生是国家最值得骄傲的精英

但卻受金錢驅使，心甘情願充當其他人的工具，做出違規的事情，不能不說是教育的缺陷、知識的悲哀。僅靠事後處罰能擋得住金錢的誘惑嗎？

但却受金钱驱使，心甘情愿充当其他人的工具，做出违规的事情，不能不说是教育的缺陷、知识的悲哀。仅靠事后处罚能挡得住金钱的诱惑吗？

词汇

枪手	槍手	qiāngshǒu	n. one who takes an examination in place of another person (lit. "shooter")
北京大学	北京大學	Běijīng dàxué	n. Peking University
研究生		yánjiūshēng	n. graduate student
研究生楼	研究生樓	yánjiūshēng lóu	n. graduate student dormitory
启事	啓事	qǐshì	n. notice; announcement
诚聘	誠聘	chéngpìn	v. to sincerely hire ("wanted")
急	急	jí	adj./adv. urgent; urgently
托福		tuōfú	TOEFL (Test of English as a Foreign Language)
代考		dàikǎo	v./n. to take an exam for somebody else
价格	價格	jiàgé	n. price
面议	面議	miànyì	v. to discuss in person
大概		dàgài	adv. probably
心虚		xīnxū	adj. with a guilty conscience; afraid of being found out
专门	專門	zhuānmén	adv. especially
注明		zhùmíng	v. to make a footnote
联系	聯繫	liánxì	v. to contact
其他		qítā	adj. other; else
著名		zhùmíng	adj. famous; celebrated
代考者		dàikǎozhě	n. people who take an

			examination for others
称	稱	chēng	v. to call; to be called
专	專	zhuān	adv. especially (=专门)
替		tì	prep. for; on behalf of
他人		tārén	n. some other persons
达成	達成	dáchéng	v. to realize; to achieve
目标	目標	mùbiāo	n. objective; target
高额	高額	gāoé	n. a large amount of money
酬劳	酬勞	chóuláo	n. compensation; reward; payment
无疑	無疑	wúyí	adv. undoubtedly
当	當	dāng	v. to play the part of; to work as
角色	角色	juésè	n. role; part
毫无	毫無	háowú	adv. not at all
违规	違規	wéiguī	v. to violate regulations
性质	性質	xìng.zhì	n. nature; quality
教务处	教務處	jiàowùchù	n. educational administration office
否认	否認	fǒurèn	v. to deny
存在		cúnzài	v. to exist
举出	舉出	jǔchū	v. to give (an example); to cite as an example
发生	發生	fāshēng	v. to happen; occur; take place
起		qǐ	mw for legal cases or

			occurrences
案		àn	n. case
表示		biǎoshì	v. to express
处理	處理	chǔlǐ	v. to punish; to deal with
严厉	嚴厲	yánlì	adj. stern; severe
化学	化學	huàxué	n. chemistry
毫不留情		háobùliúqíng	v. to show no mercy whatsoever
开除	開除	kāichú	v. to expel; to discharge; to kick out
上网	上網	shàngwǎng	v. to log on to the Internet
发布	發布	fābù	v. to announce; to issue
通告		tōnggào	n. public notice; announcement
是否		shìfǒu	adv. whether or not; yes or no
防止		fángzhǐ	v. to prevent
范围	範圍	fànwéi	n. scope; extent; range
管		guǎn	v. to supervise; to manage
比较	比較	bǐjiào	adv. relatively; fairly
首先		shǒuxiān	conj. in the first place; first of all
校内		xiàonèi	n. inside the university
进行	進行	jìnxíng	v. to carry on/out; to conduct
难以	難以	nányǐ	adv. difficult to
查找		cházhǎo	v. to investigate; to look into

其次		qícì	conj. next; second
即使		jíshǐ	conj. even; even though
人数	人數	rénshù	n. number of people
众多	眾多	zhòngduō	adj. multitudinous; numerous
考场	考場	kǎochǎng	n. examination hall or room
精力		jīnglì	n. energy; vigor
逐一		zhúyī	adv. one by one
查看		chákàn	v. to look over; to examine
假		jiǎ	adj. fake
证件	證件	zhèngjiàn	n. credentials; papers; certificates
四处	四處	sìchù	n. all around; everywhere
泛滥	泛濫	fànlàn	v. to overflow; to spread unchecked
身分证	身分證	shēnfènzhèng	n. identity card
足以		zúyǐ	adv. enough; sufficiently
以假乱真	以假亂真	yǐ jiǎ luàn zhēn	v. to pass off a fake as genuine; to mix the spurious with the genuine
一一		yīyī	adv. one by one; one after another
识别	識別	shíbié	v. to discern; to distinguish
再说		zàishuō	conj. furthermore; besides
张贴	張貼	zhāngtiē	v. to put up (poster/etc.)
广告	廣告	guǎnggào	n. advertisement

贴	貼	tiē	v. to paste; to glue; to post
时时	時時	shíshí	adv. constantly; often
监督	監督	jiāndū	v. to supervise
事先		shìxiān	adv. in advance; beforehand
采取	採取	cǎiqǔ	v. to take; to adopt
有效		yǒuxiào	adj. effective; valid
措施		cuòshī	n. measure; step
制止		zhìzhǐ	v. to stop; to put an end to
几乎	幾乎	jīhū	adv. almost; nearly
给予		gěiyǔ	v. to give to
制裁		zhìcái	v. to place sanctions upon
解决	解決	jiějué	v. to solve; to settle
光		guāng	adv. only
靠		kào	v. to rely on
惩罚	懲罰	chéngfá	v/n. to punish
机制	機制	jīzhì	n. mechanism
改革		gǎigé	n/v. reform
高等		gāoděng	adj. higher; advanced
院校		yuànxiào	n. colleges and universities
值得	值得	zhídé	v. to be worth; to deserve
骄傲	驕傲	jiāoào	adj. proud
精英		jīngyīng	n. elite

驱使	驅使	qūshǐ	v/n. to prompt; to urge
心甘情愿	心甘情願	xīn'gān qíngyuàn	v. to be totally willing to; to be perfectly happy to
充当	充當	chōngdāng	v. to work as; to play the part of
工具		gōngjù	n. tool; instrument
教育	教育	jiàoyù	n. education
缺陷		quēxiàn	n. flaw; defect
知识	知識	zhī.shí	n. knowledge
悲哀		bēiāi	n. sorrow
事后	事後	shìhòu	n. afterwards
处罚	處罰	chǔfá	v./n. to punish; penalty
挡得住	擋得住	dǎng.de zhù	v. to be able to block; to be able to keep off
诱惑	誘惑	yòuhuò	n. temptation

词语例句

1. 诚聘　　　　　　　　　　　wanted!

❖ 诚聘（急）八月托福男代考！

Male "shooter" for TOEFL in August wanted(urgent)!

1) 诚聘有经验保姆！

Experienced babysitter wanted!

2) 诚聘英语家教！

English tutor wanted!

2. 专门　　　　　　　　　　　specially

❖ 启事下面还专门用英文注明……。

Under the notice it is specially noted in English that ….

1) 这家商店是专门卖旅游方面的书籍。

This shop specializes in selling books on traveling.

2) 参加一些心理测试不需要有专门的知识。

Specialized knowledge is not necessary to take a psychological test.

3. A又称B　　　　　　　　　A is also called B

❖ 代考者又称"枪手"。

People who take an examination in place of another person are also called "shooters."

1) 纽约又称"大苹果"。

New York is nicknamed "The Big Apple."

2) 电脑在中国又称"电子计算机"。

Computers are also called "electric calculating machines" in China.

4. 毫无Noun；毫不+Verb/adj　　　not … at all

❖ 同样毫无疑问的是，学生们对这类事情的违规性质十分清楚。

It is without doubt that college students know very well that this kind of business is against the university's regulations.

1) 考试以前他已经做了充分的准备，所以考试的时候毫不紧张。

He was not nervous in the test at all because he had prepared sufficiently before the test.

2) 学校发现（她代人考"托福"）后毫不留情地把她开除了。

She was expelled from the school without mercy after it was discovered that she took the TOEFL for someone else.

3) 他对能不能找到工作毫无信心。

He was not confident of finding a job at all.

5. 首先…；其次…   first …; then …

❖ 首先，是考试不一定在校内进行，难以查找；其次，人数众多，老师没有那么多精力和时间去逐一查看。

First, the examination does not necessarily take place on campus, so it is difficult to search (for "shooters"), secondly, people taking examination are numerous, the teachers don't have that much energy and time to check one by one.

1) 我认为小学生不应该做生意。首先，这样做会影响他们的学习成绩；其次，这种生意经也会使他们接受金钱万能的观念。

I think primary school students should not do business because first, doing business will affect their academic grades; second, these tricks of business will also make them accept the concept of " money is omnipotent ".

2) 在家长会上，老师首先向家长介绍学生的情况。其次，希望家长配合老师注意学生的道德培养。

During the parents' meeting, the teacher first gave the parents an introduction on how their kids behave, then she hope that parents work with teacher to pay attention to students' moral development.

6. 难以   difficult to; hard to

❖ 首先是考试不一定是在校内进行，难以查找。

First, the examination does not necessarily take place on campus, so it is difficult to search (for "shooters").

1) 他中文说的那么好，让人难以相信他只学了三个月。

He speaks Chinese so well that it is hard to believe that he has studied it for only three months.

2) 如果不是亲眼看到，真难以想象世界上还有那么落后的地方。

If I had not seen it with my own eyes, it would be hard to imagine that there were such backward places in this world.

7. adj 则… ；adj 则…

❖ 考试的人太多，每个考场少则30-40人，多则60人。

There are too many people taking the test: even the less crowded testing halls had 30 to 40 people in them, while some had as many as 60.

1) 学校一旦发现学生替人代考，轻则警告，重则开除。

As soon as the school found out students were taking exams in place of others, it gave light punishment with warnings and heavy ones with expulsions.

2) 他每年总要在纽约住一段时间，长则半年，短则一个月 。

Every year he lives for a period of time in New York, sometimes as much as half a year, sometimes as little as a month.

8. 足以   enough; sufficiently

❖ …，而且他的假身分证足以以假乱真。

…, moreover his fake identity card (is so real that) can be taken for a genuine one.

1) 你吃的安眠药足以让一头大象睡着了。

The sleeping pills you've taken are sufficient to make an elephant fall asleep.

2) 他挣钱不多，可是足以满足自己的需要。

He does not earn a large salary but it is adequate for his needs.

9. 给予   to give (usu. with abstract nouns as direct objects)

❖ 所以, 事先采取有效措施制止这一行为几乎无法做到，只能在发现后给予严厉制裁。

So there is almost no way to take effective actions beforehand to prevent this kind of behavior, the only thing they can do is to give them severe punishment after they were caught.

1) 每次我遇到困难的时候，家人和朋友总是给予我最大的帮助。

   Every time when I encounter difficulty, my family and friends always give me all the help they can.

2) 很多人希望政府能对儿童乞丐的问题给予充分的重视。

   A lot of people hoped government could pay ample attention to the issue of children beggars.

练习

I.　　Rewrite the sentence using the expressions provided.

1. 他画的《蒙娜·丽莎》跟达·芬奇画的简直完全一样，没有人看得出是假的。（以假乱真；足以）
2. 学高级中文的学生总是不太多，最多的时候有十个，最少的时候也就三四个。（adj 则；adj 则）

II.　　Fill in the blank with the most appropriate word. Each word should be used only once.

心虚	否认	毫无疑问	时时	是否
难以	一一	防止		

　　在公共汽车上，你的钱包被偷了，要想知道是谁偷的，有一个办法。虽然跟别人一样，小偷也 ①____ 偷了钱包，可因为他 ②____，不敢看你的眼睛，所以要是谁不愿意面对你，③____，他就是小偷。

　　可是有时候，由于车上人多，④____ ⑤____ 查看，很可能找不到小偷。所以 ⑥____ 钱包被偷的最好办法就是 ⑦____ 做好准备，查看钱包 ⑧____ 还在身上。

①_____ ②_____ ③_____ ④_____ ⑤_____ ⑥_____ ⑦_____

⑧_____

III.　　Composition

你是美国某大学东亚系的系主任，要写一份"招聘启事"，聘请一名中文老师。请你想一想，这位老师要符合什么条件？。请参考下面加州大学的招聘启事。

> Chinese Lecturer
>
> CALIFORNIA STATE UNIVERSITY, LONG BEACH.
>
> The department of Asian and Asian American Studies invites applications for a full-time lectureship in Chinese for a three-year appointment. Ph.D. or Ed. D. in a field related to Chinese Language Studies/Education at the time of

appointment and potential for effective teaching and scholarship. Candidates must have native or near native language competency in Chinese, as well as substantial knowledge and appreciation of Chinese culture. Applicants should have the ability to communicate and work effectively with an ethnically and culturally diverse campus community. Desired qualifications include expertise in the field of second language acquisition or other related fields. Candidates with training, experience, or interest in heritage language teaching and learning will be given preference. Also preferred are candidates who have expertise in instructional technology or in writing grant proposals with a record of receiving grants. The selection process will commence on March 19, 2001, and continues until the position is filled. Send a letter of application, resume, official transcript and 3 letters of recommendation to Dr. xx, Search Committee Chair, Asian and Asian American Studies Department, CSULB, Long Beach, CA 90840-1002. An EEO/AA employer.

IV. Answer the following questions.

1. 在美国，为别人代考的事情普遍不普遍？如果一旦被发现，会受到什么制裁？为什么在美国考试的枪手并不普遍？跟教育制度和社会情况有什么关系？

2. 托福考试在中国这么热，反映了一个什么问题？

3. 每年中国都有成千上万的大学毕业生到美国留学，这对中国有什么好处？有什么坏处？

4. 谈谈美国学校里"作弊"（zuòbì: cheat）的情形。

1999年8月5日《人民日报》

第二十課

贍養老人是子女應盡的責任

我國《婚姻法》明確規定，成年子女有贍養扶助老人的義務。但是，近年來人民法院受理的農村贍養老人案件有所增加，有的地區約佔民事案件的10%。由此看出，目前農村老年人的生活還存在一定的困難。

如果到我國北方農村走走，就會發現不少老人住在簡陋的小房子裏。據了解，造成這種狀況的原因是：有的是子女嫌棄老人，不願跟老人住在一起；有的是幾個子女成家後已經把家產全部分光，根本沒有老人的份ㄦ，老人被迫另建小房子住。

老年人失去勞動能力後，種地就成了一大難題。老年人只好求助於子女，把土地分給子女耕種，秋後要糧食。少數子女分地時嫌少，給糧時怕多，使老人要糧食如同要飯一樣難。

1999年8月5日《人民日报》

第二十课

赡养老人是子女应尽的责任

我国《婚姻法》明确规定，成年子女有赡养扶助老人的义务。但是，近年来人民法院受理的农村赡养老人案件有所增加，有的地区约占民事案件的10%。由此看出，目前农村老年人的生活还存在一定的困难。

如果到我国北方农村走走，就会发现不少老人住在简陋的小房子里。据了解，造成这种状况的原因是：有的是子女嫌弃老人，不愿跟老人住在一起；有的是几个子女成家后已经把家产全部分光，根本没有老人的份儿，老人被迫另建小房子住。

老年人失去劳动能力后，种地就成了一大难题。老年人只好求助于子女，把土地分给子女耕种，秋后要粮食。少数子女分地时嫌少，给粮时怕多，使老人要粮食如同要饭一样难。

　　一些子女，忘記當年父母把自己養育成人的辛苦，眼看父母已經步入老年人的行列，需要子女的照顧，卻互相推委，不願贍養老人。

　　當今農村有一種習慣是隨著幾個子女成家，父母的財產也被分光。子女不願或沒能力贍養老人，往往讓老人輪流到幾個子女家中生活。有的甚至把老兩口儿分開，一家養一個。這種方法看起來似乎合理，但因爲老人沒有一個固定的住處，心裏很不踏實，他們並沒有享受到子孫滿堂的天倫之樂，伴隨他們的卻是孤獨和寂寞。

　　總之，由於各地經濟條件、老人的性格、子女的道德修養等不一樣，老年人的生活狀況存在很大差異，尤其是農村中部分老年人的生活狀況令人擔憂。希望天下做子女的都能讓父母在清靜和諧的環境中安度晚年。

　　一些子女，忘记当年父母把自己养育成人的辛苦，眼看父母已经步入老年人的行列，需要子女的照顾，却互相推委，不愿赡养老人。

　　当今农村有一种习惯是随着几个子女成家，父母的财产也被分光。子女不愿或没能力赡养老人，往往让老人轮流到几个子女家中生活。有的甚至把老两口儿分开，一家养一个。这种方法看起来似乎合理，但因为老人没有一个固定的住处，心里很不踏实，他们并没有享受到子孙满堂的天伦之乐，伴随他们的却是孤独和寂寞。

　　总之，由于各地经济条件、老人的性格、子女的道德修养等不一样，老年人的生活状况存在很大差异，尤其是农村中部分老年人的生活状况令人担忧。希望天下做子女的都能让父母在清静和谐的环境中安度晚年。

词汇

赡养	贍養	shànyǎng	v. to support (parents); to provide for (parents)
老人	老人	lǎorén	n. one's aged parents or grandparents
应尽的	應盡的	yīngjìn.de	adj. bounden (duty); obligatory
责任	責任	zérèn	n. responsibility
婚姻法		hūnyīnfǎ	n. marriage law
明确	明確	míngquè	adv. clearly
规定	規定	guīdìng	v. to stipulate; to provide
成年		chéngnián	v./n. to grow up; grow-up
子女		zǐnǚ	n. sons and daughters; children
扶助		fúzhù	v. to assist
义务	義務	yì.wù	n. duty; obligation
近年来		jìnniánlái	in recent years
法院		fǎyuàn	n. court
受理		shòulǐ	v. to accept (a case)
农村	農村	nóngcūn	n. rural area; countryside
案件	案件	ànjiàn	n. case
有所	有所	yǒusuǒ	adv. to some extent; somewhat
地区	地區	dìqū	n. area; district; region
约	約	yuē	adv. approximately
占	佔	zhàn	v. to constitute; to make up

民事		mínshì	adj. relating to civil law; civil
由此		yóucǐ	conj. from this
存在		cúnzài	v. to exist
一定		yídìng	adj. certain
北方		běifāng	n. north; northern part of the country
简陋	簡陋	jiǎnlòu	adj. simple and crude
状况	狀況	zhuàngkuàng	n. condition; situation
嫌弃	嫌棄	xiánqì	v. to dislike; to mind; to complain of
成家		chéngjiā	v. to get married; to start a family
家产	家產	jiāchǎn	n. family property
分光		fēn'guāng	v. to divide up
份儿		fènr	n. share
被迫		bèipò	v. to be forced
另		lìng	adv./adj. another; other
建		jiàn	v. to build
失去		shīqù	v. to lose
种地	種地	zhòngdì	v. to cultivate land
难题	難題	nántí	n. difficult problem; tough question
求助于	求助於	qiúzhùyú	v. to seek for help; to resort to
土地		tǔdì	n. land
耕种	耕種	gēngzhòng	v. to plant; to cultivate; to sow
秋后	秋後	qiūhòu	n. after the autumn harvest

粮食	糧食	liáng.shí	n. grain; cereals; food
少数	少數	shǎoshù	n. a few; a small number of
嫌	嫌	xián	v. to dislike; to mind
粮（食）	糧（食）	liáng(.shí)	n. grain; cereals; food
如同		rútóng	prep. like; similar to
要饭		yàofàn	v. to beg (for food or money)
忘记	忘記	wàngjì	v. to forget
当年	當年	dāngnián	n. in those years
养育	養育	yǎngyù	v. to bring up; to rear
成人		chéngrén	v./n. to grow up; to become full-grown
辛苦		xīnkǔ	n. hardships
眼看		yǎnkàn	v. to watch (sth. happen) without making any effort to help
步入		bùrù	v. to walk into
行列		hángliè	n. line or row (of people, vehicles, etc.); procession; lineup
需要		xūyào	v. to need
照顾	照顧	zhào.gù	v./n. to take care; care
互相		hùxiāng	adv. each other
推委	推委	tuīwěi	v. to shirk responsibility; to shift responsibility onto others
当今	當今	dāngjīn	n. present time; today
随着	隨著	suí.zhe	prep. along with; in the wake of
财产	財産	cáichǎn	n. property; fortune

轮流	輪流	lúnliú	adv. take turns; do sth. in turn
甚至		shènzhì	adv. even (to the point of)
老两口儿		lǎoliǎngkǒur	n. old couple
合理		hélǐ	adj. reasonable
固定		gùdìng	adj. fixed; regular
住处	住處	zhùchù	n. dwelling (place); residence
踏实	踏實	tā.shí	adj. free from anxiety
享受		xiǎngshòu	v. to enjoy
子孙满堂	子孫滿堂	zǐsūn mǎntáng	ph. (of a person) be blessed with many children
天伦之乐	天倫之樂	tiānlún zhīlè	n. family happiness
伴随	伴隨	bànsuí	v. to accompany
孤独	孤獨	gūdú	adj. lonely; solitary
性格		xìnggé	n. disposition; temperament
修养	修養	xiūyǎng	n. self-possession
差异	差異	chāyì	n. difference
担忧	擔憂	dānyōu	v. to worry
天下		tiānxià	n. in the world
清静	清静	qīngjìng	adj. quiet
和谐	和諧	héxié	adj. harmonious
安度		āndù	v. to spend (one's remaining years) in happiness
晚年		wǎnnián	n. old age; one's later years

词语例句

1. 有所   **to some extent; somewhat**

❖ 人民法院受理的农村赡养老人案件有所增加。

The cases heard in the people's court of old people in rural areas not getting support from their children increased to some extent.

1) 经过一段时间的学习，她的中文水平有所提高。

After a period of studying, her Chinese improved to some extent.

2) 近期两国的关系有所改善。

Recently the relations between these two countries have improved to some extent.

2. 由此   **from this; therefrom**

❖ 由此看出目前农村老年人的生活还存在一定的困难。

Judging from this, there still exist certain difficulties in the lives of old people in the villages.

1) 她的中文跟一个月以前完全不同了，由此看来，这个语言培训班的效果真的不错。

Her Chinese is completely different from that of a month before, judging from this, this language program is really effective.

2) 要是你一定要这样做，由此产生的后果由你自己负责。

If you insist on doing it in this way, you will be responsible for all the consequences afterwards.

3. 另 + Verb   **other; another**

❖ 老人被迫另建小房子住。

The elders were forced to build another house to live in.

1) 我们本来决定星期日去长城，可是大部分人都不能去，所以我们只好另选一个日子。

We originally planned to go to the Great Wall on Sunday, but most people couldn't make it, so we had to choose another date.

2) 今天没有时间了，我们另约个时间再谈吧。

We don't have time today. Let's set up another time to discuss it.

4. 据　　　　　　　　　　　　　　　according to

❖ 据了解，造成这种状况的主要原因…。

As I understood it, it was … that led up to this.

1) 据报道，每年有两百万人死于爱滋病。

According to the report, two million people die of AIDS each year.

2) 据学过中文的人说，开始的时候很难。

People who have studied Chinese say that it was very difficult at the beginning.

5. 求助于　　　　　　　　　　　turn to sb. for help

❖ 有的老年人只好求助于子女。

Some elderly people had to turn to their children for help.

1) 有的妇女受到丈夫的虐待以后，只好求助于妇联。

Some women had no choice but to turn to the Women's Union for help after they were abused by their husbands.

2) 要是你不能给我一个满意的答复，我只好求助于法律手段。

If you can't give me a satisfying answer, I will have no choice but to turn to the law.

6. 嫌　　　　　　　　　　　　　dislike; mind

❖ 少数子女分地时嫌少，给粮时怕多。

A small number of children dislike receiving little when being given land , but worry about giving too much grain to their parents.

1) 我不想租这间房子，主要嫌它太旧，也离学校太远。

I don't feel like renting this room mainly because I find it too old and too far away from school.

2) 她父母反对她的婚事，主要是嫌她的男朋友是农村人，嫌他没有钱。

Her parents opposed her marrying that man because they thought he was from a rural area and had no money.

7. 甚至　　　　　　　　　　　　**even (to the point of)**

❖ 子女往往让老人轮流到几个子女家中生活，有的甚至把老两口儿分开。

The children often let their parents take turns living with them, some even go so far as to break the old couples up.

1) 他失去了生活的兴趣，甚至想自杀。

He lost faith in life, and even thought of committing suicide.

2) 中国的孩子为父母上学，为父母考试，甚至为父母结婚。

Chinese children go to school for their parents, take the exam for their parents, they even get married for their parents.

8. 眼看　　　　　　　　　　　　**watch helplessly**

❖ 眼看父母已经步入老年人行列，需要子女照顾，却互相推委。

While their parents grew old and began to need their care, they just looked on passively and push the responsibility onto each other.

1) 旁边的人眼看着她的钱包被偷走，也不说一句话。

People next to her just looked on passively and didn't say a word while her purse was stolen.

2) 眼看考试结束的时间就要到了，可是我还有一半没有做完。

The time for the exam will soon be up, but I still have half of it to do.

练习

I. Choose the phrase that is closest in meaning to the underlined phrase in the sentence.

(   ) 1. 近年来人民法院受理的农村瞻养老人案件<u>有所增加</u>。

　　　　　　a. 增加了很多　　b. 增加了一些　　c. 增加了很少

(   ) 2. 老年人只好<u>求助于子女</u>。

　　　　　　a. 请子女帮助他们 b. 帮助子女　　　 c. 请别人帮助子女

(   ) 3. 有些人不愿给父母粮食，使父母要粮食<u>如同</u>要饭一样难。

　　　　　　a. 如果　　　　　b. 相同　　　　　c. 好象

(   ) 4. 子女<u>成家</u>后把家产分光，没有老人的份儿。

　　　　　　a. 结婚　　　　　b. 长大　　　　　c. 养育成人

II. Complete the following sentences using the expression provided.

1. 开车以前喝了太多酒，所以他不能控制自己，……。（眼看）

2. 要是你不喜欢这份礼物，那我……。（另）

3. 有时孩子不愿跟父母一块住，因为……。（嫌）

4. 现在在报上也能看到批评政府的文章了，……。（由此看出）

III. Read the following passage and summarize it in Chinese.

What is neglect of elders? Neglect can be intentional or unintentional. If a relative or caregiver deliberately fails to give an elder what he or she needs, this is intentional neglect, which is a crime. Either way, neglect means that an elder is suffering from deprivation or abandonment. Neglect can involve a failure to meet basic needs, such as food, housing, medicine, clothing or physical aids. Sometimes caregivers fail to keep elders clean and comfortable. An elder who is being neglected may be left alone, even if he or she needs supervision to be safe. Elders can be deprived of essential medical services like doctor's appointments. This is also neglect.

IV. Answer the following questions.

1. 中国一向是个重视孝道的国家，但从这篇文章看来，中国农村老人的生活是非常困难的，孩子为什么不照顾老人的生活了？是不是孩子越来越自私了？

2. 要想改善中国老人的生活，应该采取什么措施？提倡传统的孝顺是不是有效的方法？

3. 老年人生活这么糟糕，政府有没有责任？

1999年7月5日《參考消息》

第二十一課

中國老人需要關懷

中國1/5的老人生活在空蕩蕩的家中。子女到大城市尋找工作，而父母卻在空空的房子中孤獨地生活著。

子女決定到其他城市尋找更好的就業機會時，沒有幾個中國父母會感到高興。在中國1.2億60歲以上父母當中，有1/5的人受到子女在外就業情況的影響。

在傳統的中國社會，老人受到年輕人的尊敬。年輕人從師長和父母那裏學到了生活哲學的基本原則。但近幾十年來，越來越多的退休老人生活在空蕩蕩的家中，盡管其中60％的人更希望跟子女共同生活。最近一項調查結果表明，子女們也希望能夠照顧自己的父母。

大部分父母和子女都認爲這種孤獨的情況是暫

1999年7月5日《参考消息》

第二十一课

中国老人需要关怀

中国1/5的老人生活在空荡荡的家中。子女到大城市寻找工作，而父母却在空空的房子中孤独地生活着。

子女决定到其他城市寻找更好的就业机会时，没有几个中国父母会感到高兴。在中国1.2亿60岁以上父母当中，有1/5的人受到子女在外就业情况的影响。

在传统的中国社会，老人受到年轻人的尊敬。年轻人从师长和父母那里学到了生活哲学的基本原则。但近几十年来，越来越多的退休老人生活在空荡荡的家中，尽管其中60％的人更希望跟子女共同生活。最近一项调查结果表明，子女们也希望能够照顾自己的父母。

大部分父母和子女都认为这种孤独的情况是暂

時的。父母希望出門在外的子女回到故鄉一家團聚，或者功成名就的子女將他們接到大城市生活。

有些年輕人企圖通過給老人錢來彌補這種離棄的行爲，但他們忘記了老人需要的是關心和照顧。

在失去子女的情況下，有些老人開始創造自己的生活方式，上海和北京在60歲以上老人之間開展的"時間儲蓄"計劃就證明了這一點。

67歲的寡婦郎淑珍在照顧著另一位95歲的孤獨老人，幫她做飯，洗澡，買東西，打掃房間，陪她散步，無微不至地陪伴著老人。

她的所有工作都記錄在一個銀行帳戶上，帳戶上累計的不是錢數而是時間；洗衣服4小時，買東西2小時，打掃房間5小時。

根據這個"時間儲蓄"計劃，郎淑珍日後無法生活自理的時候，她將有權得到與現在"投資"的同等時間的照料和服務。

比起農村的老人來，城市的情況要好些。農村的老人不得不眼睜睜地看著子女到大城市謀生，將他們孤零零地留在空蕩蕩的家中。

时的。父母希望出门在外的子女回到故乡一家团聚，或者功成名就的子女将他们接到大城市生活。

有些年轻人企图通过给老人钱来弥补这种离弃的行为，但他们忘记了老人需要的是关心和照顾。

在失去子女的情况下，有些老人开始创造自己的生活方式，上海和北京在60岁以上老人之间开展的"时间储蓄"计划就证明了这一点。

67岁的寡妇郎淑珍在照顾着另一位95岁的孤独老人，帮她做饭，洗澡，买东西，打扫房间，陪她散步，无微不至地陪伴着老人。

她的所有工作都记录在一个银行帐户上，帐户上累计的不是钱数而是时间；洗衣服4小时，买东西2小时，打扫房间5小时。

根据这个"时间储蓄"计划，郎淑珍日后无法生活自理的时候，她将有权得到与现在"投资"的同等时间的照料和服务。

比起农村的老人来，城市的情况要好些。农村的老人不得不眼睁睁地看着子女到大城市谋生，将他们孤零零地留在空荡荡的家中。

词汇

关怀	關懷	guānhuái	v. show love care; show concern for
生活		shēnghuó	v./n. to live; life
空荡荡	空蕩蕩	kōngdàng.dàng	adj. empty; deserted
寻找	尋找	xúnzhǎo	v. to seek; to look for
空		kōng	adj. empty
孤独	孤獨	gūdú	adj. solitary; lonely
就业	就業	jiùyè	v. to get or take up a job
感到		gǎndào	v. to feel; to sense
亿	億	yì	num. hundred million
以上		yǐshàng	n. more than; over
当中	當中	dāngzhōng	prep. among
在外		zàiwài	=在外面
尊敬		zūnjìng	v. to respect
师长	師長	shīzhǎng	n. teachers and elders
生活哲学	生活哲學	shēnghuó zhéxué	n. philosophy of life
基本		jīběn	adj. basic; fundamental
原则	原則	yuánzé	n. principle
退休		tuìxiū	v. to retire
共同		gòngtóng	adv. jointly
调查	調查	diàochá	n. survey

结果	結果	jiéguǒ	n. result; outcome
能够	能夠	nénggòu	v. can; be able to; be capable of
暂时	暫時	zànshí	adv. temporarily
出门	出門	chūmén	v. to be away from home
故乡	故鄉	gùxiāng	n. birthplace;
团聚	團聚	tuánjù	v. to reunite
功成名就		gōngchéng míngjiù	ph. (of a person's career) to be successful and famous
企图	企圖	qǐtú	v. to attempt
弥补	彌補	míbǔ	v. to make up; to make good
离弃	離棄	líqì	v. to abandon; to desert
忘记	忘記	wàngjì	v. to forget
关心	關心	guānxīn	v. to be concerned about
失去		shīqù	v. to lose
创造	創造	chuàngzào	v. to create
生活方式		shēnghuó fāngshì	n. way of life; life style
之间	之間	zhījiān	prep. between
开展	開展	kāizhǎn	v. to develop; to launch
储蓄	儲蓄	chǔxù	v. to save; to deposit
证明	證明	zhèngmíng	v. to prove; to testify
郎淑珍		Láng Shūzhēn	n. a person's name
打扫	打掃	dǎsǎo	v. to sweep; to clean

陪		péi	v. to accompany
散步		sànbù	v. to go for a walk
无微不至	無微不至	wúwēibúzhì	ph. in every possible way; meticulously
陪伴		péibàn	v. to accompany
记录	記錄	jìlù	v. to take notes; to keep minute; to record
帐户	帳户	zhànghù	n. account
累计	累計	lěijì	v. to add up; accumulate
日后	日後	rìhòu	n. in days to come
自理		zìlǐ	v. to take care of or provide for oneself
投资	投資	tóuzī	v. to invest
同等		tóngděng	adj. of the same class, quantity, etc.
照料	照料	zhàoliào	v. to take care of
服务	服務	fúwù	n./v. service; be in the serve of
不得不		bù.de .bù	adv. have no choice but ; cannot but
眼睁睁	眼睜睜	yǎnzhēngzhēng	adv. look on helplessly
谋生	謀生	móushēng	v. to make a living
孤零零		gūlínglíng	adj. solitary; lonely

词语例句

1. **空荡荡**　　　　　　　　　　　**empty**

❖ 中国1/5的老人生活在"空荡荡的家"中。

1/5 of Chinese old people is now living in an "empty home."

1) 屋子里黑乎乎的，我什么也看不见。

The room is quite dark, and I can't see anything.

2) 那个孩子真可爱，脸总是红扑扑的。

That kid who has a reddish face is really cute.

2. **而**　　　　　　　　　　　　　**while**

❖ 子女到大城市寻找工作，而父母却在空空的房子中孤独地生活。

Parents live lonely in the empty houses while their children go to big cities to look for job opportunities.

1) 中国老人喜欢遛鸟，而美国老人喜欢遛狗。

Elderly Chinese like to take their birds for a walk, while American old people like walking a dog.

2) 你喜欢运动，而我呢，愿意看书。

You like sports while I'd rather read.

3. **在…当中**　　　　　　　　　**among; in the middle of**

❖ 在1.2亿中国60岁以上的父母当中，有1/5的人受到子女在外就业情况的影响。

One-fifth of the a hundred and twenty million Chinese parents over sixty years old have been subject to the effect of their children working in a different place.

1) 在所有学过的课文中，老夫少妻给我留下最深的印象。

Of all the lessons I've learned, that of old husbands and young wives has make the deepest impression on me.

2) 据报道，在每一百个美国人当中，就有一个人被抢劫过。

One out of every hundred American has been robbed, according to the press.

练习

I. Choose the most appropriate word for each blank and fill in with its
    Chinese equivalent.

    retire   make up   reunite   empty   take care of oneself
    in every possible way   lose

1. 春节的时候，中国人的传统是一家人_____在一起，吃一顿饭。
2. 中国政府规定，女性55岁就可以_____。
3. 希望你能给我一个机会，让我_____所做的错事。
4. 自从他在战争中_____双手以后，他的生活就不能_____，幸亏
   妻子_____照顾他。
5. 自从儿子上大学以后，她每天没有事情可做，心里觉得_____的
   。

II. Make a sentence using the underlined expression.

1. 农村的老人只好<u>眼睁睁</u>地看着子女不可避免地到大城市谋生。
2. 年轻人<u>从</u>师长和父母<u>那里学</u>到了生活哲学的基本原则。
3. 子女决定到其他城市寻找更好的就业机会时，<u>没有几个</u>中国父母
   会感到高兴。
4. <u>根据</u>这个"时间储蓄"<u>计划</u>，她以后有权得到同等时间的照料。
5. <u>在</u>中国所有的父母<u>当中</u>，五分之一的人受到子女在外就业情况的
   影响。

III. Choose the correct answer.

1. 保护环境和发展经济【同等；相同】重要。
2. 有些学生【关心；关怀】的不是学到了什么，而是成绩。
3. 在我的所有的老师【之间；之中】，我最喜欢的是那个总是带着
   笑容的老师。

IV. Answer the question using the expressions given.
    什么是"时间储蓄计划"？（在…情况下，在外，无法；之间；
    开展；打扫；买；陪；记录；帐户；不是，而是；日后；有权；
    照顾；服务；创造）

V.　　Answer the following questions.

1. 在你看来，这个"时间储蓄计划"会不会成功？
2. 比较中国老年人和美国老年人的生活，有什么不同？
3. 中国老年人越来越孤单寂寞了，这是孩子的责任吗？
4. 孩子不照顾老人是经济问题还是道德问题？
5. 美国有什么样的老人问题？政府是怎么解决这个问题的？

1999年11月5日《人民日報》（海外版）

第二十二課
老夫少妻爲何增多？

3年前，27歲年輕活潑的方小姐嫁給了比她大20歲的李先生，不少親戚朋友對這個婚姻持否定態度，認爲方小姐是圖李先生有錢有地位，有的甚至說，瞧著吧，不出三年，方小姐就得鬧離婚。三年過去了，現在的方小姐，整天和李先生一起出出進進，與李先生的兒子也相處得很和睦。問起她嫁給"老夫"三年的感受，方小姐說："其實，當初我也挺猶豫，他不僅比我大20歲，而且我一嫁過去就得給他15歲的兒子當後媽。可李先生的才華、經濟實力、辦事能力讓我特別傾心，而且知道怎麼疼我。那些和我年齡差不多的男孩兒雖然也愛我，卻並不懂得怎麼愛護我。"

像方小姐李先生這樣"老夫少妻"的家庭近年來正逐漸增多。據報載，進入90年代後，男大女

1999年11月5日《人民日报》（海外版）

第二十二课

老夫少妻为何增多？

　　3年前，二十七岁年轻活泼的方小姐嫁给了比她大20岁的李先生，不少亲戚朋友对这个婚姻持否定态度，认为方小姐是图李先生有钱有地位，有的甚至说，瞧着吧，不出三年，方小姐就得闹离婚。三年过去了，现在的方小姐，整天和李先生一起出出进进，与李先生的儿子也相处得很和睦。问起她嫁给"老夫"三年的感受，方小姐说："其实，当初我也挺犹豫，他不仅比我大20岁，而且我一嫁过去就得给他15岁的儿子当后妈。可李先生的才华、经济实力、办事能力让我特别倾心，而且知道怎么疼我。那些和我年龄差不多的男孩儿虽然也爱我，却并不懂得怎么爱护我。"

　　像方小姐李先生这样"老夫少妻"的家庭近年来正逐渐增多。据报载，进入90年代后，男大女

5歲的比例最高，達48％，男大女10歲以上的比例也比1987年增加10％。

分析男女結婚年齡差距拉大的原因，首先是因爲經濟的緣故。新中國成立以後，提倡婦女解放，女人從家庭走向社會，經濟獨立。男女同工同酬，收入差別不大。夫妻雙方自食其力，誰也不靠誰養活，在這樣的經濟環境下，男女自然選擇年齡差不多的對象結婚。因此，60年代至80年代結婚的夫妻大多數年齡差距只有二三歲。

改革開放以後，人們的收入差距逐步拉大，一些事業成功的男人或因爲忙於事業未婚，或離婚準備再娶，這些男人雖然早已過了傳統觀念中結婚的年齡，但因爲他們有較強的經濟實力，往往成爲年輕女性選擇的目標。這與近年來金錢在價值觀中所佔分量越來越重也有很大關係。

"老夫少妻"婚姻比例的增加固然與經濟因素有直接關係，但現實社會裏有相當一部分知識女性找比自己大很多的男性並不是爲了錢，而是被年長的成熟的男人的學識、能力、體貼所吸引。

5岁的比例最高，达48%，男大女10岁以上的比例也比1987年增加10%。

分析男女结婚年龄差距拉大的原因，首先是因为经济的缘故。新中国成立以后，提倡妇女解放，女人从家庭走向社会，经济独立。男女同工同酬，收入差别不大。夫妻双方自食其力，谁也不靠谁养活，在这样的经济环境下，男女自然选择年龄差不多的对象结婚。因此，60年代至80年代结婚的夫妻大多数年龄差距只有二三岁。

改革开放以后，人们的收入差距逐步拉大，一些事业成功的男人或因为忙于事业未婚，或离婚准备再娶，这些男人虽然早已过了传统观念中结婚的年龄，但因为他们有较强的经济实力，往往成为年轻女性选择的目标。这与近年来金钱在价值观中所占分量越来越重也有很大关系。

"老夫少妻"婚姻比例的增加固然与经济因素有直接关系，但现实社会里有相当一部分知识女性找比自己大很多的男性并不是为了钱，而是被年长的成熟的男人的学识、能力、体贴所吸引。

　　除了以上這些以外，社會寬容度的增加也是促使 " 老夫少妻 " 增多的原因之一。現在大家覺得嫁甚麼人完全是個人的事，跟別人是沒有關係的。" 老夫少妻 " 的增加，表明社會允許多元化價值觀的存在。

　　除了以上这些以外，社会宽容度的增加也是促使"老夫少妻"增多的原因之一。现在大家觉得嫁什么人完全是个人的事，跟别人是没有关系的。"老夫少妻"的增加，表明社会允许多元化价值观的存在。

词汇

老夫		lǎofū	n. old husband
少妻		shàoqī	n. young wife
为何	爲何	wèihé	conj. why
增多		zēngduō	v. to grow in number; to increase
年轻	年輕	niánqīng	adj. young
活泼	活潑	huó.pō	adj. lively
方		fāng	n. a surname
小姐		xiǎojiě	n. Miss
嫁		jià	v. to marry (only for woman)
李		lǐ	n. a surname
不少		bùshǎo	adj. many; not few
亲戚	親戚	qīn.qī	n. relative
婚姻		hūnyīn	n. marriage
持		chí	v. to hold
否定		fǒudìng	adj. negative
图	圖	tú	v. to seek; to pursue
地位		dìwèi	n. status
瞧着吧	瞧著吧	qiáo.zhe.ba	ph. just wait and see
不出		bùchū	prep. within
闹	鬧	nào	v. to make a big fuss in request for or in protest of (sth.)

离婚	離婚	líhūn	v. to divorce
过去	過去	guò.qù	v. to pass by; to go by
整天		zhěngtiān	n. all day; day and night
出出进进	出出進進	chūchūjìnjìn	v. to pass in and out; to get in and out
相处	相處	xiāngchǔ	v. to get along
和睦		hémù	adj. harmonious; in peace
感受		gǎnshòu	n. feeling; experience
当初	當初	dāngchū	n. at first; originally
挺		tǐng	adv. quite; very
犹豫	猶豫	yóuyù	v./adj. hesitate; hesitant
后妈	後媽	hòumā	n. stepmother
才华	才華	cáihuá	n. brilliance of mind; genius
实力	實力	shílì	n. strength; actual strength
办事	辦事	bànshì	v. to perform work; to handle business; to manage an affair
倾心	傾心	qīngxīn	v. to admire wholeheartedly
疼		téng	v. to love dearly
懂得		dǒngdé	v. to understand; to know
爱护	愛護	àihù	v. to love and protect
逐渐	逐漸	zhújiàn	adv. gradually; progressively
据报载	據報載	jùbàozǎi	ph. according to newspaper's report
比例		bǐlì	n. proportion

达	達	dá	v. to reach (a place or a figure such as a price or quantity)
差距		chājù	n. the difference (in distance; amount; progress, etc.); disparity; gap
拉大		lādà	v. to expand; to enlarge
成立		chénglì	v. to found; to establish
妇女解放		fùnǚjiěfàng	ph. emancipation of women; women's liberation
走		zǒu	v. to walk; to go
向		xiàng	prep. to; towards
同工同酬		tónggōngtóngchóu	ph. equal pay for equal work
收入		shōurù	n. income; revenue
夫妻		fūqī	n. husband and wife
双方	雙方	shuāngfāng	n. both parties
自食其力		zìshíqílì	ph. to support oneself by one's own labor
靠		kào	v. to depend on
养活	養活	yǎng.huó	v. to support; to provide for
自然		zìrán	adv. naturally
选择	選擇	xuǎnzé	v. to choose; to select
对象	對象	duìxiàng	n. object; target (here, a partner for marriage)
至		zhì	prep. to; till; until
大多数	大多數	dàduōshù	n. great majority; at large

改革开放	改革開放	gǎigékāifàng	ph. "reform and open up"
逐步		zhúbù	adv. step by step; gradually
事业	事業	shìyè	n. career; enterprise
成功		chénggōng	v./adj. succeed; to be a success; successful
忙于	忙於	mángyú	v. to be busy with
未婚		wèihūn	v. to be single; to be unmarried
再		zài	suf. re-doing; again
娶		qǔ	v. to take as wife
目标	目標	mùbiāo	n. objective
价值观	價值觀	jiàzhíguān	n. value system
固然		gùrán	conj. no doubt even though; it is true that
直接	直接	zhíjiē	adj. direct
现实	現實	xiànshí	adj. real; actual
知识女性	知識女性	zhīshínǚxìng	n. educated women
年长	年長	niánzhǎng	adj. older in age; senior
成熟		chéngshú	adj. mature
学识	學識	xuéshí	n. scholarly attainments; learned wisdom
体贴	體貼	tǐtiē	v./adj. to show every consideration to; thoughtful; considerate
吸引		xīyǐn	v. to attract
宽容度	寬容度	kuānróngdù	n. degree of tolerance

促使		cùshǐ	v. to cause; to compel; to urge
表明		biǎomíng	v. to indicate
允许	允許	yúnxǔ	v. to permit; to allow
多元化		duōyuánhuà	adj. diversified
存在		cúnzài	v./n. to exist; existence

词语例句

1. 图   **seek; pursue**

❖ 他们认为方小姐是图李先生有钱有地位。

They believed that Miss Fang was solely going after Mr. Li's money and status.

1) 我跟你结婚，不图你的钱，就图你老实，孝敬父母。

I'm marrying you not for your money, but because you are honest and you respect your parents.

2) 这个房子又小又贵，住在这儿只是图方便。

This house is small and expensive, I'm only living here because it is convenient.

2. 不出…就…   **within**

❖ 不出三年，方小姐就得离婚。

She will surely get a divorce within the next three years.

1) 他这个人，总是说脏话，不出三句话，就是一句"他妈的"。

He is always swearing. He can't say even three sentences without saying " damn it!"

2) 在这儿吃饭很方便，不出十米，就有好几家饭馆儿。

It is very convenient to eat here. There are several restaurants within ten meters.

3. 犹豫   **hesitate; hesitant**

❖ 其实，当初我也挺犹豫。

Actually I was quite hesitant at first,

1) 我请她看电影的时候，她犹豫了一下，然后同意了。

When I asked her to a movie, she hesitated a moment and then accepted.

2) 中国的父母不舍得为自己花钱，可是为了孩子的教育，花钱的时候一点儿都不犹豫。

Chinese parents are unwilling to spend money on themselves, but when it comes to their children's education, they don't hesitate at all.

4. 懂得   **understand; know**

❖ 那些跟我年龄差不多的男孩儿虽然也爱我，却并不懂得怎么爱护我。

Although those boys who are around the same age as me might love me, but they don't know how to take care of me.

1) 被惯坏的独生子女根本不懂得怎么孝敬父母，也不懂得怎么跟别人相处。

The only child who is spoiled doesn't know how to respect his parents, nor does he know how to get along with other people.

2) 他虽然年纪很小，可是却懂得照顾别人。

He may be young, but he knows how to take care of others.

5. 谁也不…谁   **neither A nor B…**

❖ 夫妻双方自食其力，谁也不靠谁养活。

A husband and wife support themselves independently, neither of them depends on the other to live.

1) 昨天他们大吵了一架，现在谁也不理谁。

They had a big fight yesterday, and now neither of them is talking to the other.

2) 表面上这两个人关系很好，其实，他们谁也不相信谁。

On the surface they have a good relationship, but in reality, neither of them trusts the other.

6. 或…或…   **or … or …**

❖ 一些事业成功的男人或因为忙于事业未婚，或离婚准备再娶…。

Some successful men are single because they have been busy with their careers or have divorced and plan to remarry….

1) 他们学习中文，或因为父母是中国人，或因为对中国的文化特别有兴趣。

They are taking Chinese because their parents are Chinese or because they are particularly interested in Chinese culture.

2) 以前，在美国的中国人或是开饭馆或是开洗衣店，而现在的中国人或是电脑程序员或是做会计。

In the past, most Chinese in America ran a restaurant or a dry cleaner, nowadays, they are computer programmers or accountants.

7. 在···所占的分量···   **play a ··· role in ···**

❖ 这与近年来金钱在价值观中所占的分量越来越重也有很大关系。

It is greatly related to the fact that in recent years the position of money among Chinese values has been rising.

1) 运动在美国人的生活中所占的分量很重。

Sports play an important role in Americans' lives.

2) 数学课在经济专业中所占的分量很重。

Mathematics is a great portion in the classes for an economic major.

8. 固然···，但···   **admittedly; even though it is true··· but···**

❖ 老夫少妻的婚姻比例增加，固然与经济因素有直接关系，但有相当一部分知识女性并不是为了钱。

It is true that money has had a direct effect on the increasing number of "young wife and old husband" marriages, but a considerable proportion of well-educated women don't marry for money.

1) 钱固然重要，但并不是生活中最重要的。

It is true that money is important, but it is not the most important thing in life.

2) 他固然做得不对，但是你也不必那么生气。

It is true that he did something wrong, but there is no need for you to be that mad about it.

练习

I.　Choose the correct answer.

（　）1. 很多父母由于_____工作，忽视了孩子的心理问题。

　　　　a. 急忙于　　　　　　b. 忙于　　　　　　c. 求助于

（　）2. 我今年已经三十岁了，早就_____上大学的年龄了。

　　　　a. 路过了　　　　　　b. 经过了　　　　　　c. 过了

（　）3. 最近我的邻居娶了一位_____。

　　　　a. 年轻小姐比他二十岁小

　　　　b. 比他小二十岁的小姐

　　　　c. 比他二十岁小的小姐

（　）4. 我觉得跟年龄大一点儿的人结婚无所谓，可是给跟我年龄差
　　　　不多的人_____后妈是不能接受的。

　　　　a. 当　　　　　　　　b. 成为　　　　　　c. 成了

（　）5. 我读了他的几篇作品以后，就一直_____。

　　　　a. 对他很倾心　　　b. 很倾心他　　　　c. 倾心

II.　Rewrite the following sentence using the expression provided.

1. 在北京交通堵塞那么严重，常常是因为司机不让行人，行人
　 也不让司机。（谁也不…谁）

2. 这种产品的质量真差，我刚用了两天就坏了。
　 （不出…就…）

3. 大学毕业后，他就自己养活自己了。（自食其力）

4. 他一直反对婚前同居。（持…态度）

III.　Choose the most appropriate word for each blank and fill in with its
　　　Chinese equivalent.

　　　　day and night　originally　　hesitate　　　expand

　　　　diversified　　according to newspaper's report

1. 科技的发展不但没有缩短富国和贫国的差距，反而_____
　 了它们之间的差距。

336

2. 学习固然重要，你也不要＿＿＿＿＿＿＿坐在图书馆里，应该运动运动。

3. 纽约的＿＿＿＿＿＿＿文化吸引了世界各地的人。

4. ＿＿＿＿＿＿＿要不是你帮了我的忙，我怎么会有今天的成绩？

5. 别＿＿＿＿＿＿＿了，机会一旦失去，就不会再来了。

6. ＿＿＿＿＿＿＿，女人的平均寿命比男人长五岁。

IV. Composition

你的儿子爱上了一个比他大二十岁的有才华、有经济实力的女人，作为母亲，你有点担心，所以你要跟他谈一谈，请用下面的生字，准备五个问题，另外再写出你的看法和建议。【为何、图、懂得、自然、固然、吸引、犹豫、差距、体贴、提醒、禁止　倾向于、持…态度】

问题一：

问题二·

问题三：

问题四·

问题五·

建议：

V. Answer the following questions.

1. 这篇文章说改革开放以前男女结婚年龄相差不多，改革开放以后，因为有了竞争，男人在事业上比较成功，于是就出现了"老夫少妻"的情形，这是不是暗示(ànshì: imply)女人竞争不过男人，你同意不同意这个看法。

2. 你见过"老夫少妻"的婚姻吗？为什么"老夫少妻"比"老妻少夫"多得多？

3. 在你看来，"老夫少妻"的增多反映妇女地位的上升还是下降？

1998年8月17日《人民日報》

第二十三課

產品質量與社會道德

現在，一次性產品越來越多了，從飯館儿裏的碗筷到賓館裏的牙刷牙膏拖鞋，從醫院裏的注射器到路邊儿穿羊肉串儿的竹簽儿等等。

對這類產品，人們不會有過高的要求，用過一次就扔了。可是這種"一次性"常常也難以保證。有一回我到山東出差，住進賓館時已經很晚了，又有些累，準備洗洗澡上床休息。我穿著"一次性"拖鞋上衛生間，鞋底軟得讓人受不了，剛走出了兩步，一隻鞋就壞了。然後我拿起"一次性"牙膏，那牙膏硬得像石頭，怎麼擠也擠不出來；我拿起牙刷來，還沒刷兩下，"啪"的一聲斷了。第二天早晨，我做的第一件事就是去買牙刷牙膏，當然還有拖鞋。

一次性產品的優點是很顯然的：衛生，不會傳

1998年8月17日《人民日报》

第二十三课
产品质量与社会道德

现在，一次性产品越来越多了，从饭馆儿里的碗筷到宾馆里的牙刷牙膏拖鞋，从医院里的注射器到路边儿穿羊肉串儿的竹签儿等等。

对这类产品，人们不会有过高的要求，用过一次就扔了。可是这种"一次性"常常也难以保证。有一回我到山东出差，住进宾馆时已经很晚了，又有些累，准备洗洗澡上床休息。我穿着"一次性"拖鞋上卫生间，鞋底软得让人受不了，刚走出了两步，一只鞋就坏了。然后我拿起"一次性"牙膏，那牙膏硬得像石头，怎么挤也挤不出来；我拿起牙刷来，还没刷两下，"啪"的一声断了。第二天早晨，我做的第一件事就是去买牙刷牙膏，当然还有拖鞋。

一次性产品的优点是很显然的：卫生，不会传染疾病。但是這一點也難以保證。人們到飯館儿吃飯，總是用"一次性"筷子，但一次性筷子不見得都那麼乾淨。有一次在一家飯館吃飯，我拿了一雙"一次性"筷子，發現上面黑乎乎的，再拿了一雙還是那樣。老板見我在那裏挑筷子，"嘿嘿"地一笑，那筷子和那笑聲都讓我覺得不舒服。

至於穿羊肉串儿的竹簽儿，就更讓人不放心了。我家門口有烤羊肉串儿的，經常有許多人在那裏買了吃。有一天晚上，十一點多鐘的時候，我路過那裏，發現地上到處都是竹簽儿，烤羊肉串儿的人正在撿。一位鄰居對我説："你看那賣羊肉串儿的人多缺德，他把竹簽儿撿回去，也不知道洗不洗，明天照樣用它來穿羊肉串儿。"

一次性產品連一次都用不了，那是產品質量問題；可是一次性產品用過了再拿給人用，那是道德問題。

染疾病。但是这一点也难以保证。人们到饭馆吃饭，总是用"一次性"筷子，但一次性筷子不见得都那么干净。有一次在一家饭馆吃饭，我拿了一双"一次性"筷子，发现上面黑乎乎的，再拿了一双还是那样。老板见我在那里挑筷子，"嘿嘿"地一笑，那筷子和那笑声都让我觉得不舒服。

至于穿羊肉串儿的竹签儿，就更让人不放心了。我家门口有烤羊肉串儿的，经常有许多人在那里买了吃。有一天晚上，十一点多钟的时候，我路过那里，发现地上到处都是竹签儿，烤羊肉串儿的人正在捡。一位邻居对我说："你看那卖羊肉串儿的人多缺德，他把竹签儿捡回去，也不知道洗不洗，明天照样用它来穿羊肉串儿。"

一次性产品连一次都用不了，那是产品质量问题；可是一次性产品用过了再拿给人用，那是道德问题。

词汇

一次性		yícìxìng	adj. disposable; one-time
产品	產品	chánpǐn	n. product
碗筷		wǎnkuài	n. bowls and chopsticks
宾馆	賓館	bīn'guǎn	n. hotel
牙刷		yáshuā	n. toothbrush
牙膏		yágāo	n. toothpaste
拖鞋		tuōxié	n. slippers
注射器		zhùshèqì	n. syringe
路边儿	路邊儿	lùbiānr	n. roadside; wayside
穿		chuān	v. to string together
羊肉串儿		yángròuchuànr	n. mutton kebob
竹签儿	竹簽儿	zhúqiānr	n. bamboo skewer
等等		děng.děng	and so on; etc.
类	類	lèi	n. kind; type
过	過	guò	adv. excessively
要求		yāoqiú	n. demand; request
扔		rēng	v. to throw away
保证	保證	bǎozhèng	v. to guarantee
山东	山東	Shāndōng	n. a province in eastern China
出差		chūchāi	v. to go on a business trip

住进	住進	zhùjìn	v. to check in
又		yòu	adv. also
有些		yǒuxiē	adv. rather
准备	準備	zhǔnbèi	v. to prepare
洗澡		xǐzǎo	v. to take a bath
休息		xiū.xī	v. to have a rest; to have a break
卫生间	衛生間	wèishēngjiān	n. bathroom
鞋底	鞋底	xiédǐ	n. sole
受不了		shòu.bùliǎo	v. cannot stand
步		bù	n. step
石头	石頭	shí.tóu	n. stone; rock
挤	擠	jǐ	v. to squeeze
刷		shuā	v. to brush
啪的一声	啪的一聲	pā.de yìshēng	onomatopoeia: a sound of clapping; slapping; a gunshot
断	斷	duàn	v. to break
优点	優點	yōudiǎn	n. strong point; merit
显然	顯然	xiǎnrán	adj. obvious; evident
卫生	衛生	wèishēng	adj. clean
传染	傳染	chuánrǎn	v. to contract or spread
疾病		jíbìng	n. disease
这一点	這一點	zhèi yì diǎn	n. this aspect

不见得	不見得	bújiàn.dé	adv. not necessarily
黑乎乎		hēihūhū	adj. blackened
嘿嘿一笑		hēi hēi yí xiào	onomatopoeia: laugh with self-pride or satisfaction
至于	至於	zhìyú	conj. as for; as to
门口儿	門口儿	ménkǒur	n. entrance; doorway
烤		kǎo	v. to barbecue; to roast
路过	路過	lùguò	v. to pass through or by (place)
到处	到處	dàochù	n. everywhere; all over
捡	撿	jiǎn	v. to pick up; to collect
邻居	鄰居	lín.jū	n. neighbor
缺德		quēdé	adj. mean; wicked
照样	照樣	zhàoyàng	adv. same as before
用不了		yòng.bùliǎo	v. cannot use

词语例句

1. 又   **in addition; moreover**

❖ 住进宾馆时已经很晚了，又有些累，准备洗洗澡上床休息。

   It was very late when I checked in and I was also quite tired, so all I wanted was to take a shower and go to sleep.

1) 他人聪明，又肯用功，自然成绩很好。

   He is smart and willing to work hard, so naturally he has good grades.

2) 天气那么热，屋里又没有空调，很不舒服。

   It is hot and there is no air conditioner in the room, so it is very uncomfortable.

2. adj. 得   **so adj. that …**

❖ 鞋底软得让人受不了。

   The soles are so soft that I can't stand it.

1) 那个学生累得上课的时候就睡着了。

   That student was so exhausted that he fell asleep in class.

2) 他紧张得一句话也说不出来。

   He is too nervous to utter even one word.

3. 刚…，就…   **no sooner … than …**

❖ 刚走出两步，一只鞋就坏了。

   No sooner had I walked a few steps than one of the slippers broke.

1) 他们刚认识一个礼拜就结婚了。

   They got married just a week after they met.

2) 我刚写完最后一个字，老师就说该交考卷了。

   I had just finished writing the last character, when the teacher said it was time to hand in our quizzes.

4. adj. 得像   **as adj. as**

❖ 那牙膏硬得像石头。

That toothpaste is as hard as a rock. (That toothpaste is so hard that as a result it is just like a rock.)

1) 那个女孩儿美得像白雪公主。

That girl is as pretty as Snow White.

2) 这个教室冷得像冰箱。

This classroom is as cold as a refrigerator.

5. 怎么…也不…　　　　　　　　　　**no matter how… , can not …**

❖ 我怎么挤（牙膏）也挤不出来。

However hard I tried, I couldn't squeeze the toothpaste out.

1) 我怎么学也学不会。

However hard I worked, I just couldn't learn it.

2) 我怎么劝他，他也不听。

I tried my best to persuade him, but he wouldn't listen to me.

3) 我怎么睡，也睡不着。

However hard I tried, I just couldn't fall asleep.

6. …，至于…　　　　　　　　　　**as for; as to**

❖ …，至于穿羊肉串的竹签儿·就更让人不放心了。

. . . , as for the bamboo skewers for mutton kebobs, that is even more worrisome.

1) 我知道他生病了，至于他生了什么病，就不清楚了。

I knew that he was sick, but as for which disease he has, I'm not sure.

2) 我愿意看他写的书，至于出版，是另外一回事。

I'm willing to read his book, but as for publishing it, that is a different matter.

7. 照样　　　　　　　　　　**same as before**

❖ 明天照样用它来穿羊肉串。

The next day he used the same skewers to string mutton kebob as usual.

1) 他每天十点睡觉，即使大考的时候，也照样十点上床。

He goes to sleep at ten every day, even during the final, he still goes to bed at ten as usual.

2) 谁看电影，都得买票，美国总统也得照样买票。

Whoever wants to see the movie has to buy a ticket, even the president of the United States of America.

练习

I.　Choose the correct answer.

1. 他正在洗澡的时候，突然听见"啪的一声"，灯【损坏；危害；坏】了。
2. 你在美国住了十年还不会说英文，真令人难以【信；想；相信】
3. 看你的手，脏【乎乎；嘿嘿；啪】的，快洗洗手。
4. 这牙刷的质量真差，我刚用了两天【才；连；就】断了。

II.　Fill in each blank with the most appropriate word.

卫生　照样　缺德　出差　传染

1. 谁这么_____，在我的新鞋上吐痰。
2. 我的邻居总是把录音机开得很大声，每次我跟他说，他总是说对不起，可是下次还是_____那么大声。
3. 由于工作的关系，他常常去外国_____。
4. 你最好离我远一点儿，我正在感冒，别_____你。
5. 街上的烤羊肉串好吃是好吃，就是有点不_____。

III.　Rewrite the sentence using the expression given.

1. 今天的数学题真难，我用了各种办法也解不开。（怎么…也…）
2. 太不象话了，食堂的馒头那么硬，简直可以当榔头了。（adj得…）
3. 你的记忆太差了，我两分钟以前告诉你的事，现在你怎么就忘了呢？（刚…就）
4. 未婚先孕的意思就是结婚以前生孩子。（还没…就…）

2000年7月21日《人民日報》

第二十四課

餐桌上的文明與野蠻

　　飲食文化作爲中華文明的特色之一，早已世界聞名。然而近年來，在我國一些地方，這種文明卻越來越帶著野蠻的味道。

　　不顧國家法令，不顧輿論的批評，一些餐館幾乎成了野生動物“博物館”。“孔雀全宴”“天鵝全宴”“紙包鴕鳥肉”“紅燒果子狸”“清炖蛇龜鷹”“香炸鱷魚條”“紅燒五腳金龍（巨蜥）”……這是一個記者不久前在廣西南寧市一些餐館中看到的菜名。在那裏，你還可以看到許多平常不容易看到的稀有動物都成了餐桌上的食物。珍稀野生動物作爲一道“主菜”，在一些場合甚至成爲某種規格、待遇的象征。

　　這種情況，實在令人震驚和憂慮。著名生物學家楊雄里說：“在南方某些地方，一些人爲了補腦，竟然用繩子捆住猴子，再用硬物敲開猴子的腦殼吃裏面的猴腦

2000年7月21日《人民日报》

第二十四课
餐桌上的文明与野蛮

　　饮食文化作为中华文明的特色之一，早已世界闻名。然而近年来，在我国一些地方，这种文明却越来越带着野蛮的味道。

　　不顾国家法令，不顾舆论的批评，一些餐馆几乎成了野生动物"博物馆"。"孔雀全宴""天鹅全宴""纸包鸵鸟肉""红烧果子狸""清炖蛇龟鹰""香炸鳄鱼条""红烧五脚金龙（巨蜥）"……这是一个记者不久前在广西南宁市一些餐馆中看到的菜名。在那里，你还可以看到许多平常不容易看到的稀有动物都成了餐桌上的食物。珍稀野生动物作为一道"主菜"，在一些场合甚至成为某种规格、待遇的象征。

　　这种情况，实在令人震惊和忧虑。著名生物学家杨雄里说："在南方某些地方，一些人为了补脑，竟然用绳子捆住猴子，再用硬物敲开猴子的脑壳吃里面的猴脑。這種行為實在愚昧之極、野蠻之至！”他甚至用“沒人性”這樣的詞句，來表達他對此類行為的憤慨。 前不久，上海有八位科學家聯名發出“不吃野生動物，提倡文明生活”的倡議，他們説：“為了給子孫後代留下一個完整而美好的世界，千萬別把我們的餐桌變成野生動物的屠宰場！”

據報道，在近1600年中，已有700多種有史料記載的動物滅絕。在國際公認的640個面臨滅絕的野生動物物種中，我國就佔了156個。保護野生動物已成為我們的嚴峻課題。

地球是人類及其他生物的共有家園。人與野生動物本是共生關係，這是我們越來越深切感受到的現實。餐桌上的野蠻再一次警告人們：保護野生動物，人人有責。

。这种行为实在愚昧之极、野蛮之至！"他甚至用"没人性"这样的词句，来表达他对此类行为的愤慨。前不久，上海有八位科学家联名发出"不吃野生动物，提倡文明生活"的倡议，他们说："为了给子孙后代留下一个完整而美好的世界，千万别把我们的餐桌变成野生动物的屠宰场！"

据报道，在近1600年中，已有700多种有史料记载的动物灭绝。在国际公认的640个面临灭绝的野生动物物种中，我国就占了156个。保护野生动物已成为我们的严峻课题。

地球是人类及其他生物的共有家园。人与野生动物本是共生关系，这是我们越来越深切感受到的现实。餐桌上的野蛮再一次警告人们：保护野生动物，人人有责。

词汇

餐桌		cānzhuō	n. dining table
文明		wénmíng	n. civilization; culture
野蛮	野蠻	yěmán	adj. barbarous; cruel
饮食	飲食	yǐnshí	n. food and drink; diet
作为	作爲	zuòwéi	prep. as
中华	中華	zhōnghuá	n. the Chinese nation
特色		tèsè	n. distinguishing feature
早已		zǎoyǐ	adv. long ago; for a long time
世界闻名	世界聞名	shìjiè wénmíng	adj. world-famous
闻名	聞名	wénmíng	adj. renowned; well-known
味道		wèi.dào	n. flavor; smell
不顾	不顧	búgù	v. to disregard
法令		fǎlìng	n. law and decrees
舆论	輿論	yúlùn	n. public opinion
餐馆	餐館	cān'guǎn	n. restaurant
几乎	幾乎	jīhū	adv. almost
野生		yěshēng	adj. wild; uncultivated
动物	動物	dòng.wù	n. animal
博物馆	博物館	bówùguǎn	n. museum
孔雀		kǒngquè	n. peacock
全		quán	adj. complete; whole

宴	宴	yàn	n. banquet; dinning party
天鹅	天鵝	tiān'é	n. swan
包		bāo	v. to wrap
鸵鸟	鴕鳥	tuóniǎo	n. ostrich
红烧	紅燒	hóngshāo	v. to braise in soy sauce
果子狸	果子狸	guǒ.zilí	n. masked civet
清炖	清炖	qīngdùn	adj. boiled in clear soup (without soy sauce)
蛇	蛇	shé	n. snake
龟	龜	guī	n. tortoise; turtle
鹰	鷹	yīng	n. hawk; eagle
香	香	xiāng	adj. appetizing; fragrant
炸	炸	zhá	v. to deep-fry
鳄鱼	鱷魚	èyú	n. crocodile
条	條	tiáo	n. strip
金	金	jīn	n. gold
龙	龍	lóng	n. dragon
巨蜥	巨蜥	jùxī	n. huge lizard
不久前		bùjiǔqián	n. before long
广西	廣西	Guǎngxī	n. a province in southern China
南宁	南寧	Nánníng	n. capital city of Guangxi
稀有		xīyǒu	adj. rare; unusual

餐		cān	n. meal
珍稀	珍稀	zhēnxī	adj. precious; rare
道		dào	MW for dishes
主菜		zhǔcài	n. main dish
场合	場合	chǎnghé	n. occasions; situations
规格	規格	guīgé	n. standard
待遇		dài.yù	n. treatment
象征		xiàngzhēng	n. symbol; token
实在	實在	shízài	adv. really; certainly; truly
忧虑	憂慮	yōulù	adj. worried; concerned
生物学家	生物學家	shēngwùxuéjiā	n. biologist
杨雄里	楊雄里	Yáng Xiónglǐ	n. name of a person
南方		nánfāng	n. south
补脑	補腦	bǔnǎo	v. to nourish the brain
竟然		jìngrán	adv. unexpectedly
绳子	繩子	shéng.zǐ	n. rope
捆住		kǔn.zhù	v. to bind; to tie
猴子		hóu.zǐ	n. monkey
硬物		yìngwù	n. hard objects
敲开	敲開	qiāo.kāi	v. to strike open
脑壳	腦殼	nǎoké	n. head (southern dialect)
脑	腦	nǎo	n. brain

愚昧	愚昧	yúmèi	adj. ignorant; benighted
之极	之極	zhījí	adv. extremely
之至		zhīzhì	adv. extremely
人性		rénxìng	n. human nature
词句	詞句	cíjù	n. words and sentences (here: expression)
表达	表達	biǎodá	v. to express
此		cǐ	= 这
行为	行爲	xíngwéi	n. behavior
愤慨	憤慨	fènkǎi	adj./n. be indignant (toward an injustice)
科学家	科學家	kēxuéjiā	n. scientist
联名	聯名	liánmíng	adv. to jointly sign; jointly
发出	發出	fāchū	v. to put forward; to raise
提倡		tíchàng	v. to advocate; to encourage
倡议	倡議	chàngyì	v/n. to propose; proposal
子孙	子孫	zǐsūn	n. descendants
后代	後代	hòudài	n. descendants; posterity
留下		liú.xià	v. to leave
完整		wánzhěng	adj. intact; complete
美好		měihǎo	adj. happy; glorious
千万	千萬	qiānwàn	adv. be sure; must
屠宰场	屠宰場	túzǎichǎng	n. slaughterhouse

报道	報道	bàodào	n. news report
近		jìn	adj. recent
史料		shǐliào	n. historical data/materials
记载	記載	jìzǎi	v/n. to record; to put down in writing
灭绝	滅絶	mièjué	v. to become extinct
国际	國際	guójì	adj. international
公认	公認	gōngrèn	v. to be generally acknowledged
面临	面臨	miànlín	v. to be faced with
物种	物種	wùzhǒng	n. species
严峻	嚴峻	yánjùn	adj. stern; severe
课题	課題	kètí	n. question for study
地球		dìqiú	n. the earth; the globe
人类	人類	rénlèi	n. human kind
生物		shēngwù	n. living thing; creature
共有		gòngyǒu	v. to jointly possesses
家园	家園	jiāyuán	n. home; homeland
本		běn	adv. originally
深切		shēnqiè	adj. heartfelt; deep
感受		gǎnshòu	n./v. experience; to feel
警告	警告	jǐnggào	v. to warn
责	責	zé	n. duty; responsibility

词语例句

1. 作为   **as**

❖ 饮食文化作为中华文明的特色之一早已世界闻名。

Chinese food culture, as one of the features of Chinese civilization, has long since been world famous.

1) 作为你的老师，我有责任指出你的错误。

As your teacher, it is my responsibility to point out your faults.

2) 珍稀野生动物作为一道主菜，在一些场合甚至成为某种规格、待遇的象征。

On some occasions serving a rare and wild animal as a main course has even become a symbol of a (high) standard and a (good) treatment.

2. 早已   **long since**

❖ 饮食文化作为中华文明的特色之一早已世界闻名。

(see 1. for translation)

1) 他早已做了决定了。

He made up his mind long ago

2) 你要的东西，我早已给你买来了。

I've long since bought all the things you want.

3. 味道   **flavor; hint**

❖ 这种文明越来越带着野蛮的味道。

This kind if civilization is more and more coming to have a hint of the savage.

1) 她的话有种讽刺的味道。

There is a touch of sarcasm in her remarks.

2) 看到自己的女朋友跟最好的朋友结婚，他心里有说不出的味道。

He had an indescribable feeling when he saw his girlfriend marrying his best friend.

4. 不顾   **regardless; disregard**

❖ （一些餐馆）不顾国家法令，不顾舆论的批评，几乎成了野生

动物的 " 博物馆 " 。

Some restaurants almost became "museum of wild animals," regardless of law and criticism of public.

1) 这个人真自私，从来不顾别人的感觉。

This person is so selfish — he never cares about other's feelings.

2) 他不顾父母的反对，坚决要去外国念书。

He is determined to go study abroad in spite of his parents' disapproval.

5. …之至；…之极   **extremely**

❖ 这种行为实在是愚昧之极，野蛮之至。

This kind of behavior really is extremely ignorant and uncivilized

1) 让你等那么久，真是抱歉之至。

I'm terribly sorry to have kept you waiting for such a long time.

2) 我对她的帮助感激之至。

I'm extremely grateful for her help.

6. 用…表达   **use … to express**

❖ 他甚至用 " 没有人性 " 这样的词句，来表达他对此类行为的愤慨。

He even used words like "inhumane" to express his anger towards this kind of behavior.

1) 我兴奋的心情很难用语言来表达。

Words can hardly express my excitement.

2) 美国用 " 马丁路德金日 " 来表达对这位民权战士的尊敬。

Americans use Martin Luther King Day to show their respect to this civil rights fighter.

练习

I.   Choose the most appropriate word for each blank and fill in with its Chinese equivalent.

        warn   as   disregard   world-famous

        jointly sign   must   record   become extinct

  1. 北京，_____一个古老的城市之一，有很多_____名胜古迹。

  2. 政府要求烟草商人在所有的烟盒上写明：政府_____市民：吸烟
     有害健康。

  3. 这种鳄鱼在世界别的地区已经_____了，只有在中国的长江地区
     还剩下不到100只。

  4. 他_____危险跳进湖水里去救那个小孩儿。

  5. 这本书详细地_____第一次世界大战是如何开始的。

  6. 最近亚洲十二个国家_____发起"让毒品远离人类"的活动。

  7. _____别在那条河里游泳，那条河里有吃人的鱼。

II.   Choose the correct answer.

1. 保护环境是地球上每个人的【责任；责】。

2. 社会学家建议家长们挤出时间，多【关心；顾】孩子的心理情况。

3. 虽然中国的人口增长速度已经放慢，但是中国的人口形势还是十分【严
    厉；严峻】。

III.   Make a sentence using the underlined expression.

1. 一些人<u>为了</u>补脑，<u>竟然</u>用硬物敲开猴子的脑袋吃猴脑，这种行为<u>实在</u>野
    蛮<u>之至</u>。

2. 饮食文化<u>作为</u>中华文明的特色<u>之一</u>，<u>早已</u>世界闻名。<u>然而</u>近年来，在我
    国<u>一些</u>地方，这种文明<u>却越来越</u>带着野蛮的味道。

IV.   Composition

    最近上海八名科学家联名向社会发出"不吃野生动物，提倡文明生
    活"的倡议。请你为他们写这份倡议书。

1999年6月30日《文匯報》

第二十五課

杭州街頭設置安全套自售機引起爭議

今年6月3日，杭州市在街上設置了兩個安全套自動售貨機。20多天來，銷售平穩，但同時也發生了一些令人不愉快的事，有一位店主竟用掛曆紙把自售機封上，只留下一個投幣口。

用掛曆紙把自售機封上的是一家髮廊的店主，雖然自售機裝在髮廊隔壁的飲食店門口，但這位店主還嫌它礙眼。現在這部機器已經被計劃生育站撤回。計劃生育站的負責人説，由於在居民區找一個合適的裝機點兒不容易，這台機器暫時還沒有重新裝回去。

杭州市計劃生育站負責人認爲，杭州是華東地區第一個推行安全套自售機的城市，一些市民由於傳統觀念的影響，存在"這種東西見不得人""設

1999年6月30日《文汇报》

第二十五课

杭州街头设置安全套自售机引起争议

今年6月3日，杭州市在街上设置了两个安全套自动售货机。20多天来，销售平稳，但同时也发生了一些令人不愉快的事，有一位店主竟用挂历纸把自售机封上，只留下一个投币口。

用挂历纸把自售机封上的是一家发廊的店主，虽然自售机装在发廊隔壁的饮食店门口，但这位店主还嫌它碍眼。现在这部机器已经被计划生育站撤回。计划生育站的负责人说，由于在居民区找一个合适的装机点儿不容易，这台机器暂时还没有重新装回去。

杭州市计划生育站负责人认为，杭州是华东地区第一个推行安全套自售机的城市，一些市民由于传统观念的影响，存在"这种东西见不得人""设在自己家門口不雅觀"等思想。除此之外，自售機的設置還引起一部分市民的擔心。認爲自售機在方便育齡婦女的同時，也給某些違法活動提供了方便。但計劃生育部門的同志跟社會學家在接受記者採訪時表示，這種憂慮是不必要的，因爲安全套在各大藥房都有，街頭自售機與違法活動沒有關係。

據了解，杭州市計劃生育部門這次在西湖區等六個地方設置了一百多個自動售貨機，所覆蓋人口超過三十萬。這種投幣一元就可以吐套的二十四小時自動售貨機比起商店來，有方便、可靠、和免於不好意思的優點。自動售貨機設置以來，平均每天吐套五百個。大部分杭州市民對這種銷售方式已經有科學認識並持歡迎態度。

有關負責人在接受採訪時表示，自售機是現代化城市文明的一種標誌。儘管有觀念上的爭議，但杭州市仍然把它列爲計劃生育優質服務的一項重要內容，大力推行。今年下半年，杭州市各區都將設置安全套自售機，總量將達一千五百台左右。隨著人民經濟水平和對生活質量要求的提高，自售機也在自己家门口不雅观"等思想。除此之外，自售机的设置还引起一部分市民的担心。认为自售机在方便育龄妇女的同时，也给某些违法活动提供了方便。但计划生育部门的同志跟社会学家在接受记者采访时表示，这种忧虑是不必要的，因为安全套在各大药房都有，街头自售机与违法活动没有关系。

据了解，杭州市计划生育部门这次在西湖区等六个地方设置了一百多个自动售货机，所覆盖人口超过三十万。这种投币一元就可以吐套的二十四小时自动售货机比起商店来，有方便、可靠、和免于不好意思的优点。自动售货机设置以来，平均每天吐套五百个。大部分杭州市民对这种销售方式已经有科学认识并持欢迎态度。

有关负责人在接受采访时表示，自售机是现代化城市文明的一种标志。尽管有观念上的争议，但杭州市仍然把它列为计划生育优质服务的一项重要内容，大力推行。今年下半年，杭州市各区都将设置安全套自售机，总量将达一千五百台左右。随着人民经济水平和对生活质量要求的提高，自售机也應該成爲人民接受並愛護的一項公物，因爲它終究關係著廣大人民的健康。

应该成为人民接受并爱护的一项公物，因为它终究关系着广大人民的健康。

词汇

杭州		Hángzhōu	n. capital city of Zhejiang Province
街头	街頭	jiētóu	n. street; street corner
设置	設置	shèzhì	v. to install; to fit; to set up
安全套		ānquántào	n. condom
自售机	自售機	zìshòujī	n. automatic vending machine
引起		yǐnqǐ	v. to give rise to; to bring about
争议	爭議	zhēngyì	n. dispute; debate; contention
自动	自動	zìdòng	adj. automatic
售货机	售貨機	shòuhuòjī	n. vending machine
销售	銷售	xiāoshòu	n. sale
平稳	平穩	píngwěn	adj. stable; smooth
发生	發生	fāshēng	v. to occur; to take place
令人		lìngrén	v. to make one (feel...)
愉快		yúkuài	adj. delight; pleasant
店主		diànzhǔ	n. owner of store
竟		jìng	adv. unexpectedly
挂历	掛曆	guàlì	n. wall calendar
封上		fēng.shàng	v. to seal
留下		liú.xià	v. to leave
投币口	投幣口	tóubìkǒu	n. coin slot

发廊	髮廊	fàláng	n. hair salon
装	裝	zhuāng	v. to install
隔壁		gébì	n. the next door
饮食店	飲食店	yīnshídiàn	n. eating house; café; snack bar
门口儿	門口儿	ménkǒur	n. entrance; entry; doorway
嫌		xián	v. to dislike; to detest; to mind
碍眼	礙眼	àiyǎn	adj. to be unpleasant to look at
部		bù	mw for machine
机器	機器	jīqì	n. machine
计划生育	計劃生育	jìhuàshēngyù	n. family planning; birth control
站		zhàn	n. center
撤回	撤回	chèhuí	v. to withdraw; to take back
负责人	負責人	fùzérén	n. person in charge
居民区	居民區	jūmínqū	n. residential district
合适	合適	héshì	adj. suitable; appropriate
装机点儿	裝機點儿	zhuāngjī.diǎnr	n. place to install vending machine
台	臺	tái	mw for engine, machine
暂时	暫時	zànshí	adv. for the moment; temporarily
重新		chóngxīn	adv. re-doing; anew
华东	華東	Huádōng	n. Eastern China

地区	地區	dìqū	n. region; area
推行		tuīxíng	v. to try to carry out (a policy, etc.)
传统	傳統	chuántǒng	n. convention; tradition
观念	觀念	guānniàn	n. concept
影响	影響	yǐngxiǎng	v. to influence; to affect
存在		cúnzài	v. to exist
见不得人	見不得人	jiàn.bù.de rén	ph. not fit to be seen or revealed; unpresentable
设	設	shè	v. to establish
不雅观	不雅觀	bù yǎguān	adj. offensive to the eye; disagreeable to the sight
除此之外		chúcǐzhīwài	conj. besides this
方便		fāngbiàn	v./adj. to make things convenient to sb.; convenient
育龄妇女	育齡婦女	yùlíng fùnǚ	n. woman of childbearing age
某些		mǒuxiē	adj. certain; some
违法	違法	wéifǎ	adj. lawless; illegal
活动	活動	huódòng	n. activity
提供		tígōng	v. to provide
部门	部門	bùmén	n. department of a large organization
社会学家	社會學家	shèhuìxuéjiā	n. sociologist
接受		jiēshòu	v. to accept
记者	記者	jìzhě	n. journalist; reporter

采访	採訪	cǎifǎng	n. (of a journalist) to interview
表示		biǎoshì	v. to express
忧虑	憂慮	yōulǜ	v./n. to fear; anxiety
必要		bìyào	adj. necessary
药房	藥房	yàofáng	n. pharmacy
西湖区	西湖區	Xīhú qū	n. name of an area or a district
覆盖	覆蓋	fùgài	v. to cover
人口		rénkǒu	n. population
超过	超過	chāoguò	v. to surpass; to exceed
万	萬	wàn	num. ten thousand
元		yuán	mw for money
吐		tǔ	v. to dispense (lit. "spit out")
商店		shāngdiàn	n. store; shop
可靠		kěkào	adj. reliable
免于	免於	miǎnyú	v. to prevent; to avoid
不好意思		bùhǎoyì.sī	v. to feel embarrassed
以来		yǐlái	prep. since
平均		píngjūn	adj. average
方式		fāngshì	n. way; fashion; manner
科学	科學	kēxué	adj. scientific
认识	認識	rèn.shí	n. understanding; knowledge

并	並	bìng	conj. and; also
持		chí	v. to hold (an opinion or attitude)
态度	態度	tài.dù	n. attitude
有关	有關	yǒuguān	adj. concerning
现代化	現代化	xiàndàihuà	adj. modernized
文明		wénmíng	n. civilization
标志	標誌	biāozhì	n. symbol; signal
尽管	盡管	jǐn'guǎn	conj. even though; in spite of
仍然		réngrán	adv. still
列为	列爲	lièwéi	v. to rank as; to list as
优质	優質	yōuzhì	n. high quality; high grade
服务	服務	fúwù	n. service
项	項	xiàng	mw for item, clauses, etc.
内容		nèiróng	n. content
大力		dàlì	adv. with great exertion
推行		tuīxíng	v. to try to carry out
将	將	jiāng	adv. be ready to; be about to
总量	總量	zǒngliàng	n. total
达	達	dá	v. to reach
随着	隨著	suí.zhe	prep. along with
人民		rénmín	n. the people

质量	質量	zhìliàng	n. quality
提高		tígāo	v. to raise; to improve
爱护	愛護	àihù	v. to take good care of
公物		gōngwù	n. public property
终究	終究	zhōngjiū	adv. eventually; in the end; in the long run
广大	廣大	guǎngdà	adj. numerous
健康		jiànkāng	n. health

词语例句

1. **重新**   **again; anew; re-**

❖ 由于在居民区找一个合适的装机点儿不容易,这台机器暂时还没有重新装回去。

Since it is not easy to find a suitable place to install the machine in the residential district, this machine has not yet been reinstalled.

1) 我不小心把名字写到生日那栏里了,我能不能再填一张表?

I wrote my name in the 'date of birth' space by accident, can I fill in a new form?

2) 因为两位总统候选人的票数太接近,美国政府只好重新数佛罗里达州的选票。

Since the two presidential candidates' votes were too close, the American government had to recount the ballots in Florida.

2. **见不得人**   **not fit to be seen**

❖ 一些市民存在"这种东西见不得人"的思想。

Some city residents have it in their mind that this kind of thing would be embarrassing if exposed.

1) 二十年以前,婚外关系还是很见不得人的事情。可是,现在很多人都觉得没有什么大不了的。

Twenty years ago, extra-marital relationships were kept hidden, but nowadays a lot of people think they are not a big deal.

2) 在有些人看来,吸毒并不是见不得人的事,相反,他们还以此为荣。

Some people are not ashamed to use drugs; on the contrary, they are proud of it.

3. **在···同时,也···**   **while**

❖ 他们认为自售机在方便育龄妇女的同时,也给某些违法活动带来方便。

They thought while the vending machine brings convenience to woman of childbearing age, it will also make it easier for some unlawful activities.

1) 教育界的人士向政府呼吁，政府在发展经济的同时，也要重视教育。

   Educators appealed to the government to focus on education and the economy simultaneously.

2) 家长在重视孩子成绩的同时，也应该关心孩子的心理健康。

   Parents should pay attention to their children's grades and at the same time be concerned about their psychological health.

4. 尽管…，但是… **even though; despite**

❖ 尽管有观念上的争议，但杭州市仍然把它列为计划生育优质服务的一项重要内容。

   Even though there was disagreement about it, Hangzhou city government went ahead and made it important part of the "High Quality Service" in family planning program.

1) 尽管美国政府采取了很多措施来阻止校园暴力，但校园暴力还是有增无减。

   Even though the American government has taken many steps to stop campus violence, it is still on the rise.

2) 尽管在很多方面我们的看法不一致，但我们还是好朋友。

   Although we don't agree with each other in many ways, we are still good friends.

5. 随着 **along with**

❖ 随着人民经济水平和对生活质量要求的提高，自售机也应该成为人民自觉接受并爱护的一项公物。

   With the rising of living standard of Chinese people and their demand for life quality, people should accept and protect vending machine as a kind of public property.

1) 随着经济的发展，许多传统的观念也都发生了改变。

Along with economic development, many traditional concepts have changed as well.

2) 人们相信随着竞争的增加，中国饭店服务的质量会进一步提高。

People believe that the quality of service in hotels will rise as competition increases.

6. 终究   **eventually; in the end**

❖ ……，因为它终究关系着广大人民的健康。

……, for it plays a great part in people's health after all.

1) 靠别人生活终究不是一个长久的法子。

It is not a permanent way to rely on other people for a living.

2) 他一定会原谅你，终究他是你父亲。

He will understand you in the end; after all, he is your father.

练习

I.　　Make a sentence using the underlined expression.

1. 他们认为自售机<u>在</u>方便育龄妇女的<u>同时</u>，<u>也</u>给某些违法活动带来方便。

2. <u>随着</u>人民对生活质量要求的提高，自售机也应该成为人民接受并爱护的一项公物。

3. 这种自售机<u>比起</u>商店<u>来</u>，<u>有</u>方便、可靠<u>的优点</u>。

4. 发廊的主人<u>嫌</u>自售机碍眼，<u>就</u>把自售机用挂历封上了。

5. 人们最终还是会接受安全套自售机的，因为它<u>终究</u>关系着人民的健康。

II.　　Choose the correct answer.

(　　)1. 找一位有名的人写推荐信非常重要，因为这_____着你能不能找到一个好工作。

　　　　　a. 有关　　　　　b.关于　　　　c.关系

(　　)2. 我打算明年_____这个大学，去别的国家旅行。

　　　　　a. 留下　　　　　b. 剩下　　　　　c. 离开

(　　)3. 我住的城市很安全，你真的_____为我担心。

　　　　　a. 没必要　　　　b. 不必须　　　　c. 不一定

(　　)4. 一些市民_____在街上设置安全套自售机会方便一些违法活动。

　　　　　a. 忧虑　　　　　b.不放心　　　　c.担心

III.　　Answer the following questions.

1. 比较香烟自售机和安全套自售机对社会道德和健康的影响。

2. 如果你是一个店主，你愿意不愿意在你的商店里放一个安全套自售机？为什么？

3. 文章中所说的"违法活动"说的是什么？

4. 普遍设置安全套自售机会不会鼓励婚前和婚外的性关系？

2000年4月21日《人民日報》

第二十六課

男人有沒有生育權？

"男人有要求妻子生育孩子的權利嗎？"

最近，重慶一個市民因妻子擅自做墮胎手術而告到法庭。這是又一個發生在夫妻之間的關於生育權的糾紛案件。

33歲的楊先生結婚4年，妻子一直不想生育。急於要孩子的楊先生就用維生素片代替避孕藥給妻子服食。3個月後，妻子懷孕。但她很快決定要去墮胎。楊先生堅決反對。情急之下，他無意中說出了懷孕的緣故。知道真相的妻子認爲楊先生的行爲不可以原諒，第二天就去醫院墮了胎，並要跟楊先生離婚。理由很簡單：楊先生侵犯了她的生育權，是變相強迫她生育子女。律師告訴楊先生，如果妻子真起訴他，他絕對敗訴。

我國的現行法律中，對男性是否有生育權沒有任何規定。那麼，男人是否也應該有生育權？

2000年4月21日《人民日报》

第二十六课

男人有没有生育权？

"男人有要求妻子生育孩子的权利吗？"

最近，重庆一个市民因妻子擅自做堕胎手术而告到法庭。这是又一个发生在夫妻之间的关于生育权的纠纷案件。

33岁的杨先生结婚4年，妻子一直不想生育。急于要孩子的杨先生就用维生素片代替避孕药给妻子服食。3个月后，妻子怀孕。但她很快决定要去堕胎。杨先生坚决反对。情急之下，他无意中说出了怀孕的缘故。知道真相的妻子认为杨先生的行为不可以原谅，第二天就去医院堕了胎，并要跟杨先生离婚。理由很简单：杨先生侵犯了她的生育权，是变相强迫她生育子女。律师告诉杨先生，如果妻子真起诉他，他绝对败诉。

我国的现行法律中，对男性是否有生育权没有任何规定。那么，男人是否也应该有生育权？

　　有的專家認爲，男人應該有生育權。生育權反映的是夫妻關係的一種權利，假如這種權利單單只有夫妻中的一方享有，在法理上存在問題。也有專家認爲《婦女兒童保障法》中保障的是婦女身處弱者地位時的權利，意思是説妻子不能在實現自己不生育自由時，剝奪了丈夫繁衍後代的權利。孩子是夫妻兩人的。誰也不能單方面決定他的命運。對懷孕以後孩子的去留問題應該是雙方共同協商後決定的。所以專家建議在法規中加入有關規定，已婚婦女的流產手術必須經丈夫同意，才可以進行。

　　而一名婦聯幹部卻認爲：法律沒有必要爲丈夫加進生育的條款。如果法律賦予男性生育權的話，那麼他就有權要求妻子生育，女性的不生育自由就無法保證了。

　　另一位女士認爲，眞如男人所願，給一半生育權，最終將導致法律的紊亂。以重慶楊先生爲例，妻子不生，有生育自由保護；丈夫讓妻子懷孕，也以生育權作爲藉口。如果保護丈夫的權利，那麼就有的专家认为，男人应该有生育权。生育权反映的是夫妻关系的一种权利，假如这种权利单单只有夫妻中的一方享有，在法理上存在问题。也有专家认为《妇女儿童保障法》中保障的是妇女身处弱者地位时的权利，意思是说妻子不能在实现自己不生育自由时，剥夺了丈夫繁衍后代的权利。孩子是夫妻两人的。谁也不能单方面决定他的命运。对怀孕以后孩子的去留问题应该是双方共同协商后决定的。所以专家建议在法规中加入有关规定，已婚妇女的流产手术必须经丈夫同意，才可以进行。

而一名妇联干部却认为：法律没有必要为丈夫加进生育的条款。如果法律赋予男性生育权的话，那么他就有权要求妻子生育，女性的不生育自由就无法保证了。

另一位女士认为，真如男人所愿，给一半生育权，最终将导致法律的紊乱。以重庆杨先生为例，妻子不生，有生育自由保护；丈夫让妻子怀孕，也以生育权作为借口。如果保护丈夫的权利，那么就侵犯了妻子的權利。保護了妻子的權利，則侵犯了丈夫的權利。如此下去，光討論是否生育子女就夠法官忙的了---這是不現實的。更有人認爲解決丈夫生育權的問題，應該是在家裏，而不是在法庭上，換一句話説，這是一個道德倫理或習俗範圍裏的問題，不應該由法律來處理。

侵犯了妻子的权利。保护了妻子的权利，则侵犯了丈夫的权利。如此下去，光讨论是否生育子女就够法官忙的了---这是不现实的。更有人认为解决丈夫生育权的问题，应该是在家里，而不是在法庭上，换一句话说，这是一个道德伦理或习俗范围里的问题，不应该由法律来处理。

词汇

生育		shēngyù	v. to give birth; to bear
权（利）	權（利）	quánlì	n. the legal right
要求		yāoqiú	v. to demand; to request
妻子		qī.zǐ	n. wife
重庆	重慶	Chóngqìng	n. name of a city in southwest China
擅自		shànzì	adv. to do sth. without authorization
堕胎	墮胎	duòtāi	v. to perform an abortion; abortion
手术	手術	shǒushù	n. surgery
告		gào	v. to accuse; to go to law against
法庭		fǎtíng	n. court
夫妻		fūqī	n. husband and wife
关于	關於	guānyú	prep. about; with regard to; concerning
纠纷	糾紛	jiūfēn	n. dispute; quarrel
案件	案件	ànjiàn	n. legal case
杨	楊	yáng	n. a surname
一直	一直	yìzhí	adv. always; all along; continuously
急于	急於	jíyú	v. to be eager/anxious to do sth.
维生素片	維生素片	wéishēngsù piàn	n. vitamin pills
代替		dàitì	v. to take the place of; to substitute for

避孕	避孕	bìyùn	n./to. contraception; to avoid conception
药	藥	yào	n. medicine
服食		fúshí	v. to take (medicine)
怀孕	懷孕	huáiyùn	v. to become pregnant
坚决	堅決	jiánjué	adv. firmly; resolutely
反对	反對	fǎnduì	v. to oppose; to be against
情急之下	情急之下	qíngjízhīxià	ph. in a moment of desperation
无意中	無意中	wúyìzhōng	adv. accidentally; inadvertently
缘故	緣故	yuángù	n. cause; reason
真相	眞相	zhēnxiàng	n. the real fact (truth)
行为	行爲	xíngwéi	n. behavior
原谅	原諒	yuánliàng	v. to forgive; to excuse
理由		lǐyóu	n. reason; grounds; argument
侵犯	侵犯	qīnfàn	v. to infringe on (one's rights)
变相	變相	biànxiàng	adv. in a disguised form; convert
强迫	強迫	qiángpò	v. to force; to compel
律师	律師	lǜshī	n. lawyer
起诉	起訴	qǐsù	v. to bring a case to court; to go to court (over sth.)
绝对	絕對	juéduì	adv. certainly; surely
败诉	敗訴	bàisù	v. to lose a lawsuit; to be cast in a lawsuit
现行	現行	xiànxíng	adj. currently in effect; in force;

			active
男性		nánxìng	n. male sex; man
是否		shìfǒu	conj. whether or not
规定	規定	guīdìng	n./v. stipulation; to stipulate; to provide
那么	那麼	nà.me	conj. then; in that case
专家	專家	zhuānjiā	n. expert
反映		fǎnyìng	v. to reflect
假如		jiǎrú	conj. supposing; in case; if
单单	單單	dāndān	adv. only
一方		yīfāng	n. one party
享有		xiǎngyǒu	v. to enjoy (rights)
法理		fǎlǐ	n. legal principle; theory of law
妇女	婦女	fùnǚ	n. woman
儿童	兒童	értóng	n. children
保障		bǎozhàng	v. to guarantee; to safeguard; to protect
身处	身處	shēnchǔ	v. to be situated in; to be in a certain condition
弱者		ruòzhě	n. the weak
地位		dìwèi	n. position; status
实现	實現	shíxiàn	v. to realize
剥夺	剝奪	bōduó	v. to deprive; to expropriate
繁衍	繁衍	fányǎn	v. to multiply; to reproduce

后代	後代	hòudài	n. descendants
单方面	單方面	dānfāngmiàn	adj. unilateral; one-sided
命运	命運	mìngyùn	n. fate
去留		qùliú	n. "go or stay" (here: give birth or get an abortion)
共同		gòngtóng	adv. jointly
协商	協商	xiéshāng	v. to talk things over; to consult
建议	建議	jiànyì	v. to suggest; to advise
法规	法規	fǎguī	n. law and regulation; code
加入		jiārù	v. to add; to put in
已婚		yǐhūn	adj. married
流产	流產	liúchǎn	v./n. miscarry; miscarriage
经	經	jīng	prep. through; after
进行	進行	jìnxíng	v. to conduct; to carry on
妇联	婦聯	Fùlián	n. The Woman's Federation
干部	幹部	gàn.bù	n. cadre
必要		bìyào	adj. necessary; indispensable
加进	加進	jiājìn	v. to add; to put in; to append
条款	條款	tiáokuǎn	n. clause; article; provisions
赋予		fùyǔ	v. to endow; to entrust
保证	保證	bǎozhèng	v. to guarantee
女士		nǚshì	n. lady; Madam

如愿	如願	rúyuàn	v. to achieve what one wishes; to have one's wish fulfilled
最终	最終	zuìzhōng	n. in the long run
导致	導致	dǎozhì	v. to give rise to
紊乱	紊亂	wěnluàn	n. disorderliness; confusion; chaos
借口	藉口	jièkǒu	n. excuse
如此下去		rúcǐxià.qù	ph. if it keeps going on
光		guāng	adv. only
法官		fǎguān	n. judge
现实	現實	xiànshí	adj. realistic; practical
伦理	倫理	lúnlǐ	n. ethics
习俗	習俗	xísú	n. custom
范围	範圍	fànwéi	n. scope; range

词语例句

1. **擅自**   **without authorization**

❖ 最近，重庆一个市民因为妻子擅自做堕胎手术而告到法庭。

❖ Recently, a Chongqing citizen brought a lawsuit against his wife because she had an abortion without consulting with him ,

1) 那个护士上班的时候擅自离开病房，导致病人的死亡。

That nurse left the ward without authorization while she was on duty, and this caused the patient's death.

2) 要是有什么事情发生，等我回来，你不能擅自做决定。

If something happen, wait until I come back; don't make any decisions yourself.

2. **adj＋于＋Verb**   **be adj to Verb**

❖ 急于要孩子的杨先生就用维生素片代替避孕药给妻子服食。

So Mr. Yang, who was anxious to have a baby, replaced his wife's contraceptive pills with vitamin pills.

1) 下班以后他急于去学校接孩子，所以一般不跟别人闲聊。

He usually doesn't chat with other people after work because he is anxious to go to pick up his child at school.

2) 因为最近忙于写毕业论文，所以没有时间给朋友打电话。

I've been busy with my thesis, so I have no time to call my friends.

3) 请你留下你的地址和电话，这样便于我们跟你联系。

Please leave your address and phone number so that it is easy for us to contact you.

4) 虽然他有学问，可是不善于表达，所以做老师不合适。

Although he is quite knowledgeable, he is not good at making himself clear, therefore, teaching is not suitable for him.

3. **无意中**   **inadvertently; by chance**

❖ 他无意中说出了怀孕的缘故。

He inadvertently told the truth about making her pregnant.

1) 今天我迟到的原因是昨天我无意中把闹钟关掉了,所以今天早上我睡过了头。

I was late because I turned off my alarm clock by accident yesterday, and so I overslept this morning.

2) 牛顿坐在树下,无意中看见一个苹果从树上掉下来,这个现象引起了他的注意。

Sitting under the tree, Newton happened to see an apple dropping from the tree; this drew his attention.

4. 是否   **whether or not**

❖ 我国的现行法律中,对男性是否有生育权没有任何规定。

Among the present laws in China, there is no such regulation about whether men should enjoy the right to have a baby.

1) 他是否能来,还不一定。

It is uncertain whether he can come or not.

2) 他们正在讨论美国人是否应该保持有枪的权利。

They are discussing whether Americans should keep the right to bear arms.

5. 假如   **if; supposing**

❖ 假如这种权利单单只有夫妻中的一方享有,在法理上存在问题。

If only one side of a couple can enjoy this kind of rights, it causes problem in the (theory of) law.

1) 假如生活欺骗了你,不要悲伤。

If life deceives you, don't be sad.

2) 假如我忘了,请提醒我一下。

Remind me in case I forget.

6. 单单   **only; solely**

❖ 假如这种权利单单只有夫妻中的一方享有,在法理上存在问题。

(see 5. for translation)

1) 那只狗为什么不咬别人,单单只咬你,一定是你先踢了它。

Why did that dog only bite you, of all people? You must have kicked it first.

2）别人都来了，单单他没来。

Everybody has arrived except him.

7. 以…为例   take …for example

❖ 另一位女士认为，真如男人所愿，给一半生育权，最终将导致法律的紊乱。以重庆杨先生为例。

Another woman believed that if men were given half of the authority to (make women) have babies as they wished, it would eventually lead to chaos in the law. Take Mr. Yang in Chongqing, for example.

1）不是所有的体态语言在不同的国家表示相同的意思，以点头为例，在一些亚洲国家，点头不表示"是"，而表示"不是"。

Not all body language means the same thing in different countries. Take the nodding of the head, for example. In some Asian countries, it means not "yes", but "No".

2）在美国很多地名是西班牙文。以佛罗里达为例，在西班牙文的意思是"鲜花之乡。"

A great many place names in the United States are actually Spanish words. Take Florida for example, which means " land of flowers" in Spanish.

8. 经   after; through; as a result of

❖ 已婚妇女的流产手术必须经丈夫同意，才可以进行。

Married woman can only get an abortion after their husband agrees to it.

1）经讨论，校董会决定录取这个成绩不好，可是很有领导能力的学生。

After discussion, the board decided to admit this student who has bad grades but has leadership talent.

2）经检查，产品的质量合格了。

After the examination, the quality of the products confirmed to be up to specifications.

9. 光…就…   only; merely

❖ 如此下去，光讨论是否生育子女就够法官忙的了。

If this keeps going on, judges will have no time to do anything but discuss

whether women or men should have the right to have babies.

1) 这个学校太贵了，每年光学费就四万多。

This school is too expensive-tuition alone costs forty thousand dollars a year!

2) 你不必告诉我他是谁，光听他的笑声我就知道。

You don't need to tell me who he is; I know just by his laughter.

练习

I.　　Fill in the blank with the most appropriate word.

经　　震惊　侵犯　决不　因…而…　　擅自　坚决　深刻
告

最近在纽约，一位华裔女高中生 ① 杀死亲生父母 ① 被 ② 到法庭。事情的原因是这位女学生交了一个黑人男朋友，而父母 ③ 反对。父母认为，她未 ④ 父母的同意，就 ⑤ 交男朋友，让他们在亲戚朋友面前很丢脸。他们也说 ⑥ 容许她跟黑人谈恋爱。女儿觉得自由和权利受到了 ⑦，绝望中，就跟男朋友一起把父母杀死。这件事 ⑧ 纽约的华人社会，引起了华人父母的 ⑨ 反思。

①____ ②____ ③____ ④____ ⑤____ ⑥____ ⑦____ ⑧____ ⑨____

II.　　Choose the correct answer.

1. 在中国现行的法律中，没有男人有没有生育权的【有关；关于】规定。

2. 有些法律专家认为没有【必要；必须】给男人生育权。

3. 给不给男人生育权不【被；由】妇联决定。

4. 在战争中，很多人【被迫；强迫】离开自己的家。

5. 在有些地方，妻子被看作是为丈夫【生育；出生】子女的工具。

III.　　Complete the following sentences with the expressions provided.

1. 我昨天在饭馆儿里要吃鸡肉，可是服务员怎么也听不懂我的话，_____。
(情急之下，只好)

2. 我不是故意要听你们两人的私事，只是_____。(无意中)

3. 所有的事情都有好的一面和坏的一面，_____。(以…为例)

4. 有些妇女认为，法律特别保护妇女和儿童其实_____。（变相）

5. A：怎么你那么生气？
   B：因为我的同屋_____。（擅自）

IV.　　Answer the following questions.

1. 你认为男人应该不应该有生育权？可能不可能男人跟女人共同享有生育权？男人享有生育权会不会侵犯女人的生育权利？

2. 如果不能男人跟女人共同享有生育权，谁应该享有？为什么？

3. 在这个事件中，你对杨先生和他的爱人的行为有什么看法？

4. 你觉得应该怎么解决这个问题？

2000年7月19日《人民日報》

第二十七課
尊重人格尊嚴

（一）人格尊嚴受到侵害

近年來，經常在報上看到侵害人格尊嚴的案件。去年，兩位小學六年級的老師爲了抬高畢業班總成績，就哄騙成績較差的學生假裝成弱智學生，並開出弱智證明，把學生推上求學無門的絕路。

還是去年，四川一個小學老師因爲幾個學生違反課堂紀律又都不敢承認，就強迫全班80多名學生集體在教室裏下跪。

今年，一名17歲的女孩儿在武漢市一個超市偷了兩包食品，商店的工作人員就用白底紅字牌寫了"偷"字掛在她的胸前，強迫她站在店門前示眾。

在上述行爲中，侵權的具體方式雖然各有不同，但都有一個共同的特點，這就是使受害人的人格尊嚴受到嚴重的損害。

2000年7月19日《人民日报》

第二十七课

尊重人格尊严

（一）人格尊严受到侵害

近年来，经常在报上看到侵害人格尊严的案件。去年，两位小学六年级的老师为了抬高毕业班总成绩，就哄骗成绩较差的学生假装成弱智学生，并开出弱智证明，把学生推上求学无门的绝路。

还是去年，四川一个小学老师因为几个学生违反课堂纪律又都不敢承认，就强迫全班80多名学生集体在教室里下跪。

今年，一名17岁的女孩儿在武汉市一个超市偷了两包食品，商店的工作人员就用白底红字牌写了"偷"字挂在她的胸前，强迫她站在店门前示众。

在上述行为中，侵权的具体方式虽然各有不同，但都有一个共同的特点，这就是使受害人的人格尊严受到严重的损害。

（二）保護人格尊嚴

上述行爲，都嚴重地侵害了人格尊嚴，都是違反法律的侵權行爲。但是不僅實施侵害行爲的教師不知道這侵害了人格尊嚴，就是在實施侵權行爲之後，受害人自己及其監護人也都不知道受害人的人格尊嚴受到了嚴重的侵害，有權要求賠償。

我國法律早就確認了人格尊嚴。《憲法》中明文規定："中華人民共和國公民的人格尊嚴不受侵犯。"

1991年12月23日，兩個女青年到北京一個超級市場購買商品。在她們交完錢準備離開時，超級市場的兩名男保安將二人攔住，並將二人推進一間倉庫，強行要求她們摘下帽子，解開衣服，打開包，進行檢查。檢查以后發現二人並沒有偷竊行爲，才讓她們走。

這一事件，正是典型的侵犯人格尊嚴的案例。它引起了公眾的憤怒。

目前重要的是，從理論上和實踐上都要加強對人格

（二）保护人格尊严

上述行为，都严重地侵害了人格尊严，都是违反法律的侵权行为。但是不仅实施侵害行为的教师不知道这侵害了人格尊严，就是在实施侵权行为之后，受害人自己及其监护人也都不知道受害人的人格尊严受到了严重的侵害，有权要求赔偿。

我国法律早就确认了人格尊严。《宪法》中明文规定："中华人民共和国公民的人格尊严不受侵犯。"

1991年12月23日，两个女青年到北京一个超级市场购买商品。在她们交完钱准备离开时，超级市场的两名男保安将二人拦住，并将二人推进一间仓库，强行要求她们摘下帽子，解开衣服，打开包，进行检查。检查以后发现二人并没有偷窃行为，才让她们走。

这一事件，正是典型的侵犯人格尊严的案例。它引起了公众的愤怒。

目前重要的是，从理论上和实践上都要加强对人格尊嚴的研究和宣傳，使更多的法律專業人士士和群眾熟悉和掌握這一法律賦予的權利，更好地保護他人、保護自己。

尊严的研究和宣传，使更多的法律专业人士士和群众熟悉和掌握这一法律赋予的权利，更好地保护他人、保护自己。

词汇

尊重		zūnzhòng	v. to respect; to esteem
人格		rén'gé	n. moral integrity
尊严	尊嚴	zūnyán	n. dignity
侵害		qīnhài	v. to encroach on(other's rights)
近年来		jìnniánlái	n. in recent years
案件		ànjiàn	n. (legal) case
抬高		táigāo	v. to raise; to increase
毕业班	畢業班	bìyèbān	n. graduating class
总	總	zǒng	adj. total; overall
哄骗	哄騙	hǒngpiàn	v. to trick; to cheat
差		chà	adj. poor; bad
假装	假裝	jiǎzhuāng	v. to pretend to be; to feign
弱智	弱智	ruòzhì	adj. mentally retarded
开	開	kāi	v. to write out
证明	證明	zhèngmíng	n. certificate; proof
推		tuī	v. to push
求学	求學	qiúxué	v. to attend school
无	無	wú	v. have not; without
绝路	絕路	juélù	n. a road to ruin; impasse
四川		Sìchuān	n. name of a province in southwest China

违反	違反	wéifǎn	v. to violate
课堂	課堂	kètáng	n. classroom
纪律	紀律	jì.lǜ	n. discipline; morale
承认	承認	chéngrèn	v. to confess
强迫	強迫	qiángpò	v. to force
集体	集體	jítǐ	adv. collectively
下跪		xiàguì	v. to kneel (on both knees)
武汉	武漢	Wǔhàn	n. capital city of Hubei province
超市		chāoshì	n. supermarket
偷		tōu	v. to steal
包		bāo	MW for wrapped things
食品		shípǐn	n. foodstuff; food
商店		shāngdiàn	n. store; shop
工作人员	工作人員	gōngzuò rényuán	n. staff
底		dǐ	n. background
牌		pái	n. plate; tablet
挂	掛	guà	v. to hang
胸		xiōng	n. chest
示众	示眾	shìzhòng	v. to publicly expose (as a punishment)
上述		shàngshù	adj. above-mentioned
侵权	侵權	qīnquán	n. tort

具体	具體	jùtǐ	adj. specific; concrete
各		gè	adv. separately; differently
共同		gòngtóng	adj. common; joint
特点	特點	tèdiǎn	n. characteristic; trait
受害人		shòuhàirén	n. victim
严重	嚴重	yánzhòng	adj. serious; grave
损害	損害	sǔnhài	n/v. to harm; to damage
保护	保護	bǎohù	v. to protect
法律		fǎlǜ	n. law
实施	實施	shíshī	v. to put into effect; to implement
教师	教師	jiàoshī	n. teacher
及		jí	conj. and
其		qí	pron. his or her
监护人	監護人	jiānhùrén	n. guardian
有权	有權	yǒuquán	adv. authoritatively
赔偿	賠償	péicháng	v/n. to compensate; to pay for; indemnification
早就		zǎojiù	adv. long since
确认	確認	quèrèn	v. to confirm; to recognize
宪法	憲法	xiànfǎ	n. constitution; charter
明文规定	明文規定	míngwén guīdìng	v. to stipulate in explicit term
公民		gōngmín	n. citizen

青年	青年	qīngnián	n. young people; youth
超级市场	超級市場	chāojí shìchǎng	n. supermarket
购买	購買	gòumǎi	v. to buy
商品		shāngpǐn	n. goods; merchandise
交		jiāo	v. to pay
离开	離開	líkāi	v. to leave
保安	保安	bǎoān	n. security personnel
将	將	jiāng	= 把
拦住	攔住	lánzhù	v. to hold back; to stop
推进	推進	tuījìn	v. to push into
仓库	倉庫	cāngkù	n. warehouse; storehouse
强行	強行	qiángxíng	adv. to do sth by force
摘下		zhāixià	v. to take off (hat, glasses, etc.)
解开	解開	jiěkāi	v. to unbutton; to untie
打开	打開	dǎkāi	v. to open
包		bāo	n. bag; sack
进行	進行	jìnxíng	v. to carry on; to conduct
检查	檢查	jiǎnchá	v. to examine; to check; to inspect
偷窃	偷竊	tōuqiè	n. theft
走	走	zǒu	v. to leave; to go away
正		zhèng	adv. precisely; exactly

典型		diǎnxíng	adj. typical
案例		ànlì	n. case
引起		yǐnqǐ	v. to give rise to; to lead to
公众	公眾	gōngzhòng	n. the public; the community
愤怒	憤怒	fènnù	adj. indignant; angry
理论	理論	lǐlùn	n. theory
实践	實踐	shíjiàn	n/v. practice
加强	加強	jiāqiáng	v. to reinforce; to strengthen
研究	研究	yánjiū	v./n. to study; to research; study; research
宣传	宣傳	xuānchuán	v/n. give publicity to; advertisement
专业人士	專業人士	zhuānyè rénshì	n. professionals
群众	群眾	qúnzhòng	n. the masses
熟悉		shú.xī	v. know sb./sth. well
掌握		zhǎngwò	v. to grasp; to master
赋予		fùyǔ	v. to endow; to entrust
他人		tārén	n. others; some other persons; another person

词语例句

1. 把…推上绝路　　　　　　　　**put… to a road to ruin**

❖ 两名小学老师为了抬高毕业班总成绩，就哄骗成绩较差的学生假装成弱智学生，并开出弱智证明，把学生推上求学无门的 绝路。

In order to raise the total grades of the graduating classes, two teachers tricked students into pretending to be mentally retarded and wrote out certificates which confirmed they were mentally retarded, making it impossible for them to continue their education.

1) 是家族之间的没有理性的仇恨把无辜的茱莉叶和罗密欧推上了绝路。

It was the irrational hatred between the two families that put the innocent Romeo and Juliet onto the road to ruin.

2) 是不公平的社会制度把他推上了绝路。

It was the unfair social system that left him at a dead end.

2. 承认　　　　　　　　　　**admit; confess**

❖ 几个学生违反了课堂纪律又不敢承认。

Several students violated the class rules and dared not admit it.

1) 克林顿不得不承认他有了婚外关系。

Clinton had no choice but to confess that he had an extra-marital relationship.

2) 我承认是我打破了玻璃。

I admit to breaking the window.

3. 明文规定　　　　　　　　**expressly stipulate**

❖ 《宪法》中明文规定：中华人民共和国公民的人格尊严不受侵犯。

The constitution expressly provides that the human dignity of citizens of the People's Republic of China must not be violated.

1) 政府明文规定，电视上不能出现烟草广告。

The government stipulates in explicit terms that tobacco advertisements are prohibited on TV.

2) 学校当局明文规定，学生打工每周不得超过十八个钟头。

The university authorities expressly stipulates that university students must not work more than eighteen hours per week.

4. 强行   **forcefully**

❖ （男保安）强行要求其摘下帽子，解开衣服，打开包，进行检查。

The security guards forcefully asked them to take off their hats, unbutton their clothes and open their purses for inspection.

1) 尽管大多数人反对这个议案，他们还是强行通过了。

They forced the bill through even though the majority opposed it.

2) 警察强行进入她的家，把她的丈夫带走。

The police forcefully entered her house and took her husband away.

5. 赋予   **to endow with**

❖ 目前重要的是，从理论上和实践上加强对人格尊严的研究和宣传，使更多的法律专业人士和群众熟悉和掌握这一法律赋予 的权利。

At the present the important thing is to enhance the study and publicity of human dignity both in theory and in practice to make more legal experts and ordinary people familiar with and able to grasp this right.

1) 总统的权力是人民赋予的，所以应该为人民服务。

A president's power comes from the people; therefore he should serve the people.

2) 人权是天赋予的，是不可剥夺的。

Human rights which are endowed by God must not be taken away.

练习

I. Choose the most appropriate word for each blank and fill in with its Chinese equivalent.

pretend to   write out a certificate

kneel(down)   publicly expose   compensate   typical

1. 如果你真的生病，不能考试，请医生给你_____。
2. 100年前，要是一个中国女人有了婚外关系，一定会受到严厉的惩罚，轻则_____，重则被杀死。
3. 他_____请父母原谅他的错。
4. 要是航空公司把你的行李弄丢了，你绝对有权要求_____。
5. 苹果馅饼可以说是最_____的美国甜点了。
6. 当路边的乞丐向行人要钱时，大部分的行人都_____没听见或没看见。

II. Make a sentence using the underlined expression.

1. 两个小学老师<u>为了</u>抬高毕业班总成绩，就<u>哄骗</u>成绩较差的学生假装成弱智学生。
2. 在上述行为中，侵权的具体方式<u>虽然</u>各有不同，<u>但都有一个共同的特点，这就是</u>使受害人的人格尊严受到严重的损害。
3. 但是<u>不仅</u>实施侵害行为的教师不知道这侵害了人格尊严，<u>就是</u>受害人自己及其监护人<u>也</u>不知道。

III. Answer the following questions.

1. 在这篇报道中，哪一件事让你最愤怒？为什么？
2. 怎么样才可以防止损害人格尊严？
3. 在美国你听过类似这样的损害人格尊严的事吗？说说你的经验。

1998年7月13日《光明日報》

第二十八課
兒童乞丐

（一）不給錢就不"放行"

在北京過街天橋、地鐵出入口或商店門口，常常可以看到一些不到10歲的小孩儿截住過往行人，不給錢就不"放行"。盡管這種沿街要錢的小孩儿很少，但他們的行爲卻給城市帶來了一種不愉快。這種不勞而獲的謀生方式更會對孩子的人格產生非常不好的影響。

一位朋友不久前告訴記者，她在北京某過街天橋被幾個看上去農村模樣的小孩儿"圍攻"，不給錢就不"放行"，給每人一角兩角也不讓走；最後，每個小孩儿都得到五角錢之後才"放行"。"這些孩子長大後怎麼辦？"

記者也曾在過街天橋上見過3個不到10歲的小孩儿向行人要錢，不給錢就"不放行"，而小孩儿

1998年7月13日《光明日报》

第二十八课
儿童乞丐

（一）不给钱就不"放行"

在北京过街天桥、地铁出入口或商店门口，常常可以看到一些不到10岁的小孩儿截住过往行人，不给钱就不"放行"。尽管这种沿街要钱的小孩儿很少，但他们的行为却给城市带来了一种不愉快。这种不劳而获的谋生方式更会对孩子的人格产生非常不好的影响。

一位朋友不久前告诉记者，她在北京某过街天桥被几个看上去农村模样的小孩儿"围攻"，不给钱就不"放行"，给每人一角两角也不让走；最后，每个小孩儿都得到五角钱之后才"放行"。"这些孩子长大后怎么办？"

记者也曾在过街天桥上见过3个不到10岁的小孩儿向行人要钱，不给钱就"不放行"，而小孩儿後面跟著兩個帶外地口音的婦女。這兩個婦女手上拎著一個過時的提包，假裝行人跟在小孩儿後面不遠的地方。

記者注意到北京動物園儿過街天橋、西單過街天橋、地鐵出入口這些外地游客多、行人多的繁華地段，一些結伴的小孩儿不斷地向行人"要錢"。在動物園儿過街天橋，三個小孩儿一邊儿喝著易拉罐儿飲料，一邊儿觀察行人。一位打扮入時的姑娘走過天橋，三個小孩儿就突然出現在這位姑娘面前，嚇了她一跳，低頭一看，一個小孩儿抱住她的腿正在"哭"；另一個小孩儿硬拉著她的花裙子不放；第三個小孩儿站在她的前面，雙手伸開，意思是不給錢就不能走。姑娘剛開始還試圖逃走，後來可能是怕小孩儿把她的裙子撕破，於是打開了錢包；她以爲這就解決了問題，誰知道其中一個孩子得到的錢和另外兩個孩子的錢數不一樣。這個小孩儿非要姑娘"補足"，姑娘不得不滿足這個小孩儿的要求。姑娘走後，小孩儿們又高興地喝起易拉罐儿來了。

后面跟着两个带外地口音的妇女。这两个妇女手上拎着一个过时的提包，假装行人跟在小孩儿后面不远的地方。

记者注意到北京动物园儿过街天桥、西单过街天桥、地铁出入口这些外地游客多、行人多的繁华地段，一些结伴的小孩儿不断地向行人"要钱"。在动物园儿过街天桥，三个小孩儿一边儿喝着易拉罐儿饮料，一边儿观察行人。一位打扮入时的姑娘走过天桥，三个小孩儿就突然出现在这位姑娘面前，吓了她一跳，低头一看，一个小孩儿抱住她的腿正在"哭"；另一个小孩儿硬拉着她的花裙子不放；第三个小孩儿站在她的前面，双手伸开，意思是不给钱就不能走。姑娘刚开始还试图逃走，后来可能是怕小孩儿把她的裙子撕破，于是打开了钱包；她以为这就解决了问题，谁知道其中一个孩子得到的钱和另外两个孩子的钱数不一样。这个小孩儿非要姑娘"补足"，姑娘不得不满足这个小孩儿的要求。姑娘走后，小孩儿们又高兴地喝起易拉罐儿来了。

（二）讓人擔心的問題

記者發現，在什麼地段要錢，向什麼人要錢，用什麼方法要錢，這些10歲左右的小孩ㄦ都很清楚。在熱鬧繁華的地段，最能截住行人的地方是天橋、地鐵出入口或商店門口，因為行人通過這些地段時，一般會自然放慢速度，加上地段狹窄，行人簡直沒有地方躲閃。記者觀察到，小孩ㄦ知道哪些人可能會給錢—打扮入時的姑娘、成對的青年男女、看上去和善以及看上去有錢的人，都是小孩ㄦ們要錢的主要對象。

記者想知道這些小孩ㄦ的有關問題：他們是從什麼地方來的？在北京住在哪裏？由什麼人帶出來的？家裏究竟窮不窮？為什麼不上學？即使記者答應給他們很多錢，這些小孩ㄦ都不回答，而且躲得遠遠的。顯然這些孩子是受過訓練的，知道要錢時應該注意什麼！

行人對這些小孩ㄦ的行為怎麼看呢？曾在西單過街天橋被"圍攻"過的一對青年男女笑著對記者說："他們哪裏是在討錢，分明是在搶錢。碰到搶

（二）让人担心的问题

记者发现，在什么地段要钱，向什么人要钱，用什么方法要钱，这些10岁左右的小孩儿都很清楚。在热闹繁华的地段，最能截住行人的地方是天桥、地铁出入口或商店门口，因为行人通过这些地段时，一般会自然放慢速度，加上地段狭窄，行人简直没有地方躲闪。记者观察到，小孩儿知道哪些人可能会给钱—打扮入时的姑娘、成对的青年男女、看上去和善以及看上去有钱的人，都是小孩儿们要钱的主要对象。

记者想知道这些小孩儿的有关问题：他们是从什么地方来的？在北京住在哪里？由什么人带出来的？家里究竟穷不穷？为什么不上学？即使记者答应给他们很多钱，这些小孩儿都不回答，而且躲得远远的。显然这些孩子是受过训练的，知道要钱时应该注意什么！

行人对这些小孩儿的行为怎么看呢？曾在西单过街天桥被"围攻"过的一对青年男女笑着对记者说："他们哪里是在讨钱，分明是在抢钱。碰到抢劫犯還可以報警或搏鬥搏鬥，被這些小孩ㄦ截住，罵不得打不得，還眞沒有辦法。"其他被截過的行人，嘴裏不停地説："這些小孩ㄦ的大人呢？"看熱鬧的人也説："這些小孩ㄦ不應該跑到北京來討錢，該上學。"

兒童向行人要錢令人擔心。一般來説，兒童討錢的原因有三點：首先，從全社會來講，社會發生變化之後，一定比例的家庭處於貧困狀態；同時，也有一些家庭並不貧困，但是卻要小孩ㄦ出門討錢；最後一個原因可能是父母帶小孩ㄦ來北京討錢是爲了"致富"。盡管沿街要錢的小孩ㄦ人數很少，但他們畢竟是小孩ㄦ，現在應該在學校讀書的。現在問題是，這個問題究竟要如何解決？又應該由哪些部門來解決呢？

劫犯还可以报警或搏斗搏斗，被这些小孩儿截住，骂不得打不得，还真没有办法。"其他被截过的行人，嘴里不停地说："这些小孩儿的大人呢？"看热闹的人也说："这些小孩儿不应该跑到北京来讨钱，该上学。"

儿童向行人要钱令人担心。一般来说，儿童讨钱的原因有三点：首先，从全社会来讲，社会发生变化之后，一定比例的家庭处于贫困状态；同时，也有一些家庭并不贫困，但是却要小孩儿出门讨钱；最后一个原因可能是父母带小孩儿来北京讨钱是为了"致富"。尽管沿街要钱的小孩儿人数很少，但他们毕竟是小孩儿，现在应该在学校读书的。现在问题是，这个问题究竟要如何解决？又应该由哪些部门来解决呢？

词汇

儿童	兒童	értóng	n. children
乞丐		qǐgài	n. beggar
过街天桥	過街天橋	guòjiē tiānqiáo	n. overhead walkway
地铁	地鐵	dìtiě	n. subway
出入口		chūrùkǒu	n. exit and entrance
商店		shāngdiàn	n. shop; store
不到		búdào	v. less than
截住		jié.zhù	v. to stop; to intercept
过往	過往	guòwǎng	n. coming and going
行人		xíngrén	n. pedestrian
放行		fàngxíng	v. to let sb. pass
尽管		jǐn'guǎn	conj. even though; despite
沿街		yánjiē	adv. along the street
行为	行爲	xíngwéi	n. behavior; conduct
却	卻	què	adv. however
城市		chéngshì	n. city
带来	帶來	dàilái	v. to bring; to bring about
愉快		yúkuài	adj. pleasant
不劳而获	不勞而獲	bù láo ér huò	v. " reap without sowing"
谋生	謀生	móushēng	v. to make a living
方式		fāngshì	n. way; style; method

人格		rén'gé	n. personality; character
产生	產生	chǎnshēng	v. to produce
影响	影響	yǐngxiǎng	n. effect
不久前		bùjiǔqián	n. not long ago
记者	記者	jìzhě	n. journalist; reporter
某		mǒu	adj. certain; some
看上去		kànshàng.qù	v. to look like
农村	農村	nóngcūn	n. rural area; village
模样	模樣	múyàng	n. appearance; look
围攻	圍攻	wéigōng	v. to attack from all sides
长大	長大	zhǎngdà	v. to grow up
曾		céng	adv. once
跟着	跟著	gēn.zhe	v. to follow;
带	帶	dài	v. to carry
外地		wàidì	n. place other than when one is
口音		kǒuyīn	n. accent
妇女	婦女	fùnǚ	n. woman
拎着	拎著	līn.zhe	v. to hold something by the arm
过时	過時	guòshí	adj. out of fashion
提包		tíbāo	n. handbag
假装	假裝	jiǎzhuāng	v. to pretend to
动物园儿	動物園儿	dòng.wùyuánr	n. zoo

西单	西單	Xīdān	n. name of an area in Beijing
游客		yóukè	n. tourist
繁华	繁華	fánhuá	adj. prosperous
地段		dìduàn	n. area
结伴	結伴	jiébàn	adv. in a group
不断	不斷	búduàn	adv. continuously; constantly
易拉罐儿	易拉罐儿	yìlāguànr	n. pop-top
饮料	飲料	yǐnliào	n. drinks
观察	觀察	guānchá	v. to observe
打扮		dǎbàn	v. to dress up
入时	入時	rùshí	adj. fashionable
姑娘		gū.niáng	n. young woman
出现	出現	chūxiàn	v. to appear
面前		miànqián	n. in front of sb.
吓一跳	嚇一跳	xiàyítiào	v. to startle or scare sb
低头	低頭	dītóu	v. to hang one's head
抱住		bào.zhù	v. to hold
腿		tuǐ	n. leg
哭		kū	v. to cry
硬		yìng	adv. obstinately
拉		lā	v. to pull
花裙子		huā qún.zǐ	n. floral skirt

不放		búfàng	v. not release; not let go one's hold
双手	雙手	shuāngshǒu	n. both hands
伸开	伸開	shēnkāi	v. to stretch
刚开始	剛開始	gāngkāishǐ	n. at the first beginning
试图	試圖	shìtú	v. to try; to attempt
怕		pà	v. to fear
撕破	撕破	sīpò	v. to tear
于是	於是	yú.shì	conj. thus; as a result; consequently
钱包	錢包	qiánbāo	n. wallet; purse
解决	解決	jiějué	v. to solve
其中		qízhōng	among them
钱数	錢數	qiánshù	n. amount of money
非要		fēiyào	adv. simply must
补足	補足	bǔzú	v. to make up the difference
不得不		bù.dé.bù	adv. have no choice but
满足	滿足	mǎnzú	v. to satisfy
向…要钱	向…要錢	xiàng …yàoqián	v. to beg money from
左右		zuǒyòu	adv. around; approximately
热闹	熱鬧	rè'.nào	adj. bustling; busy
通过	通過	tōngguò	v. to pass by
一般		yìbān	adv. generally speaking

放慢		fàngmàn	v. to slow down
速度		sùdù	n. speed
加上		jiā.shàng	conj. plus; in addition
狭窄	狹窄	xiázhǎi	adj. narrow
简直	簡直	jiǎnzhí	adv. simply
无处	無處	wúchù	no place
躲闪	躲閃	duǒshǎn	v. to dodge; to hide
成对	成對	chéngduì	n. in pair
青年		qīngnián	n. young people
和善		héshàn	adj. kind and genial
究竟		jiūjìng	adv. actually; exactly
即使		jíshǐ	adv. even though
答应	答應	dā.yìng	v. to promise; to agree
显然	顯然	xiǎnrán	adv./adj. clearly; clear
训练	訓練	xùnliàn	v. to train
讨钱	討錢	tǎoqián	v. to beg money
分明		fēnmíng	adv. clearly; evidently
抢	搶	qiǎng	v. to pillage
碰到		pèng.dào	v. to run into
抢劫犯	搶劫犯	qiǎngjiéfàn	n. mugger
报警	報警	bàojǐng	v. to report (an incident) to police

搏斗	搏鬥	bódòu	v. to fight; to wrestle
拦住	攔住	lán.zhù	v. to hold back
打不得		dǎ.bù.dé	ph. cannot hit
骂	罵	mà	v. to scold; to abuse
其他		qítā	adj. other; else
不停地		bùtíng.de	adv. continuously
看热闹	看熱鬧	kànrè.nào	v. to watch the fun
首先		shǒuxiān	n. first of all
一定		yídìng	adv. certain
比例		bǐlì	n. proportion; ratio
贫困	貧困	pínkùn	adj. impoverished; poor
致富		zhìfù	v. to get rich
毕竟	畢竟	bìjìng	adv. after all
读书	讀書	dúshū	v. to attend school
如何		rúhé	adv. how
部门	部門	bùmén	n. department of a larger organization

词语例句

1. 尽管…，但是…   **though; even though**

❖ 尽管这种沿街要钱的小孩儿很少，但他们的行为却给社会带来一种不愉快。

Though mot many children begged for money on the roadside, their behaviors brought unpleasantness to the city.

1) 尽管实行人口政策已经二十年了，可中国的人口还在继续增长。

Though China has implemented a family planning policy for twenty years, the population of China is still rising.

2) 尽管我认识他已经很多年了，然而我还是不了解他。

Although I've known him for many years, I still don't understand him.

2. 曾   **once; ever; before**

❖ 记者也曾在某过街天桥上见过三个不到十岁的孩子向行人要钱。

One time I saw three kids under ten years old asking people on the overhead walkway for money.

1) 四十年前，他曾参加过第二次世界大战。

He fought in World War II forty years ago.

2) 自从大学毕业以后，我就不曾见过他。

I have not seen him since we graduated form college.

3. Verb到

❖ 记者注意到北京动物园儿过街天桥、西单过街天桥、地铁出入口这些外地游客多、行人多的繁华地段，一些结伴的小孩儿不断地向行人要钱。

I noticed that in the flourishing and busy places, like the Beijing zoo walkway, Xidan overhead walkway, and subway exits where there are a lot of tourists and pedestrians, some children would beg for money.

1) 记者观察到小孩儿们知道哪些人可能会给钱。

I noticed that the children beggars knew who would possibly give them money.

2）后来我了解到他当乞丐是被迫的。

I found later that he was forced to be a beggar.

4. 硬　　　　　　　　　　　　　　　**obstinately**

❖ 另一个小孩儿硬拉住他的花裙子不放。

Another child firmly pulled on her skirt and wouldn't let he go.

1）她明明很累，可是硬说不累。

She looked clearly tired, but she insisted that she wasn't

2）我对中文没什么兴趣，可是父母硬要我学。

I'm not interested in learning Chinese, but my parents (obstinately) want me to study anyway.

5. 加上　　　　　　　　　　　　　　**in addition**

❖ 因为行人通过这些地段时，一般会自然放慢速度，加上地段狭窄，行人简直没有地方躲闪。

People naturally slow down when they go through these places, since they are narrow and there is nowhere to hide.

1）他住得比较远，加上交通不太方便，所以很少来。

Since he lives quite far away, and additionally transportation is inconvenient, he seldom comes.

2）这个电影不太有意思，再加上没有字幕，很多地方我看不懂，所以只看了一半就睡着了。

This movie was not interesting. Moreover, because there were no subtitles, I couldn't understand most of it, so I fell asleep halfway through.

6. 由　　　　　　　　　　　　　　　**by; through**

❖ 记者想知道这些小孩儿由什么人带出来？

I want to know, who brought these kids here?

" 由 " introduce the action here. It is usually expressed in the following pattern: (receiver of action) ＋由 ＋ (doeser of action) + verb

Listed below are some verbs that can be used in the 由 pattern and can not be used in the 被 pattern.

1) 儿童乞丐的问题应该由社会和政府一起解决。

The government and society should work together to solve the problem of child beggars.

2) 以前中国人跟谁结婚由父母决定，他们不能自己决定。

Before, Chinese people were not able to decide whom to marry; which was decided by their parents.

3) 这个会议由新校长主持。

The meeting will be presided over by the new principal.

4) 这件事应该由法院处理。

Leave this matter for to the court to handle.

7. 毕竟　　　　　　　　　　　after all; at last

❖ 但他们毕竟是小孩儿，现在应该在学校读书。

After all, they are still kids and are supposed to study in school now.

1) 虽然他很聪明，可是毕竟刚来，对工作还不熟悉。

Although he is smart, after all, he is new to the work and isn't good to it yet.

2) 他虽然不好，可是毕竟是我弟弟，我得照顾他。

Although he did misbehave, he is my brother after all; I have to take care of him.

练习

I.　Choose the correct answer.

(　　) 1. 当孩子告诉父母，他不继续上学了，_____。

a. 孩子吓了一跳　　b. 父母吓了一跳　　c. 父母吓了孩子一跳

(　　) 2. 我不认识路，请你走在前面，_____。

a. 我跟在你后面　　b. 你跟在我后面　　c. 你跟着我

(　　) 3. 你说得太快了，我听不懂，请你_____。

a. 说得慢　　　　　b. 慢速度　　　　　c. 放慢速度

(　　) 4. 我上大学时靠奖学金过日子，很少_____父母要钱。

a. 从　　　　　　　b. 由　　　　　　　c. 向

(　　) 5. 我们中学的电脑都是_____那家公司免费提供的。

a. 由　　　　　　　b. 给　　　　　　　c. 被

II.　　Make a sentence using the underlined expressions.

1. 姑娘<u>以为</u>给了钱就能走，<u>谁知道</u>因为孩子们的钱数不一样，他们非要她补足。

2. 你<u>哪里</u>是来帮我的，<u>分明</u>是来给我找麻烦的。

3. 第三个孩子站在她的前面，双手伸开，<u>意思是</u>不给钱就不能走。

4. <u>即使</u>记者答应给他们很多钱，这些孩子都不回答。

5. <u>尽管</u>要钱的小孩人数很少，可是他们<u>毕竟</u>是小孩，应该在学校里读书。

III.　　Choose the most appropriate word for each blank and fill in with its Chinese equivalent.

　　reap without sowing　accent　　　　pretend to　　stop　tear
　　obstinately　　prosperous

1. "快_____那个人，他偷了我的钱包。"一个老人大声喊着。

2. 你的南方_____那么重，别人一听就听出来了。

3. 这是新书，你看的时候小心一点儿，别_____了。

4. 昨天我本来很不想看电影，可是女朋友_____要我去，没办法只好在电影院里睡了一个多小时。

5. 有些年轻人不想努力工作，却总想过_____的生活。

6. 年轻人多半喜欢住在_____的大城市里。

7. 他的脾气真好，即使别人当面笑他，他也_____听不懂。

IV.　　Answer the question using the expressions provided.

1. 哪些人是儿童乞丐要钱的主要对象？为什么？（看上去；模样；入时；成对；和善；训练；往往；怕；即使）

2. 为什么有时候儿童乞丐会让人觉得很不愉快？（突然；面前；吓一跳；抱住；拉住；非要；要不然；甚至；抢）

V.　　Answer the following questions.

1. 从社会安全，孩子的人格发展，孩子的将来等方面谈谈儿童做乞丐有什么坏处？

2. 中国乞丐跟美国乞丐有什么不同？

3. 你遇到乞丐以后怎么办？

4. 给儿童乞丐钱是不是帮助他们最好的办法？为什么？

1999年6月1日《人民日報》（海外版）

第二十九課

中國要控制吸煙率上升趨勢

　　今天是世界衛生組織發起的第12個世界無煙日。中國副總理李嵐清發表書面講話，表示要把控制吸煙作爲政府的職責，採取更有效的措施控制吸煙率上升的趨勢。

　　李嵐清在講話中指出，中國政府從1979年以來一直大力提倡控制吸煙的工作，成績顯著。但全國的吸煙率，特別是青少年和婦女的吸煙率仍在持續上升，因爲吸煙得病和死亡的人數也在上升，中國控制吸煙的任務仍然很艱巨。

　　中國現有3.2億人吸煙。1996年的調查表明，與1984年相比，中國人吸煙率上升了3.74%，開始吸煙的年齡提前了3歲，吸煙者每日平均吸煙量增加了2支，青少年吸煙率上升明顯。近年來中國因肺癌而死亡的人數每年以4.5%的速度增加。

1999年6月1日《人民日报》（海外版）

第二十九课

中国要控制吸烟率上升趋势

今天是世界卫生组织发起的第12个世界无烟日。中国副总理李岚清发表书面讲话，表示要把控制吸烟作为政府的职责，采取更有效的措施控制吸烟率上升的趋势。

李岚清在讲话中指出，中国政府从1979年以来一直大力提倡控制吸烟的工作，成绩显著。但全国的吸烟率，特别是青少年和妇女的吸烟率仍在持续上升，因为吸烟得病和死亡的人数也在上升，中国控制吸烟的任务仍然很艰巨。

中国现有3.2亿人吸烟。1996年的调查表明，与1984年相比，中国人吸烟率上升了3.74%，开始吸烟的年龄提前了3岁，吸烟者每日平均吸烟量增加了2支，青少年吸烟率上升明显。近年来中国因肺癌而死亡的人数每年以4.5%的速度增加。

中國在20年前開始正式展開控制吸煙的工作，包括吸煙危害健康的教育，立法以及在公共場所禁止吸煙等措施。衛生部部長張文康說，全國已有85個城市頒布在公共場所禁止吸煙的規定；自1991年起逐步取消新聞媒體上的煙草廣告，北京等10個城市首先成爲"無煙草廣告城市"；1997年還在北京成功地舉辦了第10屆世界煙草與健康大會。

但他強調，中國必須認識到控制吸煙工作面臨的巨大考驗和挑戰，"特別是有些發達國家的煙草商因爲在國內受到限制和責難，就轉向中國等發展中國家推銷香煙，誘惑青少年吸洋煙。"

張文康要求繼續開展"無煙學校"等活動，使全國2億多學生逐步擺脫煙草危害；同時倡導公務人員、教師帶頭不吸煙，不敬煙；主動戒煙並宣傳吸煙危害健康的知識。

今年世界無煙日的主題是"戒煙"，口號是"放棄香煙"。這一主題的目的是使人們提高對吸煙危害健康的認識，強調戒煙工作的重要性。

中国在20年前开始正式展开控制吸烟的工作，包括吸烟危害健康的教育，立法以及在公共场所禁止吸烟等措施。卫生部部长张文康说，全国已有85个城市颁布在公共场所禁止吸烟的规定；自1991年起逐步取消新闻媒体上的烟草广告，北京等10个城市首先成为"无烟草广告城市"；1997年还在北京成功地举办了第10届世界烟草与健康大会。

但他强调，中国必须认识到控制吸烟工作面临的巨大考验和挑战，"特别是有些发达国家的烟草商因为在国内受到限制和责难，就转向中国等发展中国家推销香烟，诱惑青少年吸洋烟。"

张文康要求继续开展"无烟学校"等活动，使全国2亿多学生逐步摆脱烟草危害；同时倡导公务人员、教师带头不吸烟，不敬烟；主动戒烟并宣传吸烟危害健康的知识。

今年世界无烟日的主题是"戒烟"，口号是"放弃香烟"。这一主题的目的是使人们提高对吸烟危害健康的认识，强调戒烟工作的重要性。

词汇

控制		kòngzhì	v. to control
吸烟	吸煙	xīyān	v. to smoke
率		lǜ	suf. rate; ratio; proposition
上升		shàngshēng	v. to rise; to ascend
趋势	趨勢	qūshì	n. trend
世界卫生组织	世界衛生組織	shìjiè wèishēng zǔzhī	n. World Health Organization
发起	發起	fāqǐ	v. to initiate; to sponsor
世界无烟日	世界無煙日	shìjiè wú yān rì	n. No Smoking Day
副		fù	pref. vice-
总理	總理	zǒnglǐ	n. premier; prime minister
李岚清	李嵐清	Lǐ Lánqīng	n. name of Chinese vice-prime minister
发表	發表	fābiǎo	v. to issue; to announce
书面	書面	shūmiàn	adj. in written form; in writing
讲话	講話	jiǎnghuà	n. speech
表示		biǎoshì	v. to express
作为	作爲	zuòwéi	v. to regard as; to take for
政府		zhèngfǔ	n. government
职责	職責	zhízé	n. duty; responsibility

采取	採取	cǎiqǔ	v. to adopt; to take
有效		yǒuxiào	adj. effective
措施		cuòshī	n. measure; step
指出		zhǐchū	v. to point out (that)
大力		dàlì	adv. devote major effort to
提倡		tíchàng	v. to advocate; to encourage
显著	顯著	xiǎnzhù	adj. notable; marked
特别		tèbié	adv. especially
青少年		qīngshàonián	n. teenager
妇女	婦女	fùnǚ	n. women
仍（然）		réng(rán)	adv. still
持续	持續	chíxù	v. to continue
死亡		sǐwáng	v. to be dead
人数	人數	rénshù	n. number of people
任务	任務	rèn.wù	n. task; undertaking
艰巨	艱巨	jiānjù	adj. extremely difficult; arduous
现（在）	現（在）	xiàn(zài)	n. now
亿	億	yì	num. hundred million
调查	調查	diàochá	n. survey
相比		xiāngbǐ	v. to compared with
年龄	年齡	nián.líng	n. age

提前		tíqián	v. to advance date
平均		píngjūn	adj. average
支		zhī	MW for long and narrow objects
明显	明顯	míngxiǎn	adj. clear; obvious
肺癌	肺癌	fèi'ái	n. lung cancer
正式		zhèngshì	adj./adv. formal; officially
展开	展開	zhǎnkāi	v. to launch; to carry out
包括		bāokuò	v. to include
危害		wēihài	v. to harm; to endanger
立法		lìfǎ	v. to enact law; to legislate
以及		yǐjí	conj. as well as; along with
公共场所	公共場所	gōnggòng chǎngsuǒ	n. public places
禁止		jìnzhǐ	v. to prohibit; to ban
卫生部	衛生部	Wèishēngbù	n. ministry of health
部长	部長	bùzhǎng	n. minister
张文康	張文康	Zhāng Wénkāng	n. a person's name
已（经）	已（經）	yǐ(.jīng)	adv. already
城市		chéngshì	n. city
颁布	頒布	bānbù	v. to promulgate
规定	規定	guīdìng	n. regulation; rule

逐步		zhúbù	adv. step by step
取消		qǔxiāo	v. to abolish; to cancel
新闻媒体	新聞媒體	xīnwén méitǐ	n. news media
烟草	煙草	yāncǎo	n. tobacco
广告	廣告	guǎnggào	n. advertisement
首先		shǒuxiān	adv. in the first place; first of all
无	無	wú	adv. not have; without
成功		chénggōng	v. to succeed
举办	舉辦	jǔbàn	v. to hold (a meeting, exhibition, etc)
届	屆	jiè	MW for meeting graduating classes
强调	強調	qiángdiào	v. to stress; to underline
必须	必須	bìxū	adv. must
面临	面臨	miànlín	v. to be faced with
巨大		jùdà	adj. tremendous; enormous
考验	考驗	kǎoyàn	n. test; trial
挑战	挑戰	tiǎozhàn	n. challenge
发达（国家）	發達（國家）	fādá(guójiā)	n. developed country
烟草商	煙草商	yāncǎoshāng	n. tobacco businessman
限制		xiànzhì	v. to restrict; confine
责难	責難	zé'nàn	v. to censure; to criticize

转向	轉向	zhuǎnxiàng	v. to turn to
发展中 （国家）	發展中 （國家）	fāzhǎnzhōng (guójiā)	n. developing country
推销	推銷	tuīxiāo	v. to promote sale to
香烟	香煙	xiāngyān	n. cigarette
诱惑	誘惑	yòuhuò	v. to tempt
洋		yáng	suf. foreign
继续	繼續	jìxù	v. to continue
开展	開展	kāizhǎn	v. to launch; to develop
活动	活動	huódòng	n. activities
摆脱	擺脱	bǎituō	v. to shake off; to get rid of
倡导	倡導	chàngdǎo	v. to advocate
公务人员	公務人員	gōngwù rényuán	n. government employees
带头	帶頭	dàitóu	v. to take the lead; to be the first
敬烟	敬煙	jìngyān	v. to offer a cigarette
主动	主動	zhǔdòng	adv. to take the initiative
戒烟	戒煙	jièyān	v. to give up smoking
宣传	宣傳	xuānchuán	v. to give publicity to
知识	知識	zhī.shí	n. knowledge
主题	主題	zhǔtí	n. theme
口号	口號	kǒuhào	n. slogan

放弃	放棄	fàngqì	v. to give up; to abandon
目的		mù.dì	n. goal

词语例句

1. **发起**　　　　　　　　　　　**initiate; sponsor**

❖ 今天是世界卫生组织发起的第十二个世界无烟日。

Today is the twelfth "No Smoking Day" initiated by World Health Organization.

1) 这次会议是由十四个国家发起的。

Fourteen countries are sponsoring this conference.

2) 为了让全社会都认识到校园暴力的严重性，他发起这次反暴力的集会。

He initiated this anti-violence rally in order to make all of society know the seriousness of campus violence.

2. **把…作为…**　　　　　　　　**take… as…**

❖ 他表示要把控制吸烟作为政府的职责。

He said the government would take on the responsibility of controlling smoking.

1) 儿童乞丐把成对的青年男女和外国人作为要钱的主要对象。

Children beggars make young couples and foreigners their main targets to ask for money.

2) 他把考上大学作为今年的主要目标。

He has set getting into colleges as this year's major goal.

3. 大力   **vigorously; energetically**

❖ 中国政府从1979年以来一直大力提倡控制吸烟的工作。

Since 1979 the Chinese government has been putting great efforts on promoting the control of smoking.

1) 最近十年中国政府大力发展电脑业。

For the past ten years the Chinese government has been making a major effort to developing its computer industries.

2) "希望工程"的目的是让没有钱的中国孩子也能上学，这个活动得到了社会的大力支持。

Project Hope, which is designed to help poor Chinese children go to school, received enthusiastic help from society.

4. 与…相比，   **compared with**

❖ 与1984年相比，中国人吸烟率上升了百分之三点四。

Compared with that of 1984, the number of Chinese smokers has increased by 3.4 percent.

1) 这两个根本不能相比。

There is no comparison between the two.

2) 中国跟先进国家相比，还有很大差距。

China still has a long way to go to catch up with the developed countries.

5. 提前   **in advance; ahead of time**

❖ 开始吸烟的年龄提前了三岁。

The age at which people start smoking is three years earlier than it used to be.

1) 要是谁不能参加星期五的考试，请提前通知我。

If any of you can't take the exam on Friday, please notify me in advance.

2) 由于他在监狱里表现很好，所以被提前释放了。

He was released before his sentence expired due to his good behavior in jail.

6. 带头   **take the lead in; be the first to**

❖ …，同时倡导公务人员、教师带头不吸烟、不敬烟。

···, at the same time, they advocate that all government functionaries and teachers take the head in not smoking and not offering cigarette.

1) 这个学生总是准备得很好，常常带头回答问题。

This student is always well prepared and often the first to answer questions.

2) 每次献血，都是他带头。

He took the lead in donating blood every time.

7. 主动   on one's own initiative

❖ ···主动戒烟并宣传吸烟危害健康的知识。

(He wants them) to quit smoking on their own accord and popularize the knowledge that smoking does harm to one's health.

1) 他每天放学回来都主动帮母亲做家务。

He helped his mother with her housework after school without being asked.

2) 这个人对别人很冷淡，从来不主动跟别人说话。

He is a cold-natured person and never talks to other people on his own accord.

8. 提高对···认识   be more aware of

❖ 这一主题的目的是使人们提高对吸烟危害健康的认识。

The purpose of this topic is to raise people's awareness that smoking is harmful to one's health.

1) 这个电影的目的是使人们提高对爱滋病的认识。

The purpose of this movie is to make people become more aware of AIDS.

2) 他写这篇文章是为了提高人们对环境保护的认识。

In order to make people more aware of the importance of protecting environment he wrote this article.

练习

I. Choose the correct answer.

( )1. 新年前夕，学校为全校学生____了一次很大的晚会。

　　　a. 开展　　　　　　b. 进行　　　　　　c. 举行

( )2. 这次帮助无家可归者的活动是由一个学生组织____的。

　　　a. 发起　　　　　　b. 发表　　　　　　c. 颁布

( )3. 由于传统习惯的影响，中国的女孩子一般不会____跟
　　　不认识的人谈话。

　　　a. 动手　　　　　　b. 主动　　　　　　c. 发起

( )4. 政府的____应该是保护人民，为人民服务，而不是控制人
　　　民。a. 职责　　　　b. 主要　　　　　　c. 趋势

( )5. 昨天新总统在电视上____讲话，表示他会努力提高人民的
　　　生活水平，改善人民的生活环境。

　　　a. 展开　　　　　　b. 发表　　　　　　c. 颁布

( )6. 这家饭馆的生意相当好，得____好几天才能订到位子。

　　　a. 提前　　　　　　b. 上升　　　　　　c. 提高

( )7. 自这个培训班成立以来，学生人数____八年超过一百人。

　　　a. 继续　　　　　　b. 持续　　　　　　c. 一向

( )8. 很多乞丐把外国游客____要钱的主要对象。

　　　a. 成为　　　　　　b. 作为　　　　　　c. 认为

( )9. 一旦吸毒，就很难____毒品的诱惑。

　　　a. 摆脱　　　　　　b. 取消　　　　　　c. 禁止

II. Fill in the blank with the most appropriate word.

　　大力　强调　显著　面临　限制　挑战　实行　艰巨

中国总理在最近的讲话中说，近二十年来，由于中国政府_____
提倡并_____计划生育政策，人口增长率_____下降了。同时，他
也_____，中国的人口工作还_____巨大的_____，"特别是农村
地区，由于在当地生孩子受到_____，有些人就跑到城里来偷偷地
生。"所以控制人口工作的任务还很_____。

III. Make a sentence using the underlined expression.

1. 中国政府表示要<u>把</u>控制吸烟<u>作为</u>政府的职责。
2. <u>与</u>1984年<u>相比</u>，中国人吸烟率上升了3%。
3. 这一主题的目的是使人们<u>提高</u>对吸烟危害健康的<u>认识</u>。
4. 中国控制吸烟的工作<u>包</u>括宣传、教育<u>以及</u>立法。

IV.　Read the following article and summarize it into Chinese.

NO SMOKING, PLEASE

At present about 38% of the Chinese population smoke. 89% of smokers are male. Every year, millions of smokers die because of illnesses which are caused by smoking tobacco.

The Chinese government receives a lot of money from sales of tobacco; in 1989 it received about 24 billion *yuan*. But in the same year, cigarette smoking cost the government even more money, about 28 billion *yuan*. Smokers cost the government a lot of money for two reasons. First, money is spent looking after people with illnesses, which have been caused by smoking. Second, many fires are caused by smokers. People who smoke in bed often fall asleep while they are smoking. The bedclothes catch fire and the whole house may be burnt down.

China produces on third of the world's cigarettes, Each day, about 220 million packets of cigarettes are smoked by Chinese. This is good news for the tobacco companies, but bad news for the health of the nation. Every year, tobacco company must persuade new people to start smoking cigarettes. This is because each year millions of smokers die from this habit.

In Britain, which has a population of only 58 million people, 110,000 people die from smoking each year. The chance is that one smoker in four will die from smoking.

In Britain, sales of cigarettes have fallen by 30% in the last ten years. Just under a third of population now smoke, about 17 million people. In the 16~19 age group, 32% of women smoke, compared to 28% of men. However, in the 20~24 age group, 39% of women smoke and 38% of men. The problem is that 300 people are dying each day from illnesses caused by smoking. Therefore, if the tobacco companies want to remain in business, they have to encourage young people to start smoking.

V.　Answer the following questions
1. 美国政府采取哪些措施控制青少年吸烟？
2. 请你分析一下为什么青少年吸烟率在上升？
3. 政府控制吸烟率是不是侵犯人民的权利？

1999年8月5日《光明日報》

第三十課

中國強烈譴責分裂中國的議案

　　中國全國人大外事委員會負責人今天發表談話，強烈譴責美國國會少數議員提出的分裂中國的議案。

　　這位負責人説，美國國會眾議院少數議員7月29日向眾議院國際關係委員會提交了一份明目張膽地主張“一中一台”“台灣獨立”的議案。這是對中國主權、領土完整的嚴重侵犯和對國際關係準則的粗暴干涉，也與美國歷屆政府奉行的一個中國的政策背道而馳。對此，我們堅決反對，強烈譴責。

　　他指出，世界上只有一個中國，中華人民共和國是代表全中國唯一的合法政府，台灣是中國領土不可分割的一部分，這是包括美國政府在內的國際社會普遍公認的事實。台灣問題完全是中國的內政

1999年8月5日《光明日报》

第三十课

中国强烈谴责分裂中国的议案

　　中国全国人大外事委员会负责人今天发表谈话，强烈谴责美国国会少数议员提出的分裂中国的议案。

　　这位负责人说，美国国会众议院少数议员7月29日向众议院国际关系委员会提交了一份明目张胆地主张"一中一台""台湾独立"的议案。这是对中国主权、领土完整的严重侵犯和对国际关系准则的粗暴干涉，也与美国历届政府奉行的一个中国的政策背道而驰。对此，我们坚决反对，强烈谴责。

　　他指出，世界上只有一个中国，中华人民共和国是代表全中国唯一的合法政府，台湾是中国领土不可分割的一部分，这是包括美国政府在内的国际社会普遍公认的事实。台湾问题完全是中国的内政。在一個中國的原則下，正式結束兩岸敵對狀態，通過談判實現 " 和平統一 " ， " 一國兩制 " 是我們解決台灣問題的基本方針，是中國各族人民的共同心願和強烈要求，也完全符合台灣同胞的願望。

我們也希望美國國會議員先生們，應該充分認識到支持 " 台獨 " 、分裂中國的嚴重性和危險性。中國人民熱愛和平，但中國的主權、領土完整決不容許侵犯。我們將不惜任何代價來捍衛祖國的主權和領土完整。中國的統一一定要實現，也一定能夠實現。任何企圖分裂中國的作法都只能搬起石頭砸自己的腳，是注定要失敗的。 "

。在一个中国的原则下，正式结束两岸敌对状态，通过谈判实现"和平统一"，"一国两制"是我们解决台湾问题的基本方针，是中国各族人民的共同心愿和强烈要求，也完全符合台湾同胞的愿望。

我们也希望美国国会议员先生们，应该充分认识到支持"台独"、分裂中国的严重性和危险性。中国人民热爱和平，但中国的主权、领土完整决不容许侵犯。我们将不惜任何代价来捍卫祖国的主权和领土完整。中国的统一一定要实现，也一定能够实现。任何企图分裂中国的作法都只能搬起石头砸自己的脚，是注定要失败的。"

词汇

强烈	強烈	qiángliè	adv. vehemently; strongly
谴责	譴責	qiǎnzé	v. to condemn
分裂	分裂	fēnliè	v. to split up; to disunite
议案	議案	yìàn	n. motion; bill
人大		réndà	n. short for "National People's Congress" （全国人民代表大会）
外事		wàishì	n. foreign affairs
委员会	委員會	wěiyuánhuì	n. committee; council
负责人	負責人	fùzérén	n. person in charge
发表	發表	fābiǎo	v. to issue; to announce
谈话	談話	tánhuà	n. statement
国会	國會	Guóhuì	n. Congress
少数	少數	shǎoshù	n. a small number of ; few
议员	議員	yìyuán	n. senator
提出		tíchū	v. to submit; to propose
众议院	眾議院	Zhòngyìyuàn	n. House of Representatives
国际	國際	guójì	n. international
提交		tíjiāo	v. to submit; to file
份		fèn	mw for documents, papers, etc.
明目张胆	明目張膽	míng mù zhāng dǎn	adv. to do evil things openly and unscrupulously; to have the impudence to do sth.

一中一台		Yīzhōng Yītái	n. a China and a Taiwan
独立	獨立	dúlì	n. independence
主权	主權	zhǔquán	n. sovereignty
领土	領土	lǐngtǔ	n. territory
完整		wánzhěng	n. integrity
严重	嚴重	yánzhòng	adj. serious; grave
侵犯		qīnfàn	v. to infringe
准则	準則	zhǔnzé	n. norm; standard
粗暴	粗暴	cūbào	adv. brutally; wantonly
干涉		gānshè	v. to interfere
历届	歷屆	lìjiè	n. all previous (sessions, government, etc.)
奉行		fèngxíng	v. to pursue (a policy)
政策		zhèngcè	n. policy
背道而驰	背道而馳	bèi dào ér chí	v. to run in the opposite direction; to run counter to
对此	對此	duìcǐ	toward this; to diverge from
坚决	堅決	jiānjué	adv. resolutely; firmly
反对	反對	fǎnduì	v. to oppose; to be against
指出		zhǐchū	v. to point out
共和国	共和國	gònghéguó	n. republic
代表		dàibiǎo	v. to represent
唯一的		wéiyī.de	adj. sole; the only one

合法		héfǎ	adj. legal
分割		fēn'gē	v. to cut apart; to separate
包括···在内		bāokuò ··· zàinèi	v. to include
普遍		pǔbiàn	adv. commonly
公认	公認	gōngrèn	v. generally acknowledged
事实	事實	shìshí	n. fact
内政		nèizhèng	n. internal affairs
原则	原則	yuánzé	n. principle
正式		zhèngshì	adv. formally; officially
结束	結束	jiéshù	v. to end
两岸	兩岸	liǎng' àn	n. across the straits
敌对	敵對	díduì	adj. hostile; antagonistic
状态	狀態	zhuàngtài	n. state of affairs
谈判	談判	tánpàn	n. negotiation
实现	實現	shíxiàn	v. to achieve
和平		hépíng	n. peace
统一	統一	tǒngyī	n. integration
一国两制	一國兩制	Yìguó liǎngzhì	n. " one country two systems"
解决	解決	jiějué	v. to solve
基本		jīběn	adj. basic
方针	方針	fāngzhēn	n. policy

各族		gèzú	n. all ethnicity
共同		gòngtóng	adj. common
心愿	心願	xīnyuàn	n. cherished desire; wish
符合		fúhé	v. to accord with; to conform to
同胞		tóngbāo	n. fellow countryman
愿望	願望	yuànwàng	n. aspiration; desire
充分		chōngfèn	adv. fully
认识到	認識到	rènshídào	v. to realize
支持		zhīchí	v. to support
台独		táidú	n. short for "台湾独立"
严重性	嚴重性	yánzhòngxìng	n. gravity
热爱	熱愛	rè'ài	v. to ardently love
决不	決不	juébù	adv. definitely not; under no circumstance
容许	容許	róngxǔ	v. to tolerate; to allow
不惜		bùxī	v. not hesitate to (do sth.); not spare
代价	代價	dàijià	n. price; cost
捍卫	捍衛	hànwèi	v. to defend; to guard
祖国	祖國	zǔguó	n. homeland; motherland
搬起	搬起	bānqǐ	v. to lift
石头	石頭	shí.tóu	n. stone

砸		zá	v. to smash; to pound
注定		zhùdìng	v. to be doomed; to be destined
失败	失敗	shībài	v. to fail

词语例句

1. 不可

❖ 台湾是中国领土不可分割的一部分。

Taiwan is an integral part of China,

1) 二十年前出国留学对大多数中国人来说还是不可想象的事情。

Studying abroad was unimaginable for most Chinese people twenty years ago.

2) 言论自由是每个人不可剥夺的权利。

Freedom of speech is an inalienable right for every person.

2. 符合   **conform to**

❖ （这）也完全符合台湾同胞的根本愿望。

This is also in keeping with the aspiration of the people of Taiwan.

1) 你说中国人没有人权，这个不符合事实。

You claimed that Chinese people do have human rights. That does not square with the facts.

2) 我们需要一个有工作经验的人，她不符合条件。

We need an experienced person, she is not in line with our needs.

3. -性

❖ 应该充分认识到支持"台独"分裂中国的严重性和危险性。

You should be fully aware of the danger and grave results of supporting "Taiwanese Independence" and the splitting of China.

1) 下雨的可能性不大。

It is not likely to rain today.

2) 批评中国人口政策的人都没有认识到中国人口问题的严重性。

People who criticize China's population policy fail to realize the serious issues of the problem is.

4. 决不   **definitely not**

❖ 中国的主权、领土完整决不容许侵犯。

China's sovereignty over her territory should not never be interfered with.

1) 他总是不达到目的决不放弃。

He never gives up until the goal has been reached

2) 中国在任何情况下决不首先使用核子武器。

Under no circumstances will the Chinese government use nuclear weapons first.

5. 不惜   **not hesitate to do**

❖ 我们将不惜任何代价来捍卫祖国的主权和领土完整。

We will defend the motherland's integrity of sovereignty and territory at any cost.

1) 为了帮助丈夫，她不惜牺牲自己的事业。

To help her husband, she is even willing to sacrifice her own career.

2) 要是美国帮助台湾独立，中国政府会不惜使用武力。

If the United States helps Taiwan to gain independence, the Chinese government will not hesitate to use military force.

6. 任何   **any; whatever**

❖ 任何企图分裂中国的作法都只能搬起石头砸自己的脚。

Any attempts to split China will be just like lifting a stone and dropping it on one's own feet.

1) 任何事情都有好的一面和坏的一面。

Everything has a good side and a bad side.

2) 任何人都有受教育的权利。

Everyone has the right to receive an education.

7. 注定   **be doomed; be destined to**

❖ （分裂中国的企图）是注定要失败的。

(The attempt to split China) is doomed to failure.

1) 你又懒又不负责，注定这辈子找不到工作。

You are lazy and irresponsible, so you are doomed to be unemployed.

2) 按照马克思理论，帝国主义是注定要灭亡的。

According to Marxism's theory, imperialism is doomed to extinction.

练习

I.   Choose the correct answer.

(   )1. 现在的社会太不象话了，在街上有些人明目张胆地＿＿＿＿。

　　　　　a. 抢钱　　　　　　b. 做生意　　　　　c. 谈恋爱

(   )2. 第二次世界大战后，德国＿＿＿＿成东德和西德。

　　　　　a. 分开　　　　　　b. 分裂　　　　　　c. 分光

(   )3. 他是家里＿＿＿＿男孩子，所以父母和祖父母把他惯坏了。

　　　　　a. 只有　　　　　　b. 只一个　　　　　c. 唯一的

(   )4. 这三千块钱只是学费，并不＿＿＿＿。

　　　　　a. 在内保险费　　b. 包括在内保险费　c. 包括保险费在内

(   )5. 大部分家长都认为小孩子不应该在学校做生意，也有＿＿＿＿家长觉得这种生意经对他们有好处。

　　　　　a. 少　　　　　　　b. 少数　　　　　　c. 没有几个

II.   Complete the following sentences using the underlined expression.

1. 中国的主权和领土完整决不容许侵犯。

　　1) 我的家庭非常保守，…。

　　2) 在没有新闻自由的社会里，…。

2. 我们也希望美国议员充分认识到支持台独的危险性。

　　1) 他所以考试考得这么好，…。

　　2) 这次去了中国，…。

3. 我们将不惜任何代价来捍卫祖国的主权和领土完整。

　　1) 为了追求金钱和财富，…。

　　2) 她为了好好照顾孩子，…。

4. 任何企图分裂中国的行径都是注定要失败的。

　　1) 平时不上课，考试以前又不准备，…。

　　2) 他又不好看，性格又奇怪…。

III.   Answer the following questions.

1. 中国政府为什么要统一台湾？中国政府希望怎么统一台湾？

2. 美国政府对台湾问题的看法？美国人对台湾独立的看法？对这个问题，中国老百姓的看法是什么？台湾老百姓的态度怎么样？

IV.　　Composition

1. " 搬起石头砸自己的脚 " 说自己主动做了一件事情，可是结果却对自己有害。中国人用这句话来形容一个人做了一件笨事。请你写一件你或者别人做过的这样的事。

2. 请你分别采访大陆和台湾的以下的这些人：大学生；汽车司机；政府官员；商人。还有美国的：中国问题专家；老百姓。请他们谈谈对台湾独立的看法。

1999年7月20日《人民日報》

第三十一課

中國人口結構發生轉變

　　自70年代初中國開始實行計劃生育以來，我國人口增長過快得到了有效控制。按1970年的生育水平推算，近30年來，全國累計少出生3億人，我國城市地區人口完成了從"高出生、高死亡、高增長"向"低出生、低死亡、高增長"的轉變；農村地區正在轉變過程中。

　　據統計，到1998年底，我國人口自然增長率已經降到9.53‰（千分之九點五三），自70年代以來第一次降到10‰（千分之十）以下，其中上海已經連續7年實現人口負增長；全國育齡婦女生育率從1970年的人均5.8下降到2.0個左右，按國際通用標準，我國已經進入低生育率國家行列。

1999年7月20日《人民日报》

第三十一课

中国人口结构发生转变

自70年代初中国开始实行计划生育以来，我国人口增长过快得到了有效控制。按1970年的生育水平推算，近30年来，全国累计少出生3亿人，我国城市地区人口完成了从"高出生、高死亡、高增长"向"低出生、低死亡、高增长"的转变；农村地区正在转变过程中。

据统计，到1998年底，我国人口自然增长率已经降到9.53‰（千分之九点五三），自70年代以来第一次降到10‰（千分之十）以下，其中上海已经连续7年实现人口负增长；全国育龄妇女生育率从1970年的人均5.8下降到2.0个左右，按国际通用标准，我国已经进入低生育率国家行列。

　　控制數量的同時，人口素質也穩步提高。由於經濟發展、生活改善和各種優生優育措施的實行，我國出生嬰兒死亡率由建國前200‰下降到目前的33‰。

　　更深刻的變化表現在人的思想上。隨著敎育水平的提高和計劃生育觀念的建立，“多子多福”“傳宗接代”的看法已經越來越淡薄了，“少生優生”正在成爲人們的自覺追求。在經濟富裕的農村，許多夫婦自願放棄生育第二個孩子，走上“少生快富”的道路。

　　國家計劃生育委員會強調，由於人口基數較大，在未來幾十年内，我國人口的年淨增量將保持在約1200萬左右，如何在滿足新增人口需求的同時，妥善處理人口、資源、環境之間的矛盾，保持經濟、社會的可持續發展，是擺在我們面前的一個十分重要的問題。

控制数量的同时，人口素质也稳步提高。由于经济发展、生活改善和各种优生优育措施的实行，我国出生婴儿死亡率由建国前200‰下降到目前的33‰。

更深刻的变化表现在人的思想上。随着教育水平的提高和计划生育观念的建立，"多子多福""传宗接代"的看法已经越来越淡薄了，"少生优生"正在成为人们的自觉追求。在经济富裕的农村，许多夫妇自愿放弃生育第二个孩子，走上"少生快富"的道路。

国家计划生育委员会强调，由于人口基数较大，在未来几十年内，我国人口的年净增量将保持在约1200万左右，如何在满足新增人口需求的同时，妥善处理人口、资源、环境之间的矛盾，保持经济、社会的可持续发展，是摆在我们面前的一个十分重要的问题。

词汇

人口		rénkǒu	n. population; the populace
结构	結構	jiégòu	n. structure; composition
转变	轉變	zhuǎnbiàn	n. transition; shift; change
实行	實行	shíxíng	v. to put into practice; to implement
计划生育	計劃生育	jìhuàshēngyù	n. family planning; birth control
自…以来	自…以來	zì … yǐlái	prep. since
增长	增長	zēngzhǎng	v. to increase; to rise; to grow
过	過	guò	adv. excessively
有效	有效	yǒuxiào	adj. effective
控制		kòngzhì	v./n. control
按		àn	prep. according to
生育		shēngyù	v. to give birth to; to generate
推算		tuīsuàn	v. to calculate
累计		lěijì	n. accumulative total; grand total
亿	億	yì	num. hundred million
城市		chéngshì	n. city
地区	地區	dìqū	n. an area; a region; a district
完成		wánchéng	v. to complete; to finish

出生		chūshēng	n./v. birth; to be born
死亡		sǐwáng	v./n. to die; death
农村	農村	nóngcūn	n. rural area; countryside
过程	過程	guòchéng	n. process; course
据	據	jù	prep. according to
统计	統計	tǒngjì	n. statistics
年底		niándǐ	n. the end of the year
降		jiàng	v. to drop; to descend
连续	連續	liánxù	adv. continuously; successively
负增长	負增長	fùzēngzhǎng	v. to decrease (only for rates)
育龄	育齡	yùlíng	adj. childbearing age
人均		rénjūn	n. per capita
下降		xiàjiàng	v. to drop off; to decrease
左右		zuǒyòu	adv. about
国际	國際	guójì	adj. international
通用		tōngyòng	adj. commonly used
标准	標準	biāozhǔn	n. standard
进入	進入	jìnrù	v. to enter into; to reach
行列		hángliè	n. ranks; a procession; queue
数量	數量	shùliàng	n. quantity; amount; number
同时	同時	tóngshí	adv. simultaneously; in the

			meantime
素质	素質	sùzhì	n. quality
稳步	穩步	wěnbù	adv. with steady step
改善		gǎishàn	v. to improve
优生优育	優生優育	yōushēngyōuyù	ph. to bear and rear better children
措施		cuòshī	n. measure
婴儿	嬰兒	yīng'ér	n. infant
由		yóu	prep. from
建国		jiàn'guó	v. to found a state; to establish a state
目前		mùqián	n. now; for the moment
深刻		shēnkè	adj. profound; deep
变化	變化	biànhuà	n. change
表现	表現	biǎoxiàn	v. to manifest; to show
思想		sīxiǎng	n. thought; thinking
随着	隨著	suí.zhe	prep. along with
建立		jiànlì	v. to establish
多子多福		duōzǐduōfú	"the more children you have, the more lucky you will be"
传宗接代	傳宗接代	chuánzōngjiēdài	"to carry on the name of the family"
淡薄	淡薄	dànbó	adj. faint; dim
自觉	自覺	zìjué	adv. consciously; on one's own initiative; of one's own

			free will
追求		zhuīqiú	v. to pursue
富裕	富裕	fùyù	adj. abundant; well-to-do; well-off
自愿	自願	zìyuàn	adv. of one's own free will
放弃	放棄	fàngqì	v. to give up
委员会	委員會	wěiyuánhuì	n. committee
强调	強調	qiángdiào	v. to highlight; to stress; to emphasize
基数	基數	jīshù	n. base
未来		wèilái	n. coming; oncoming
净增量	淨增量	jìngzēngliàng	n. net increase; net growth
如何		rúhé	adv. how
满足		mǎnzú	v. to satisfy; to meet
新		xīn	adv. newly
需求		xūqiú	n. demand; requirement
妥善	妥善	tuǒshàn	adv. properly; well-arranged
处理	處理	chǔlǐ	v. to deal with; to handle
资源	資源	zīyuán	n. resources
矛盾		máodùn	n. contradiction
可持续发展	可持續發展	kěchíxùfāzhǎn	n. sustainable growth
摆	擺	bǎi	v. to place

词语例句

1. 得到   **get; receive**

❖ 我国人口增长过快得到了有效控制。

The rapid growth of China's population has been effectively controlled.

1) 中国的人口政策得到了联合国的高度赞扬。

China's population policy was highly praised by the UN.

2) 由于得到了及时的治疗，他的病很快就好了。

He recovered quickly due to his prompt medical treatment.

2. 按   **according to**

❖ 按1970年的生育水平推算，……。

Calculated from the 1970 birth rate, …….

1) 按国际通用标准，中国已经进入低生育率国家行列。

According to international standards, China has joined the ranks of those countries with low birth rate.

2) 按中国的大学规定，体育考试不及格的学生不能毕业。

According to the regulations of universities in China, students who fail in physical education can not graduate from the university.

3. 少（多）+ Verb+ Number

❖ 按1970年的生育水平推算，近三十年来，全国累计少出生3亿人。

Calculated from the 1970 birth rate, three hundred million people were not born for the past thirty years.

1) 这个售货员多收了我一百块钱。

This salesclerk overcharged me by 100 *kuai*.

2) 要是你每天少抽一支烟，就会健康得多。

You will be much healthier if you smoke one cigarette less a day.

4. 连续   **continuous; successive**

❖ 其中上海已经连续七年实现人口负增长。

The population growth rate of Shanghai has been decreasing for seven continuous years.

1）已经连续下了三天雨了。

It has been raining for three successive days.

2）为了准备考试，他连续两天没有睡觉了。

He didn't get any sleep for three continuous days because he was preparing for the examination.

练习

I.　　Translation

1. According to sociologists at Harvard University, modern marriage is becoming more about romance and the search for a soul mate than about child rearing and family. At the end of the 19th century, 75% of American households included children under the age of 18. By the 1960's only 48.7% of families had kids living at home, and by 1998 that number had dropped to 33.9%.

2. In 1989 the natural growth rate of China's population was 14 ‰, in 1995 the natural growth rate was 10.5 ‰. Because of the enactment of family planning, between 1989 and 1995 the decrease in the number of births nationwide was 13 million. According to the latest statistics, the total population of China was 1.25 billion by the end of 1997.

II.　　Rewrite the following sentence using the expressions given.

1. 十年前他当总统的时候，国家的经济开始快速增长，现在还是这样。（自…至今，一直）

2. 虽然她从来不告诉别人自己的年龄，可是因为她1960年大学毕业，所以我想她大概快五十岁了。（按…推算）

3. 越来越多的人接受"老夫少妻"这样的婚姻，说明社会的宽容度真是增加了。（表现在…上）

4. 新政府面临的最严重的问题是如何降低失业率。（摆在…面前）

5. 自从十年前韩国人的年平均收入超过8000美元，韩国就成了一个发达国家。（进入…行列）

III.　　Read the following passage and summarize it in Chinese.
　　　　China at 2050

　　Since the establishment of the People's Republic in 1949, China has gone through some of the most dramatic changes in its history. Analysts believe the next 50 years will bring another series of radical shifts in China, affecting its people, its government and the world. Population is one of the major issues challenging China in the next half-century.

　　"In the next 50 years, China will have to face three population 'peaks,'" said Mr. Wang, a professor at Beijing University. Wang said that in 2020 China's working population, age 15 to 64, will total around 1 billion. "That means we will have to create a lot of new jobs," he said.

By 2030 China's population is expected to reach 1.6 billion, prompting concerns about food supply. And, Wang said, the third peak will be in 2040, when about 320 million Chinese will be 60 or older.

"People who are 20 now will be 60 and ready to retire in 2040," said Wang, "During the 40 years in between, they will have to accumulate wealth for their retirement life. So it is urgent for them to start planning now."

China's population also is expected to become more urbanized in the next 50 years. "Eighty percent of the population will move to urban areas." Wang predicated. "They will not rely on agriculture for their livelihood. That's a fundamental change in society: 500 million people will move, changing their lives, changing culture, changing values."

1999年8月3日《光明日報》

第三十二課

中國對核裁軍的立場

　　爲期三天的1999年禁止原子彈國際會議3日在日本廣島開幕。中國代表在會上發表講話，重申了中國在核裁軍問題上的立場。

　　中國代表說："中國在核裁軍問題上始終採取負責任的態度，這就是：

　　第一，中國從擁有核武器的第一天起就鄭重聲明，中國在任何時候、任何情況下都不首先使用核武器。

　　第二，中國從未在境外部署過核武器，也從未對別國使用或威脅使用核武器。

　　第三，中國在發展核武器方面歷來採取最克制的態度。中國進行的核試驗、擁有的核武器的數量十分有限。在印度和巴基斯坦進行核試驗後，中國方面明確表示無意恢復核試驗。

1999年8月3日《光明日报》

第三十二 课

中国对核裁军的立场

为期三天的1999年禁止原子弹国际会议 3 日在日本广岛开幕。中国代表在会上发表讲话,重申了中国在核裁军问题上的立场。

中国代表说:"中国在核裁军问题上始终采取负责任的态度,这就是:

第一,中国从拥有核武器的第一天起就郑重声明,中国在任何时候、任何情况下都不首先使用核武器。

第二,中国从未在境外部署过核武器,也从未对别国使用或威胁使用核武器。

第三,中国在发展核武器方面历来采取最克制的态度。中国进行的核试验、拥有的核武器的数量十分有限。在印度和巴基斯坦进行核试验后,中国方面明确表示无意恢复核试验。

第四，中國一貫積極支持全面禁止和徹底銷毀核武器。"

他說："中國的國防政策具有自衛性質。中國不謀求霸權，不進行擴張，不在外國駐軍，不搞軍事同盟，不參加軍備競賽，中國軍費開支一直處於較低水平。"

他在駁斥所謂的"中國威脅論"時說："中國是維護亞洲和世界和平的重要力量。中國一心一意地從事和平建設。中國的發展只會增強世界的和平，促進各國共同發展。中國不發展，長期處於貧窮落後狀態，對人類才是威脅。"

第四，中国一贯积极支持全面禁止和彻底销毁核武器。"

他说："中国的国防政策具有自卫性质。中国不谋求霸权，不进行扩张，不在外国驻军，不搞军事同盟，不参加军备竞赛，中国军费开支一直处于较低水平。"

他在驳斥所谓的"中国威胁论"时说："中国是维护亚洲和世界和平的重要力量。中国一心一意地从事和平建设。中国的发展只会增强世界的和平，促进各国共同发展。中国不发展，长期处于贫穷落后状态，对人类才是威胁。"

词汇

核裁军	核裁軍	hécáijūn	n. Nuclear Disarmament
立场	立場	lìchǎng	n. position; stand (point)
为期	爲期	wéiqī	v. to last for (a certain duration)
禁止		jìnzhǐ	v. to prohibit
原子弹	原子彈	yuánzǐdàn	n. atomic bomb
会议	會議	huìyì	n. meeting; conference
广岛	廣島	Guǎngdǎo	n. Hiroshima
开幕	開幕	kāimù	v. (of a meeting, exhibition, etc) to open; to inaugurate
代表		dàibiǎo	n. delegate; representative
发表	發表	fābiǎo	v. to deliver (a speech)
讲话	講話	jiǎnghuà	n. speech
重申		chóngshēn	v. to reiterate
始终	始終	shǐzhōng	adv. from beginning to end; throughout
采取	採取	cǎiqǔ	v. to adopt; to assume (a certain attitude)
负责任	負責任	fùzérèn	adj. responsible
拥有	擁有	yōngyǒu	v. to possess; to own
核武器		héwǔqì	n. nuclear weapon
郑重	鄭重	zhèngzhòng	adv. solemnly
声明	聲明	shēngmíng	v. to declare

首先		shǒuxiān	adv. first
使用		shǐyòng	v. to use; to put to use
从未	從未	cóngwèi	adv. have never
境外		jìngwài	n. outside the border
部署		bùshǔ	v. to deploy
别国	別國	biéguó	n. ＝别的国家
威胁	威脅	wēixié	v. to threaten
历来	歷來	lìlái	adv. always; all through the ages; throughout the history of
克制		kèzhì	v. to restrain; take a firm hold on
核试验	核試驗	héshìyàn	n. nuclear test
数量	數量	shùliàng	n. quantity
有限		yǒuxiàn	adj. limited
印度		Yìndù	n. India
巴基斯坦		Bājīsītǎn	n. Pakistan
进行	進行	jìnxíng	v. to conduct
明确	明確	míngquè	adv. clearly; unequivocally
无意	無意	wúyì	adv. have no intention (of doing sth.); to have no interest in
恢复	恢復	huīfù	v. to resume
一贯	一貫	yíguàn	adv. consistently
积极	積極	jījí	adv. actively; positively

支持		zhīchí	v. to support
全面		quánmiàn	adv. fully; in full; in all-round manner
彻底	徹底	chèdǐ	adv./adj. thoroughly; thorough
销毁	銷毀	xiāohuǐ	v. to destroy by burning or melting
国防	國防	guófáng	n. national defense
具有		jùyǒu	v. to have; to possess; to be provided with
自卫	自衛	zìwèi	n./v. self-defense; self-protection; to be in self-defense
性质	性質	xìng.zhì	n. nature; quality
谋求	謀求	móuqiú	v. to seek; to try to get; to try for
霸权	霸權	bàquán	n. hegemony; supremacy
扩张	擴張	kuòzhāng	v. to extend; to expand
驻军	駐軍	zhùjūn	v. to station troops
搞		gǎo	v. to do; to be engaged in
军事	軍事	jūnshì	n. military
同盟		tóngméng	n. alliance; league
军备竞赛	軍備競賽	jūnbèijìngsài	n. arm race
军费	軍費	jūnfèi	n. military expenditure
开支	開支	kāiizhī	n. expenses; expenditure
驳斥	駁斥	bóchì	v. to refute

所谓的	所謂的	suǒwèi.de	adj. so called
论	論	lùn	suf. theory; an "ism"
维护	維護	wéihù	v. to maintain; to safeguard
亚洲	亞洲	Yàzhōu	n. Asia
和平		hépíng	n. peace
一心一意		yìxīnyíyì	ph. wholeheartedly; single-mindedly; to bend on doing sth.
从事	從事	cóngshì	v. to be engaged in
建设	建設	jiànshè	n./v. development; built; construct
增强	增強	zēngqiáng	v. to reinforce; to strengthen
促进	促進	cùjìn	v. to promote; to help advance
贫穷	貧窮	pínqióng	adj. impoverished; destitute; needy
落后	落後	luòhòu	adj. backward; less developed
状态	狀態	zhuàngtài	n. state (of affairs)
人类	人類	rénlèi	n. mankind; humanity

词语例句

1. 为期   **for a period of time**

❖ 为期三天的 1999 年禁止原子弹国际会议 3 日在日本广岛开幕。

The three-day 1999 international conference on Prohibition of Atomic Bombs was inaugurated in Hiroshima on the 3rd (of this month).

1) 这个语言培训班为期两个月。

This language program is scheduled to last two months.

2) 为期半个月的奥林匹克运动会今天在悉尼结束了。

The Olympics Games, which lasted half a month, finished today in Sydney.

2. 始终   **from beginning to end**

❖ 中国在核裁军问题上始终采取负责任的态度。

The Chinese government has taken a responsible position on nuclear disarmament all along.

1) 虽然试验已经失败了很多次了，可是他始终没有失去信心。

Although his experiments failed many times, he didn't lose his faith.

2) 在手术过程中，病人始终是清醒的。

The patient remained conscious throughout the operation.

3. 从…起   **since; from**

❖ 中国从拥有核武器的第一天起就郑重声明…

The Chinese government solemnly declared from the first day they possessed nuclear weapons that …

1) 我从认识他的第一天起就发现他有很多奇怪的习惯。

I noticed from the first day I knew him that he had many odd habits.

2) 从他第一眼看到这个长头发女孩儿起，他就爱上了她。

At first sight of this long-haired girl, he fell in love with her.

4. 无意   **have no intention to**

❖ 中国方面明确表示无意恢复核试验。

The Chinese government clearly said that they had no intention of resuming nuclear experiments.

1) 我只是路过，无意要偷听你们的秘密。

I was just passing by and had no intention of eavesdropping.

2) 他公开表示无意参加总统竞选。

He openly stated that he had no intention to enter the presidential election.

5. 一贯   **consistently; all along**

❖ 中国一贯积极支持全面禁止和彻底销毁核武器。

The Chinese government has consistently supported the complete and thorough destruction of nuclear weapons enthusiastically.

1) 他对人一贯很诚实。

He is always honest in his attitude towards others.

2) 中国政府一贯主张国家不分大小，一律平等。

The Chinese government has always held that all nations, big or small, are equal.

6. 搞   **do; work; manage, etc.**

❖ 中国不搞军事同盟。

China never enters into any military alliance.

1) 这么晚你还不睡觉，你在搞什么嘛？

It is so late and you still haven't fallen asleep; what on earth are you doing?

2) 学期结束的时候，我们要搞个晚会。

We will hold a party when this semester ends.

7. 所谓的   **so-called**

❖ 他在驳斥所谓的"中国威胁论"时说…

In refuting the so-called "China Threat Theory", he said …

1) 他到了那儿才发现这个所谓的"古迹"只有一百年的历史。

When he arrived, he found that the so-called historic site turned out to be only 100 years old.

2) 她所谓的"爱情"其实是"爱钱。"

Her so-called "love" is in fact a "love of money."

8. …论 …theory

❖ 他在驳斥所谓的"中国威胁论"时说，…。

In refuting the so-called "China Threat Theory", he said, ….

1) 台湾总统提出"两国论"导致台湾跟大陆关系紧张。

The "state-to-state" concept, which was put forward by Taiwan's president , has made for the tense relation between the Mainland and Taiwan.

2) 文化大革命的时候，"读书无用论"曾经很流行。

The idea that "study leads to no use" was very popular during the Culture Revolution.

9. 一心一意 wholeheartedly

❖ 中国一心一意从事和平建设。

China is wholeheartedly working for peace.

1) 自从她结婚后，就辞去工作，一心一意做起家庭主妇来。

After getting married, she quit her job, and wholeheartedly worked as a housewife.

2) 他一心一意要上名牌大学。

He was dead set on going to a famous university.

练习

I.   Make a sentence using the underlined expression.

1. 中国<u>从</u>拥有核武器的<u>第一天起就</u>郑重声明在任何时候都不首先使用核武器。

2. 中国<u>从未</u>在境外部署过核武器，<u>也从未</u>对别国使用或威胁使用核武器。

3. 中国<u>在</u>发展核武器<u>方面</u><u>历来</u>采取最克制的态度。

4. 中国不发展，长期<u>处于</u>贫穷落后<u>状态</u>，对人类才是威胁。

II.   Choose the most appropriate word for each blank and fill in with its Chinese equivalent.

have no intention of (doing) all the time outside the border promote

develop possess   responsible   resume   ally   to have

1. 我们应该把这个工作交给_____的人去做。

2. 最近五年去_____旅游的中国人显著增加。

3. 对学校组织的任何活动，她都表示_____参加。

4. 在政治经济文化上英国一向是美国的_____。

5. 这两个国家曾经中断过外交关系，可是很快就_____。

6. 中国_____十三亿人口，九百六十万平方公里土地。

7. 这种自动售货机_____方便可靠的优点。

8. 他的妻子死了十年了，可是他还_____想着她。

9. 中国总理访问美国将_____两国之间的合作。

10. 中国政府决定中国当前最主要的任务是发展经济，把中国_____成社会主义的现代化强国。

III.   Answer the following questions.

有人说，核武器是世界不安全的原因；也有人说，核武器正是世界安全的原因，你同意哪种说法？为什么？

Pinyin Index

拼音索引

The entries are in *pinyin* and arranged in alphabetical order. The number following each entry indicates the page on which it appears.

本索引以汉语拼音查索，按字母顺序排列。各词条后的号码显示该词条出现的页码。

A

ài, 爱, to love, 122
àihù, 爱护, to love and protect, 329
àihù, 爱护, to take good care of, 371
àilǐbùlǐ, 爱理不理, to look cold and indifferent, 217
àiqíng, 爱情, romantic love, 136
àiyǎn, 碍眼, to be unpleasant to look at, 367
āndù, 安度, to spend (one's remaining years) in happiness, 307
ānmiányào, 安眠药, sleeping pill, 166
ānquán, 安全, safe, 26
ānquánmào, 安全帽, safety helmet, 28
ānquántào, 安全套, condom, 366
àn, 按, according to, 456
àn, 案, case, 290
àndì, 暗地, secretly, 179
ànjiàn, 案件, case, 304
ànjiàn, 案件, legal case, 382
ànlì, 案例, case, 402
àn.zi, 案子, legal case, 112

B

Bājīsītǎn, 巴基斯坦, Pakistan, 469
bǎ, 把, MW for things with handles, 237
bàquán, 霸权, hegemony; supremacy, 470
bǎi, 摆, to place, 459
bǎituō, 摆脱, to shake off; to get rid of, 432
bàisù, 败诉, to lose a lawsuit; to be cast in a lawsuit, 383
bān, 班, MW for scheduled transport vehicles, 24
bānbù, 颁布, to promulgate, 430
bānjí, 班级, a class or a level in school, 236
bānqǐ, 搬起, to lift, 445
bānzhǔrèn, 班主任, the head-teacher of the class, 214
bànfǎ, 办法, way, means, 151
bàn'gōngshì, 办公室, office, 100
bànshì, 办事, to handle affairs, 216
bànshì, 办事, to perform work; to handle business, 329
bànshù, 半数, half (the number), 256
bànsuí, 伴随, to accompany, 307
bāngmáng, 帮忙, to help; to do a favor, 212
bāo, 包, bag; sack, 401
bāo, 包, MW for wrapped things, 399
bāo, 包, to wrap, 353
bāokuò, 包括, to include, 430
bāokuò…zàinèi, 包括…在内, to include, 444
bǎoān, 保安, security personnel, 401
bǎoguì, 宝贵, valuable; precious, 217
bǎohù, 保护, to protect, 74
bǎoshǒu, 保守, conservative, 55
bǎoxiǎn, 保险, insurance, 41
bǎoxiǎntào, 保险套, condom, 166, 258
bǎozhàng, 保障, to safeguard, 384
bǎozhèng, 保证, to guarantee, 26
bào, 报, to sign up, 275
bàochóu, 报酬, reward; pay, 213, 275
bàodào, 报道, news report, 356
bàodǎo, 报导, to report, 150
bàojǐng, 报警, to report (an incident) to police, 418
bàoxíng, 暴行, violent conduct, 239
bàozhǐ, 报纸, newspaper, 150

bào.zhù, 抱住, to hold, 416
bēi, 杯, cup glass, 74
bēiāi, 悲哀, sorrow, 293
bēijù, 悲剧, tragedy, 234
běifāng, 北方, north; northern part of the country, 305
Běijīng, 北京, Beijing, 8
Běijīng dàxué, 北京大学, Peking University, 288
Běijīng Yīkē Dàxué, 北京医科大学, Beijing Medical University, 256
bèi dào ér chí, 背道而驰, to run in the opposite direction; to run counter to, 443
bèigàorén, 被告人, defendant; the accused, 241
bèipò, 被迫, to be forced, 305
běn, 本, originally, 356
běn, 本, this, 243
běnkē, 本科, undergraduate, 256
bǐ.huà, 比划, to make hand gestures, 166
bǐjiào, 比较, to compare, 112
bǐjiào, 比较, relatively, fairly, 25
bǐlì, 比例, proportion, 274, 329
bìjìng, 毕竟, after all, 419
bìrán, 必然, be bound to; inevitable, 240
bìshǔ, 避暑, to go away for summer, 272
bìxū, 必须, must, 431
bìyào, 必要, necessary, 369
bìyèbān, 毕业班, graduating class, 398
bìyùn, 避孕, contraception, 383, 167
biānr, 边儿, side; edge, 25
biàn, 变, to become different, to change, 135
biàn, 便, then, 241
biànchéng, 变成, to become; to turn into, 216
biànhuà, 变化, change, transformation, 57, 458
biànlùn, 辩论, debate; argument, 217
biànxiàng, 变相, in a disguised form; convert, 383
biāozhì, 标志, symbol; signal, 370
biāozhǔn, 标准, standard, criterion, 55
biǎomiàn.shang, 表面上, on the surface, in name only, 100
biǎomíng, 表明, to indicate, 332
biǎomíng, 表明, to make clear, 257
biǎoshì, 表示, to express, 215
biǎoshì, 表示, to show, to indicate, 111
biǎoxiàn, 表现, performance, 214
biǎoxiàn, 表现, to manifest; to show, 458
biéguó, 别国, other country, 469
bīn'guǎn, 宾馆, hotel, 342
bìng, 并, and; also, 370
bìngfáng, 病房, sickroom, 40
bōduó, 剥夺, to deprive of, 242
bóchì, 驳斥, to refute, 470
bówùguǎn, 博物馆, museum, 352
bódòu, 搏斗, to fight; to wrestle, 419
búbì, 不必, need not, 42, 215
búdào, 不到, less than, 414
búduàn, 不断, continuously; constantly, 416
búfàng, 不放, not release; not let go one's hold, 417
búgù, 不顾, to disregard, 352
búguò, 不过, merely, only, 87
bújiàn, 不见, to disappear, 178
bújiàn.dé, 不见得, not necessarily, 344, 72
búxiànghuà, 不像话, ridiculous, 166
bú yàojǐn, 不要紧, it doesn't matter, 136
bú zhìyú, 不至于, cannot or be unlikely to go so far as to, 153
bǔnǎo, 补脑, to nourish the brain, 354
bǔzú, 补足, to make up the difference, 417

E

F

G

H

K

L

M

miǎnyú, 免于, to prevent; to avoid, 369
miànlín, 面临, to face; to confront, 259, 356
miànqián, 面前, in front of sb., 416
miànyì, 面议, to discuss in person, 288
mièjué, 灭绝, to become extinct, 355
Mín'guó, 民国, Republic of China, 54
mínshì, 民事, relating to civil law; civil, 305
míng.bái, 明白, to understand; to catch on, 217
míng mù zhāng dǎn, 明目张胆, to do evil things openly and unscrupulously; to have the impudence to do sth., 442
míngquè, 明确, clearly, 304, 469
míngtiān, 明天, tomorrow, 87
míngwén guīdìng, 明文规定, to stipulate in explicit term, 400
míngxiǎn, 明显, clear; obvious, 430
míngxìnpiànr, 明信片儿, postcard, 180
mìng, 命, one's life, 41
mìngyùn, 命运, fate, 385
móuqiú, 谋求, to seek; to try to get; to try for, 470
móushēng, 谋生, to make a living, 318
mǒu, 某, certain; some, 415
mǒuxiē, 某些, certain; some, 368, 258
múyàng, 模样, appearance; look, 415
mǔ(.qīn), 母（亲）, mother, 234
mùbiāo, 目标, goal; aim, 275
mùbiāo, 目标, objective, 331
mùbiāo, 目标, objective; target, 237, 289
mùbǐng láng.tóu, 木柄榔头, a hammer with a wood shaft, 238
mù.dì, 目的, goal, 433
mùqián, 目前, at present; for the time being, 257, 178
mùqián, 目前, now; for the moment, 458, 73

N

ná, 拿, to hold; to take, 120
ná, 拿, to receive, 100
nà.me, 那么, then; in that case, 384
nán, 男, man; male, 134
nándào, 难道, could it be that?, 73
nánfāng, 南方, south, 354
nánrén, 男人, men, 135
nántí, 难题, difficult problem; tough question, 305
nánwàng, 难忘, memorable, 9
nánxìng, 男性, male sex; men, 384
nányǐ, 难以, difficult to, 290
nǎo, 脑, brain, 354
nǎoké, 脑壳, head, 354
nào, 闹, to make a big fuss in request for or in protest of (sth.), 328
nèikù, 内裤, underpants, panties, 74
nèiróng, 内容, content, 370
nèizhèng, 内政, internal affairs, 444
nénggàn, 能干, capable, able, competent, 152
nénggòu, 能够, can; be able to; be capable of, 317
nénglì, 能力, ability, 100, 277
nián, 黏, sticky, 72
niándǐ, 年底, the end of the year, 457
niánjí, 年级, grade; year (in school, etc), 178
nián.jì, 年纪, age, 135
nián.líng, 年龄, age, 197, 429, 136, 256
niánqīng, 年轻, young, 134
niánzhǎng, 年长, older in age; senior, 331; 137
niúfèn, 牛粪, cow dung, 134

Niǔyuē, 纽约, New York, 8
nóngcūn, 农村, rural area; countryside, 304
nòng, 弄, to make, 98
nǔlì, 努力, efforts; hard work, 236
nǔlì, 努力, to strive; to endeavor, 199
nǔlì, 努力, to work hard; to make great effort, 99
nǔ, 女, woman; female, 134
nǔpéng.yǒu, 女朋友, girlfriend, 150
nǔrén, 女人, women, 135
nǔshēng, 女生, girl student; schoolgirl, 213
nǔshì, 女士, Lady; Madam, 385

O

ó, 噢, intj. of surprise, 9

P

pā.de yìshēng, 啪的一声, onomatopoeia: a sound of clapping; slapping; a gunshot, 343
pà, 怕, to fear, 417
pà, 怕, to be afraid of, 24
pái, 牌, plate; tablet, 399
pái, 排, row, 213
páiduì, 排队, to stand in line, 24
páimíng, 排名, to rank as, 236
pán.zi, 盘子, plate; tray, 55
pànchǔ, 判处, to sentence; to condemn, 241
pànduàn, 判断, to judge, 214
pànjué, 判决, court decision; judgement, 241
pàng, 胖, fat, 27
pǎobù, 跑步, to jog, 86
péi, 陪, to accompany, 318
péi, 赔, to compensate, to pay for, 110
péibàn, 陪伴, to accompany, 318
péicháng, 赔偿, to compensate, 400
péiyǎng, 培养, to develop; to foster, 180
pèihé, 配合, to work with; to cooperate, 214
pèng, 碰, to encounter, to run into, 87
pèng.dào, 碰到, to run into, 418
piānshí, 偏食, to be partial to a limited variety of food, 196
pián.yí, 便宜, cheap, 26
piào.liàng, 漂亮, beautiful, 54
pīnmìng, 拼命, to do sth. desperately; with all one's might, 199
pínfùbùjūn, 贫富不均, great difference in wealth between the rich and the poor, 99
pínkùn, 贫困, impoverished; poor, 419
pínqióng, 贫穷, impoverished; destitute; needy, 471
pǐndé, 品德, moral character, 181
pǐnxuéjiānyōu, 品学兼优, of good character and scholarship, 238
píngjūn, 平均, average, 197, 256, 369, 430, 135
Píngshān, 平山, a place in Hebei province, 273
píngshí, 平时, ordinarily; in normal times, 238
píngwěn, 平稳, stable; smooth, 366
píng.zi, 瓶子, bottle, 75
pǔbiàn, 普遍, commonly, 444, 134
pǔtōng, 普通, ordinary; common, 235, 42

Q

qijiān, 期间, time; period, 180

R

S

tèdiǎn, 特点, characteristic; trait, 400

tèsè, 特色, distinguishing feature, quality, 352

tèshū, 特殊, special; particular, 272

téng, 疼, to love dearly, 329

tī, 踢, to play; to kick, 237

tí, 题, question in a test or assignment, 213

tíbāo, 提包, handbag, 415

tíchàng, 提倡, to advocate, 74

tíchū, 提出, to put forward; to pose, 237

tíchū, 提出, to submit; to propose, 442

tígāo, 提高, to improve; to enhance, 195, 153

tígāo, 提高, to increase; to improve, 276

tígōng, 提供, to provide, 368

tíjiāo, 提交, to submit; to file, 442

tíqián, 提前, to advance date, 430

tíxǐng, 提醒, to remind, 237

tǐlì, 体力, physical strength, 135

tǐtiē, 体贴, to show consideration for, to give every care to, 135

tǐyàn, 体验, to personally experience(a kind of life), 10

tì, 替, for; on behalf of, 289

tiān'é, 天鹅, swan, 353

tiānlún zhīlè, 天伦之乐, family happiness, 307

tiānqì, 天气, weather, 11

tiānshù, 天数, number of days, 28

tiānxià, 天下, in the world, 307

tiānxiàshì, 天下事, things in the world, 121

tiānzhēn, 天真, innocent, 215

tiáo, 条, MW for clauses, 242

tiáo, 条, MW for long, narrow things, 98

tiáo, 条, strip, 353

tiáojiàn, 条件, condition; term, 73, 180

tiáokuǎn, 条款, clause; article, 385

tiǎozhàn, 挑战, challenge, 431

tiē, 贴, to paste; to glue; to post, 292

tiě, 铁, iron, 241

tīngshuō, 听说, to hear that, heard of, 87

tǐng, 挺, quite; very, 329, 41

tōnggào, 通告, public notice; announcement, 290

tōngguò, 通过, by means of; through, 179

tōngguò, 通过, to pass by, 417

tōngxíngzhèng, 通行证, pass; permit, 212

tōngyòng, 通用, commonly used, 457

tóngbāo, 同胞, fellow countryman, 445

tóngděng, 同等, of the same class, quantity, etc., 318

tónggōngtóngchóu, 同工同酬, equal pay for equal work, 330

tóngméng, 同盟, alliance; league, 470

tóngqíngxīn, 同情心, sympathy, compassion, 98

tóngshí, 同时, simultaneously; in the meantime, 457

tongyàng, 同样, same, 10

tóngyì, 同意, to agree, 56

tǒngjì, 统计, statistics, 457

tǒngyī, 统一, integration, 444

tōu, 偷, to steal, 86

tōuqiè, 偷窃, theft, 401, 87

tóubìkǒu, 投币口, coin slot, 366

tóubù, 头部, head, 242

tóupiào, 投票, to cast a vote, 153

tóurù, 投入, to put into; to invest in, 195

tóuzī, 投资, to invest, 318

tú, 图, to seek; to pursue, 328

túzǎichǎng, 屠宰场, slaughterhouse, 355

tǔ, 吐, to dispense (lit. spit out), 369

tǔdì, 土地, land, 305

tuánjù, 团聚, to reunite, 317

tuī, 推, to push, 398

tuī, 推, to shift, to defuse, 99

tuījìn, 推进, to push into, 401

tuīsuàn, 推算, to calculate, 456

tuīwěi, 推委, to shirk responsibility; to shift responsibility onto others, 306

tuīxiāo, 推销, to promote sale to, 432

tuīxíng, 推行, to try to carry out (a policy, etc.), 368

tuǐ, 腿, leg, 40

tuìxiū, 退休, to retire, 316

tuōfú, 托福, TOEFL, 288

tuōxié, 拖鞋, slippers, 342

tuóniǎo, 鸵鸟, ostrich, 353

tuǒshàn, 妥善, properly; well-arranged, 459

W

wàichū, 外出, to go out, 276

wàidì, 外地, place other than where one is, 415, 235

wàiguóyǔ, 外国语, foreign language, 276

wài.miàn, 外面, outside, 86

wàishì, 外事, foreign affairs, 442

wánbèi, 完备, complete, perfect, 150

wánchéng, 完成, to complete; to finish, 456

wánquán, 完全, completely, 10

wányìr, 玩艺儿, plaything, 166

wánzhěng, 完整, intact; complete, 355

wǎn, 碗, bowl, 56

wǎnkuài, 碗筷, bowls and chopsticks, 342

wǎnnián, 晚年, old age; one's later years, 307

wǎn.shàng, 晚上, evening, (at) night, 86

wàn, 万, num. ten thousand, 194, 369

wànyī, 万一, if by any chance, 25

wǎng, 往, to go toward, 56

wǎnglái, 往来, intercourse; contact, 180

wǎngwǎng, 往往, more often than not, 135

wǎngyè, 网页, web page, 275

wàngjì, 忘记, to forget, 306, 317

wàngzǐ chénglóng, 望子成龙, wish for one's children to be successful, 239

wēihài, 危害, to harm; to endanger, 430

wēixiǎn, 危险, dangerous, 258, 25

wēixié, 威胁, to threaten; threat, 259

wéi, 围, to surround, to enclose, 9

wéifǎ, 违法, lawless; illegal, 368

wéifǎn, 违反, to violate, 399

wéigōng, 围攻, to attack from all sides, 415

wéiguī, 违规, to violate regulations, 289

wéihù, 维护, to defend; to safeguard, 243

wéihù, 维护, to maintain; to safeguard, 471

wéilìshìtú, 唯利是图, to be intent on nothing but money, 215

wéiqī, 为期, to last for (a certain duration), 468

wéishēngsù piàn, 维生素片, vitamin pills, 382

wéiyī.de, 唯一的, sole; the only one, 443

wéizhù, 围住, to surround; to enclose, 98

wěi.qū, 委屈, feel wronged, 237

wěiyuánhuì, 委员会, committee, 459, 442

wèi, 为, for, 42

wèi, 未, not; not yet, 242

wèi.dào, 味道, flavor; smell, 352

wèihé, 为何, why, 328

wèihūn, 未婚, to be single; to be unmarried, 331

X

Y

Z

zhuóxiǎng, 着想, to give consideration to, 87
zīyuán, 资源, resources, 73, 459
zǐnǚ, 子女, sons and daughters; children, 304
zǐsūn, 子孙, descendants, 355
zǐsūn mǎntáng, 子孙满堂, be blessed with many children, 307
zìcóng, 自从, since, ever since, 120
zìdòng, 自动, automatic, 166, 366
zìgǔ, 自古, since ancient time, 111
zìjué, 自觉, consciously; on one's own initiative, 458
zìlǐ, 自理, to take care of or provide for oneself, 318
zìrán, 自然, naturally, 330
zìshēn, 自身, self; oneself, 195
zìshíqílì, 自食其力, to support oneself by one's own labor, 330
zìshòujī, 自售机, automatic vending machine, 366
zìsī, 自私, selfish, 214
zìtiáo, 字条, brief note, 239
zìwèi, 自卫, self-defense; self-protection, 470
zìwǒ bǎohù, 自我保护, self-protection, 258
zìxíngchē, 自行车, bicycle, bike, 24
zì … yǐlái, 自…以来, since, 456
zìyóu, 自由, freedom, 257
zìyóuhuà, 自由化, to liberalize, 258
zìyuàn, 自愿, of one's own free will, 458
zǒng, 总, total; overall, 398
zǒng, 总, always, invariably, 10
zǒnglǐ, 总理, premier; prime minister, 428
zǒngliàng, 总量, total, 370
zǒngtǒng, 总统, president, 150
zǒngzhī, 总之, in a word; in short, 216
zǒu, 走, to leave; to go away, 401
zǒu, 走, to walk; to go, 330
zū, 租, to rent, 24, 178
zūjīn, 租金, rental fee, 28
zúqiú, 足球, football, 237
zúyǐ, 足以, enough; sufficient, 291
zǔài, 阻碍, to hinder, to impede, 100
zǔguó, 祖国, homeland; motherland, 445
zǔ.zhī, 组织, to organize; to arrange, 153, 216
zuǐ, 嘴, mouth, 56
zuìjìn, 最近, recently, 74
zuìzhōng, 最终, in the long run, 386
zūnjìng, 尊敬, to respect, 316
zūnyán, 尊严, dignity, 398
zūnzhòng, 尊重, to respect; to esteem, 398
zuótiān, 昨天, yesterday, 24
zuò, 坐, to sit, 24
zuò.fǎ 做法, way of doing or making a thing, 100
zuòshēng.yì, 做生意, to do business, 178
zuòwéi, 作为, as, 352
zuòwéi, 作为, to regard as; to take for, 428
zuòyè, 作业, assignment, 213
zuòyòng, 作用, effect; function, 152
zuǒyòu, 左右, about, 457
zuǒyòu, 左右, about; or so, 258
zuǒyòu, 左右, around; approximately, 417

English Index

英文索引

The entries are in English and arranged in alphabetical order. The number following each entry indicates the page on which it appears.

本索引以英文词汇查索，按字母顺序排列。各词条后的号码显示该词条出现的页码。

English Index

A

a bit, a little, 点, diǎn, 12
a China and a Taiwan, 一中一台, yìzhōngyìtái, 443
a class or a level in school, 班级, bānjí, 236
a dime, 毛, máo, 98
a few; a small number of, 少数, shǎoshù, 306
a great event, an important matter, 大事, dàshì, 110
a hammer with a wood shaft, 木柄榔头, mùbǐng láng.tóu, 238
a large amount of money, 高额, gāoé, 289
a large number of; great deal of, 大批, dàpī, 274
a large number; a great quantity, 大量, dàliàng, 195
a respectful form of address for a service
    worker, 师傅, shī.fù, 27
a road to ruin; impasse, 绝路, juélù, 398
a small number of; few, 少数, shǎoshù, 442
a strong point; what one is specially good at; a specialty,
    特长, tècháng, 276
ability, 能力, nénglì, 100
about; concerning, 关于, guānyú, 195
about; ...or so, 左右, zuǒyòu, 258
above-mentioned, 上述, shàngshù, 399
abnormal; unusual, 异常, yìcháng, 194
absolutely, 绝对, juéduì, 257
abundant; well-to-do, 富裕, fùyù, 459
accent, 口音, kǒuyīn, 415
acceptable, 可以接受的, kě.yǐ jiēshòu, 257
accident, 事故, shìgù, 110
accidentally, 无意中, wúyìzhōng, 383
according to, 按, àn, 456
according to, 据, jù, 457
according to, 依照, yīzhào, 242
according to law, 依法, yīfǎ, 243
according to newspaper's report, 据报载, jùbàozǎi, 329
account, 帐户, zhànghù, 318
accumulative total, 累计, lěijì, 456
across the straits, 两岸, liǎng' àn, 444
actively; positively, 积极, jījí, 469
activity, 活动, huódòng, 368
actually, in fact, 其实, qíshí, 11
actually; exactly, 究竟, jiūjìng, 418
advanced, 先进, xiānjìn, 167
advantage, 好处, hǎochù, 73
advertisement, 广告, guǎnggào, 74
after all, 毕竟, bìjìng, 419
after the autumn harvest, 秋后, qiūhòu, 305
afterwards, 事后, shìhòu, 293
again, 再, zài, 8
age, 年龄, niánlíng, 136
age, 年纪, niánjì, 135
airconditioning, 空调, kōngtiáo, 11
airport, 机场, jīchǎng, 8
alike, 一样, yíyàng, 9
all along, 一直, yìzhí, 382
all around; everywhere, 四处, sìchù, 291
all day; day and night, 整天, zhěngtiān, 329
all ethnicity, 各族, gèzú, 445
all one's life, 一辈子, yíbèi.zǐ, 87
all one's life, 一生, yìshēng, 111
all previous (sessions, government, etc.), 历届, lìjiè, 443
all the time; always, 一直, yìzhí, 238
all walks of life; all circles, 各界, gèjiè, 234
all, any, 凡是, fán.shì, 100

all; everything, 一切, yíqiè, 277
alliance; league, 同盟, tóngméng, 470
almost; almost the same, 差不多, chà.bu duō, 11
almost; nearly, 几乎, jīhū, 292
along the street, 沿街, yánjiē, 414
along with; in the wake of, 随着, suí.zhe, 306
already, 已（经）, yǐ(.jīng), 430
also, 又, yòu, 343
always, invariably, 总, zǒng, 10
always; all the time, 一向, yíxiàng, 238
always; all through the ages, 历来, lìlái, 469
ambulance, 救护车, jiùhùchē, 41
among, 当中, dāngzhōng, 316
among (them, which, ect.), 其中, qízhōng, 256
among; between, 之间, zhijiān, 237
amount of money, 钱数, qiánshù, 417
amount of physical activity, 活动量, huódòngliàng, 196
an area; a region, 地区, dìqū, 456
analysis, 分析, fēn.xī, 194
ancient, old, 古老, gǔlǎo, 9
ancient, 古代, gǔdài, 9
and, 及, jí, 400
and; also, 并, bìng, 370
and so on, 等等, děngděng, 342
angry, 生气, shēngqì, 179
animal, 动物, dòng.wù, 352
another; other, 另, lìng, 305
any, whatever, 任何, rènhé, 99
apart from, 离, lí, 24
aphrodisiacs, 春药, chūnyào, 167
appearance; look, 模样, múyàng, 415
appetizing; fragrant, 香, xiāng, 353
approximately, 约, yuē, 304
area, 地段, dìduàn, 416
area; district; region, 地区, dìqū, 304
arm race, 军备竞赛, jūnbèijìngsài, 470
around; approximately, 左右, zuǒyòu, 417
as, 作为, zuòwéi, 352
as far as is possible; to the best of one's ability,
    尽可能, jìnkě'néng, 199
as for, 至于, zhìyú, 152
as usual, 照常, zhàocháng, 240
as well as; along with, 以及, yǐjí, 430
Asia, 亚洲, Yàzhōu, 471
aspect; side; area, 方面, fāngmiàn, 195
aspiration; desire, 愿望, yuànwàng, 445
assignment, 作业, zuòyè, 213
association; relationship; contact, 交往, jiāowǎng, 212
at (the) most, 顶多, dǐngduō, 87
at a very young age, 小小年纪, xiǎoxiǎoniánjì, 215
at all, simply, 根本, gēnběn, 121
at any time and any place, 随时随地, suíshísuídì, 167
at first; in the beginning; originally, 起先, qǐxiān, 214
at first; originally, 当初, dāngchū, 329
at least, 至少, zhìshǎo, 120
at once; right away, 马上, mǎshàng, 213
at present, 目前, mùqián, 73
at present time; today, 当今, dāngjīn, 257
at the first beginning, 刚开始, gāngkāishǐ, 417
at the present; at the moment, 目前, mùqián, 178
atomic bomb, 原子弹, yuánzǐdàn, 468
attitude, 态度, tài.dù, 99
authoritatively, 有权, yǒuquán, 400
automatic, 自动, zìdòng, 166

diligent; hardworking, 勤劳, qínláo, 198
dining table, 餐桌, cānzhuō, 352
direct, 直接, zhíjiē, 331
direct; immediate, 直接, zhíjiē, 198
direction, 方向, fāngxiàng, 73
disadvantage, 坏处, huàichù, 73
disappointed, 失望, shīwàng, 213
discipline; morale, 纪律, jìlǜ, 399
discussion; debate, 讨论, tǎolùn, 212
disease, 疾病, jíbìng, 343
distinguishing feature/quality, 特色, tèsè, 352
disgusting, 恶心, ěxīn, 56
disorderliness; chaos, 紊乱, wěnluàn, 386
disorderly; chaotic, 混乱, hùnluàn, 258
disposable; one-time, 一次性, yícìxìng, 342
disposition; temperament, 性格, xìnggé, 307
dispute; debate; contention, 争议, zhēngyì, 366
dispute; quarrel, 纠纷, jiūfēn, 382
disturbance, 风波, fēngbō, 216
diversified, 多元化, duōyuánhuà, 332
do as one pleases, 随便, suíbiàn, 167
do what, 干嘛, gànmá, 272
doesn't matter, 无所谓, wúsuǒwèi, 41
doorway; entrance, 门口, ménkǒu, 27
dormitory, 宿舍, sùshè, 26
dragon, 龙, lóng, 353
dress; attire, 穿着, chuānzhuó, 54
drinks, 饮料, yǐnliào, 416
driver, 司机, sījī, 41
duty; obligation, 义务, yì.wù, 217
duty; responsibility, 责, zé, 356
duty; responsibility, 职责, zhízé, 428
dwelling (place); residence, 住处, zhùchù, 307

E

each other, 互相, hùxiāng, 306
eager; anxious, 心切, xīnqiè, 239
ear, 耳朵, ěr.duō, 214
Eastern China, 华东, Huádōng, 367
easy, 容易, róng.yì, 56
eating house, 饮食店, yǐnshídiàn, 367
economy, 经济, jīngjì, 73
educated women, 知识女性, zhīshínǚxìng, 331
education, 教育, jiàoyù, 195
educational administration office, 教务处, jiàowùchù, 289
effect, 影响, yǐngxiǎng, 415
effect; function, 作用, zuòyòng, 152
effective; valid, 有效, yǒuxiào, 151
efforts; hard work, 努力, nǔlì, 236
electronic mail, 电子邮件, diàn.zǐyóujiàn, 120
elite, 精英, jīngyīng, 292
email, 伊妹儿, yīmèir, 122
emancipation of women; women's liberation, 妇女解放, fùnǚjiěfàng, 330
emperor, 皇帝, huángdì, 9
empty, 空, kōng, 316
empty; deserted, 空荡荡, kōng.dàng.dàng, 316
end of semester (here: final examination), 期末, qīmò, 236
energy; vigor, 精力, jīnglì, 195
enough; sufficient, 足以, zúyǐ, 291
enthusiastic; zealous, 热心, rèxīn, 239
entrance; doorway, 门口, ménkǒur, 344

environment, 环境, huánjìng, 73
equal pay for equal work, 同工同酬, tónggōngtóngchóu, 330
equipment, 设备, shèbèi, 42
especially, 特别, tèbié, 27
especially, 尤其, yóuqí, 56
especially, 专, zhuān, 289
especially, 专门, zhuānmén, 288
ethics, 伦理, lúnlǐ, 386
eve, 前夕, qiánxī, 180
even, 连, lián, 179
even (to the point of), 甚至, shènzhì, 87
even (to the point of), 甚至于, shènzhìyú, 74
even more, 更加, gèngjiā, 198
even more, 还, hái, 8
even though; despite, 尽管, jǐn'guǎn, 72
even, even if, even though, 即使, jíshǐ, 136
evening; (at night), 晚上, wǎn.shàng, 86
eventually; in the end; in the long run, 终究, zhōngjiū, 371
everywhere; all over, 到处, dàochù, 344
examination hall or room, 考场, kǎochǎng, 291
example, 例子, lì.zǐ, 57
excessively; over, 过, guò, 196
exciting, 刺激, cìjī, 11
excuse, 借口, jièkǒu, 386
exit and entrance, 出入口, chūrùkǒu, 414
expenses; expenditure, 开支, kāizhī, 470
expensive, 贵, guì, 25
experience, 经验, jīngyàn, 276
expert, 专家, zhuānjiā, 239
extensive, 广泛, guǎngfàn, 120
extent, stage, 地步, dìbù, 167
extremely, 之极, zhījí, 354
extremely, 之至, zhīzhì, 354
extremely difficult; arduous, 艰巨, jiānjù, 429
extremely; very, 十分, shífēn, 240

F

face to face, 当面, dāngmiàn, 151
fact, 事实, shìshí, 198
faint; dim, 淡薄, dànbó, 458
fair, 公平, gōngpíng, 98
fake, 假, jiǎ, 291
familiar, 熟, shú, 25
family happiness, 天伦之乐, tiānlún zhīlè, 307
family planning; birth control, 计划生育, jìhuàshēngyù, 367
family property, 家产, jiāchǎn, 305
family; household, 家庭, jiātíng, 194
famous; celebrated, 著名, zhùmíng, 288
far, 远, yuǎn, 24
fashion; way; manner, 方式, fāngshì, 258
fashionable, 入时, rùshí, 416
fat; corpulent; obese, 肥胖, féipàng, 196
fate, 命运, mìngyùn, 385
father, 父(亲), fù(.qīn), 235
father and daughter, 父女, fùnǚ, 134
fat, 胖, pàng, 27
fault, mistake, 过错, guòcuò, 99
fear of disturbance in the rear, 后顾之忧, hòu gù zhīyōu, 275

English Index

feel wronged, 委屈, wěi.qū, 237

feeling, 感觉, gǎnjué, 121

fellow countryman, 同胞, tóngbāo, 445

ferociously, 狠狠, hěnhěn, 236

few days ago, 前些日子, qiánxiērì.zǐ, 178

few, little, 少, shǎo, 73

financially poor, 穷, qióng, 136

fire disaster, 火灾, huǒzāi, 87

firmly, resolutely, 坚决, jiānjué, 383

first of all, 首先, shǒuxiān, 419

first rate; high-class, 高档, gāodàng, 56

first time, 首次, shǒucì, 257

first trial, 一审, yìshěn, 241

first year in junior high school, 初一, chūyī, 179

fitting (of clothes), 合身, héshēn, 54

fixed; regular, 固定, gùdìng, 307

flavor; smell, 味道, wèi.dào, 352

flaw; defect, 缺陷, quēxiàn, 293

floral skirt, 花裙子, huā qún.zǐ, 416

food and drink, 饮食, yǐnshí, 55

foodstuff, food, 食品, shípǐn, 57

football, 足球, zúqiú, 237

for, 为, wèi, 42

for example; such as, 如, rú, 259

for the moment, 一时, yìshí, 136

for the moment; temporarily, 暂时, zànshí, 367

for; by, 以, yǐ, 178

for; on behalf of, 替, tì, 289

foreign, 洋, yáng, 432

foreign affairs, 外事, wàishì, 442

foreign language, 外国语, wàiguóyǔ, 276

forest, 森林, sēnlín, 74

forever, 永远, yǒngyuǎn, 101

form, 形式, xíngshì, 272

formal; officially, 正式, zhèngshì, 430

fragile, 脆弱, cuìruò, 239

France, 法国, Fǎguó, 197

free from anxiety, 踏实, tā.shí, 307

free of charge, 免费, miǎnfèi, 120

freedom, 自由, zìyóu, 257

frequently; often, 经常, jīngcháng, 179

fresh flower, 鲜花, xiānhuā, 134

fresh flower sticking in cow dung --- what a waste!,
         鲜花插在牛粪上, xiānhuā chā zài niúfèn.shàng,
         134

from, 由, yóu, 458

from beginning to end; throughout, 始终, shǐzhōng, 468

from now on, 今后, jīnhòu, 213

from this, 由此, yóucǐ, 305

frugal, 节俭, jiéjiǎn, 238

fruits; achievements, 成果, chéngguǒ, 198

fully, 充分, chōngfèn, 276

fully; in full; in all-round manner, 全面, quánmiàn, 470

fun, 好玩, hǎowán, 11

furthermore; besides, 再说, zàishuō, 291

G

gains; harvests, 收获, shōuhuò, 273

garbage, 垃圾, lājī, 74

generally acknowledged, 公认, gōngrèn, 444

generally speaking, 一般来说, yìbānláishuō, 55

generally speaking, 一般, yìbān, 418

girl student; schoolgirl, 女生, nǚshēng, 213

girlfriend, 女朋友, nǚpéng.yǒu, 150

give publicity to; advertisement, 宣传, xuānchuán, 402

go or stay, 去留, qùliú, 385

goal, 目的, mùdì, 433

goal; aim, 目标, mùbiāo, 275

gold, 金, jīn, 353

good, 好好的, hǎohāo.de, 98

good business sense; the tricks of the trade,
         生意经, shēngyìjīng, 180

goods; merchandise, 商品, shāngpǐn, 401

government, 政府, zhèngfǔ, 428

government employees, 公务人员, gōngwù rényuán, 432

government work unit, 机关, jīguān, 216

grade; year (in school, etc), 年级, niánjí, 178

gradually, 渐渐, jiànjiàn, 112

gradually; progressively, 逐渐, zhújiàn, 329

graduate student, 研究生, yánjiūshēng, 288

graduate student dormitory, 研究生楼, yánjiūshēng lóu,
         288

graduating class, 毕业班, bìyèbān, 398

grain; cereals; food, 粮（食）, liáng(.shí), 306

grain; cereals; food, 粮食, liáng.shí, 306

gravity, 严重性, yánzhòngxìng, 445

great difference in wealth between the rich
         and the poor, 贫富不均, pínfùbùjūn, 99

great majority; at large, 大多数, dàduōshù, 330

green light, 绿灯, lǜdēng, 40

grocery, 杂货店, záhuòdiàn, 166

Guangdong, 广东, Guǎngdōng, 274

Guangxi, 广西, Guǎngxī, 353

guardian, 监护人, jiānhùrén, 400

H

habit, 习惯, xíguàn, 99

hair salon, 发廊, fàláng, 367

half (the number), 半数, bànshù, 256

handbag, 提包, tíbāo, 415

handbook; manual, 手册, shǒucè, 276

happy, fortunate; felicity, 幸福, xìngfú, 135

happy; glorious, 美好, měihǎo, 355

hard objects, 硬物, yìngwù, 354

hard sleeper, 硬卧, yìngwò, 11

hardships, 辛苦, xīnkǔ, 306

harmful; unwholesome, 不良, bùliáng, 240

harmonious, 和睦, hémù, 197

harmonious, 和谐, héxié, 112

have never, 从未, cóngwèi, 469

have no choice but ; cannot but, 不得不, bù.dé.bù, 318

have no intention (of doing sth.); to have no interest in,
         无意, wúyì, 469

have not; without, 无, wú, 398

hawk; eagle, 鹰, yīng, 353

head, 脑壳, nǎoké, 354

head, 头部, tóubù, 242

head of state, 元首, yuánshǒu, 151

health; healthy, 健康, jiànkāng, 195

heart; soul; spirit, 心灵, xīnlíng, 215

heartfelt; deep, 深切, shēnqiè, 356

heavy, 重, zhòng, 196

heavy pressure, 重压, zhòngyā, 237

heavy; weighty, 沉重, chénzhòng, 234
Hebei, 河北, Héběi, 273
hegemony; supremacy, 霸权, bàquán, 470
hero, 英雄, yīngxióng, 217
hesitate; hesitant, 犹豫, yóuyù, 329
high, 高, gāo, 135
high quality; high grade, 优质, yōuzhì, 370
high school and elementary school students,
    中小学生, zhōng xiǎo xuéshēng, 178
higher; advanced, 高等, gāoděng, 292
Hiroshima, 广岛, Guǎngdǎo, 468
his; her; its; such, 其, qí, 241
historical date/ materials, 史料, shǐliào, 355
home; homeland, 家园, jiāyuán, 356
homeland; motherland, 祖国, zǔguó, 445
homicide; murder; manslaughter, 凶杀, xiōngshā, 240
honest, 诚实, chéngshí, 152
honors class; advanced class, 重点班, zhòngdiǎnbān, 236
hopelessness; despair, 绝望, juéwàng, 237
hospital, 医院, yīyuàn, 40
hostile; antagonistic, 敌对, díduì, 444
hotel, 宾馆, bīn'guǎn, 342
hotel, 旅馆, lǚguǎn, 10
house, 房子, fáng.zǐ, 9
House of representatives, 众议院, zhòngyìyuàn, 442
household chores; housework, 家务, jiāwù, 197
how, 如何, rúhé, 419
however, 却, què, 414
however, 然而, rán'ér, 214
however, 则, zé, 217
huge lizard, 巨蜥, jùxī, 353
human kind, 人类, rénlèi, 356
human nature, 人性, rénxìng, 354
human rights, 人权, rénquán, 110
hundred million, 亿, yì, 73
husband, 丈夫, zhàng.fù, 136
husband and wife, 夫妻, fūqī, 330
hygiene, 卫生, wèishēng, 55

I

idea, 主意, zhǔ.yì, 27
ideal, 理想, lǐxiǎng, 135
identity card, 身分证, shēnfènzhèng, 291
ideology; thoughts, 思想, sīxiǎng, 273
if by any chance, 万一, wànyī, 25
if it keeps going on, 如此下去, rúcǐxià.qù, 386
if; supposing; in case, 假如, jiǎrú, 384
ignorant, 愚昧, yúmèi, 354
illegal, 非法, fēifǎ, 242
important, 重要, zhòngyào, 87
important, 要紧, yàojǐn, 42
impoverished; destitute; needy, 贫穷, pínqióng, 471
impoverished; poor, 贫困, pínkùn, 419
impression, 印象, yìnxiàng, 9
improvement, progress, 进步, jìnbù, 72
in a certain manner; according to a certain principle,
    从, cóng, 242
in a disguised form; convert, 变相, biànxiàng, 383
in a group, 结伴, jiébàn, 416
in a moment of desperation, 情急之下, qíngjízhīxià, 213
in a word; in short, 总之, zǒngzhī, 216
in addition; over and above, 另外, lìngwài, 196

in advance; beforehand, 事先, shìxiān, 292
in days to come, 日后, rìhòu, 318
in every possible way; meticulously,
    无微不至, wúwēibúzhì, 318
in front of sb., 面前, miànqián, 416
in pair, 成对, chéngduì, 418
in reality; in actual fact, 实际上, shíjì.shàng, 75
in recent years, 近年来, jìnniánlái, 196
in the first place; first of all, 首先, shǒuxiān, 290
in the long run, 最终, zuìzhōng, 386
in the past, formerly, 从前, cóngqián, 100
in the process of; in the middle of, 正在, zhèngzài, 238
in the world, 天下, tiānxià, 307
in those years, 当年, dāngnián, 306
in view of; in consideration of, 鉴于, jiànyú, 243
in written form; in writing, 书面, shūmiàn, 428
incident; event, 事件, shìjiàn, 234
income, earnings, 收入, shōurù, 135
increasingly; day by day, 日益, rìyì, 199
indeed; really, 确实, quèshí, 137
independence, 独立, dúlì, 443
India, 印度, Yìndù, 469
Indian person, 印度人, Yìndùrén, 54
indignant; angry, 愤怒, fènnù, 401
individual, 个体, gètǐ, 41
individual (person), 个人, gèrén, 99
induced abortion, 人工流产, réngōng liúchǎn, 259
inevitable, unavoidable, 不可避免, bùkěbìmiǎn, 112
inevitable, unavoidable, 免不了, miǎn.buliǎo, 99
infant, 婴儿, yīng'ér, 458
influence, 影响, yǐngxiǎng, 55
information, news, 信息, xìnxī, 120
innocent, 天真, tiānzhēn, 215
inside the university, 校内, xiàonèi, 290
inside; interior, 里面, lǐ.miàn, 86
insurance, 保险, bǎoxiǎn, 41
intact; complete, 完整, wánzhěng, 355
integration, 统一, tǒngyī, 444
intellectual property right, 知识产权, zhī.shíchǎnquán, 112
intense; fierce, 激烈, jīliè, 199
intercourse; contact, 往来, wǎnglái, 180
interesting, 有趣, yǒuqù, 56
intermediate, 中级, zhōngjí, 241
internal affairs, 内政, nèizhèng, 444
international, 国际, guójì, 356
Internet, 互联网, Hùliánwǎng, 121
interpreter; translator, 翻译, fānyì, 275
intj. of surprise, 噢, ó, 9
introduce; introduction, 介绍, jièshào, 275
introspection; self-examination, 反思, fǎnsī, 234
iron, 铁, tiě, 243
-ism, 论, lùn, 471
it doesn't matter, 不要紧, bú yàojǐn, 136
it is said, 据说, jùshuō, 41
it looks, it appears, it
looks as if, 看来, kànlái, 100
it seems that; it appears that; it appears as if, 似乎, sìhū, 197
it would be better to, 不如, bùrú, 153
it's nothing, 没事儿, méishìr, 28

J

objective; target, 目标, mùbiāo, 237
obstacle; bar; handicap, 障碍, zhàng'ài, 194
obstinately, 硬, yìng, 416
obvious; evident, 显然, xiǎnrán, 343
occasion, situation, 场合, chǎnghé, 354
occupation, 职业, zhíyè, 111
of good character and scholarship,
    品学兼优, pǐnxuéjiānyōu, 238
of one's own free will, 自愿, zìyuàn, 458
of the same class, quantity, etc., 同等, tóngděng, 318
of this generation; present-day, 当代, dāngdài, 275
offensive to the eye, 不雅观, bù yǎguān, 368
office, 办公室, bàn'gōngshì, 100
old age; one's later years, 晚年, wǎnnián, 307
old couple, 老两口儿, lǎoliǎngkǒur, 307
old husband, 老夫, lǎofū, 328
old husband and young wife, 老夫少妻, lǎofūshàoqī, 134
old man; old chap, 老头儿, lǎotóur, 134
old; used; worn, 旧, jiù, 26
older in age; senior, 年长, niánzhǎng, 137
older sister and younger sister; sisters, 姐妹, jiěmèi, 179
on one's way, 一路上, yílù.shàng, 8
on the contrary, 反而, fǎn'ér, 152
on the surface, in name only, 表面上, biǎomiàn.shang, 100
once, 曾, céng, 415
once, 一旦, yídàn, 87
once again; for the second time, 再次, zàicì, 237
one act two gains, 一举两得, yìjǔliǎngdé, 27
one by one, 逐一, zhúyī, 291
one by one; one after another, 一一, yīyī, 291
one country two systems, 一国两制, yìguó liǎngzhì, 444
one full year of life, 周岁, zhōusuì, 242
one of ....., ... 之一, ... zhīyī, 111
one party, 一方, yìfāng, 384
one who ..., ... 者, ... zhě, 99
one who takes an examination in place of another person (lit.
    shooter), 枪手, qiāngshǒu, 288
one wishes one could, 恨不得, hèn.bùdé, 153
one's aged parents orgrandparents, 老人, lǎorén, 304
one's life, 命, mìng, 41
one's own (children, parents), 亲生, qīnshēng, 234
one-time, 一次性, yícì.xìng, 72
only, 光, guāng, 292
only, 才, cái, 26
only, 只有, zhǐyǒu, 25
only, 单单, dāndān, 384
only; alone, 仅仅, jǐnjǐn, 240
only if, unless, 除非, chúfēi, 111
open; liberal, 开放, kāifàng, 257
open-minded, liberal, 开通, kāitōng, 167
opposite; contrary, 相反, xiāngfǎn, 217
or, 或, huò, 214
order; law and order, 秩序, zhì.xù, 273
ordinarily; in normal times, 平时, píngshí, 238
ordinary; common, 普通, pǔtōng, 235
organization, 组织, zǔzhī, 153
originally, 本, běn, 356
ostrich, 鸵鸟, tuóniǎo, 353
other country, 别国, biéguó, 469
other; else, 其他, qítā, 288
others; some other persons; another person, 他人, tārén,
    402
otherwise, 要不然, yào.bùrán, 40
otherwise; if not, 否则, fǒuzé, 277

other, 其他, qítā, 42
out of date, 落伍, luòwǔ, 121
out of fashion, 过时, guòshí, 415
out of marriage, 婚外, hūn wài, 167
outdoor education, 野外求生, yěwài qiú shēng, 11
outside, 外面, wài.miàn, 86
outside, 在外, zàiwài, 316
outside the border, 境外, jìngwài, 469
over and above, 以上, yǐshàng, 257
overhead walkway, 过街天桥, guòjiē tiānqiáo, 414
owing to; due to, 由于, yóuyú, 197
owner of store, 店主, diànzhǔ, 366

P

painstaking; hardworking, 刻苦, kèkǔ, 238
Pakistan, 巴基斯坦, Bājīsītǎn, 469
paper, 纸, zhǐ, 74
paper towel; tissue paper, 纸巾, zhǐjīn, 74
parents, 父母, fùmǔ, 10
parents' meeting, 家长会, jiāzhǎnghuì, 214
part, 部分, bù.fēn, 178
part. for showing obviousness, 咯, .lo, 111
part. indicates that sth is obvious, 嘛, ma, 134
part-work and part-study program, 勤工俭学,
    qín' gōngjiǎn xué, 275
pass; permit, 通行证, tōngxíngzhèng, 212
peace, 和平, hépíng, 444
peacock, 孔雀, kǒngquè, 352
pedestrian, 行人, xíngrén, 41
Peking University, 北京大学, Běijīng dàxué, 288
people who take an examination for others,
    代考者, dàikǎozhě, 288
per capita, 人均, rénjūn, 457
perfect; desirable; ideal, 理想, lǐxiǎng, 240
performance, 表现, biǎoxiàn, 214
perhaps, maybe, 说不定, shuō.búdìng, 167
perhaps, probably, 也许, yěxǔ, 24
period (of time), 时期, shíqī, 180
person in charge, 负责人, fùzérén, 367
personal, 人身, rénshēn, 243
personality; character, 人格, rén'gé, 415
personnel; staff, 人员, rényuán, 258
pharmacy, 药房, yàofáng, 369
phase; stage, 阶段, jiēduàn, 258
phenomenon, 现象, xiànxiàng, 57
philosophy of life, 生活哲学, shēnghuó zhéxué, 316
physical exercise, 运动, yùndòng, 26
physical labor, 劳动, láodòng, 196
physical strength, 体力, tǐlì, 135
place, 地, dì, 274
place other than when one is, 外地, wàidì, 415, 235
place to install vending machine,
    装机点儿, zhuāngjī.diǎnr, 367
plastics, 塑料, sùliào, 74
plate; tablet, 牌, pái, 399
plate; tray, 盘子, pán.zǐ, 55
plaything, 玩艺儿, wányìr, 166
pleasant, 愉快, yúkuài, 414
plus; in addition, 加上, jiā.shàng, 418
pocket money; incidental expenses, 零花钱, línghuāqián,
    277

police, 警察, jǐngchá, 41
policy, 方针, fāngzhēn, 444
policy, 政策, zhèngcè, 243
politics, 政治, zhèngzhì, 152
poor, inferior, 差, chà, 72
pop-top, 易拉罐儿, yìlāguànr, 75
popular, 热, rè, 276
population, 人口, rénkǒu, 73
pornography, 色情, sèqíng, 240
position; stand (point), 立场, lìchǎng, 468
position; status, 地位, dìwèi, 384
postcard, 明信片儿, míngxìnpiànr, 180
practical; pragmatic, 实用, shíyòng, 54
practice, 实践, shíjiàn, 402
precious; rare, 珍稀, zhēnxī, 353
precisely; exactly, 正, zhèng, 401
premarital, 婚前, hūnqián, 256
prep course, 辅导班, fǔdǎobān, 274
present time; today, 当今, dāngjīn, 306
president, 总统, zǒngtǒng, 150
pressure, 压力, yālì, 197
price, 价格, jiàgé, 288
price; cost, 代价, dàijià, 100
principal; headmaster, 校长, xiàozhǎng, 212
principle, 原则, yuánzé, 316
printer, 打印机, dǎyìnjī, 121
privacy, 隐私, yǐnsī, 152
probably, 大概, dàgài, 41
problem; question, 问题, wèntí, 27
process; course, 过程, guòchéng, 457
product, 产品, chǎnpǐn, 72
profession, 行业, hángyè, 111
professionals, 专业人士, zhuānyè rénshì, 402
profound; deep, 深刻, shēnkè, 234
profoundly, 深深, shēnshēn, 237
properly; well-arranged, 妥善, tuǒshàn, 459
properly, 财产, cáichǎn, 87
proportion, 比例, bǐlì, 274
prosperous, 繁华, fánhuá, 416
proud, 骄傲, jiāoào, 292
province, 省, shěng, 234
psychological disorder, 心理障碍, xīnlǐ zhàng'ài, 194
psychology, 心理, xīnlǐ, 194
public bus, 公共汽车, gōnggòngqìchē, 24
public bus, 公交车, gōngjiāochē, 25
public notice; announcement, 通告, tōnggào, 290
public opinion, 舆论, yúlùn, 352
public places, 公共场所, gōnggòng chǎngsuǒ, 430
public property, 公物, gōngwù, 371
public security; public order, 治安, zhìān, 243
public, common, 公, gōng, 56

Q

Qing dynasty, 清朝, Qīngcháo, 54
Qinghai, a province in northwest China, 青海, Qīnghǎi, 274
Qipao, 旗袍, qípáo, 54
quality, 素质, sùzhì, 195
quality, 质量, zhìliàng, 72
quantity; amount, 数量, shùliàng, 457

question for study, 课题, kètí, 356
question in a test or assignment, 题, tí, 213
question; doubt, 疑问, yíwèn, 272
quiet, 清静, qīngjìng, 307
quiet and gentle, 文静, wénjìng, 238
quite, 挺, tǐng, 41
quite a few, 好几, hǎo.jǐ, 110
quite; considerable, 相当, xiāngdāng, 259
quite; very, 挺, tǐng, 329

R

ranks; a procession; queue, 行列, hángliè, 457
rare, strange, unusual and seldom seen, 稀奇, xīqí, 110
rare; unusual, 稀有, xīyǒu, 353
rate; ratio; proposition, 率, lǜ, 428
rather, 有些, yǒuxiē, 343
rather than, 与其, yǔqí, 153
rather, a bit too, 未免, wèimiǎn, 11
reading matter; reading, 读物, dúwù, 240
ready-made, 现成, xiànchéng, 54
real; actual, 现实, xiànshí, 331
realistic; practical, 现实, xiànshí, 386
really; certainly; truly, 实在, shízài, 354
reap without sowing, 不劳而获, bù láo ér huò, 414
reason; justtification, 理由, lǐyóu, 55
reasonable, equitable, 合理, hélǐ, 99
recent, 近, jìn, 355
recently, 最近, zuìjìn, 74
re-doing; again, 再, zài, 331
re-doing; anew, 重新, chóngxīn, 367
reform, 改良, gǎiliáng, 57
reform, 改革, gǎigé, 292
reform and open up, 改革开放, gǎigékāifàng, 331
region; area, 地区, dìqū, 368
regulation; rule, 规定, guīdìng, 430
relating to civil law; civil, 民事, mínshì, 305
relations; sexual relations, 关系, guān.xì, 151
relative, 亲戚, qīn.qī, 328
relatively, 较, jiào, 258
relatively, fairly, 比较, bǐjiào, 25
reliable, 可靠, kěkào, 369
reluctantly; unwillingly, 勉强, miǎnqiǎng, 214
renowned; well-known, 闻名, wénmíng, 352
rental fee, 出租费, chūzūfèi, 178
rental fee, 租金, zūjīn, 28
reporter, journalist, 记者, jìzhě, 151
repressive; depressive, 压抑, yāyì, 237
republic, 共和国, gònghéguó, 443
Republic of China, 民国, Mín'guó, 54
request, 要求, yāoqiú, 152
researcher, 研究者, yánjiūzhě, 257
resentful; dissatisfied, 不满, bùmǎn, 241
residential district, 居民区, jūmínqū, 367
resolutely; firmly, 坚决, jiānjué, 443
resources, 资源, zīyuán, 459
response, 反应, fǎn.yìng, 214
responsibility, blame, 责任, zérèn, 99
responsible, 负责任, fùzérèn, 99
restaurant, 餐馆, cān'guǎn, 352
restaurant; hotel, 饭店, fàndiàn, 72
result; consequence, 结果, jiéguǒ, 57

result; outcome, 结果, jiéguǒ, 257
results (of work or study), 成绩, chéng.jī, 181
reward; pay, 报酬, bàochóu, 213
rice gruel, congee, 稀饭, xīfàn, 101
ridiculous, 不像话, bù xiànghuà, 166
right, 权, quán, 152
right, 权利, quánlì, 137
roadside; wayside, 路边儿, lùbiānr, 342
role; part, 角色, juésè, 289
romantic love, 爱情, àiqíng, 136
rope, 绳子, shéng.zi, 354
row, 排, pái, 213
rule and order; rule of law, 法治, fǎzhì, 111
rule of people, 人治, rénzhì, 112
rule, regualtion, 规则, guīzé, 25
rural area; countryside, 农村, nóngcūn, 304

S

safe, 安全, ānquán, 26
safety helmet, 安全帽, ānquánmào, 28
sale, 销售, xiāoshòu, 366
sales, 销路, xiāolù, 153
same as before, 照样, zhàoyàng, 344
same, 同样, tóngyàng, 10
sanction, 制裁, zhìcái, 150
scandal, 丑闻, chǒuwén, 150
scenic spot, 风景区, fēngjǐngqū, 75
scholarly attainments; learned wisdom, 学识, xuéshí, 331
science and technology, 科技, kējì, 121
scientific, scientific knowledge, 科学, kēxué, 273
scientist, 科学家, kēxuéjiā, 355
scope; extent; range, 范围, fànwéi, 290
scope; extent; range, 范围, fànwéi, 386
second rate, 中档, zhōngdàng, 26
second year in high school, 高二, gāoèr, 235
secretly, 暗地, àndì, 179
security personnel, 保安, bǎoān, 401
seed, 种子, zhǒng.zi, 236
seem to be, 好像, hǎoxiàng, 54
self; oneself, 自身, zìshēn, 195
self-defense; self-protection, 自卫, zìwèi, 470
selfish, 自私, zìsī, 214
self-possession, 修养, xiūyǎng, 307
self-protection, 自我保护, ziwǒ bǎohù, 258
semester, 学期, xuéqī, 212
senator, 议员, yìyuán, 442
senior high school, 高中, gāozhōng, 236
sense; awareness, 意识, yì.shí, 215
separately; differently, 各, gè, 399
serious; grave, 严重, yánzhòng, 400
seriousness; gravity, 严重性, yánzhòngxìng, 259
serious, 严重, yánzhòng, 40
service, 服务, fúwù, 370
service; be in the serve of, 服务, fúwù, 318
set term of imprisonment, 有期徒刑, yǒuqī túxíng, 241
severe, 严峻, yánjùn, 356
sex; sexual, 性, xìng, 167
sexual intercourse, 性行为, xìng xíngwéi, 256
Shangdong, 山东, Shāndǒng, 342
Shanghai, 上海, Shànghǎi, 8
Shanxi, 陕西, Shǎnxī, 273

share, 份儿, fènr, 305
shop, store, 店, diàn, 27
shop; store, 商店, shāngdiàn, 414
short (in length, duration, height), 短, duǎn, 135
should, 该, gāi, 166
should, 应当, yīngdāng, 242
show love care; show concern for, 关怀, guānhuái, 316
Sichuan, 四川, Sìchuān, 398
sickroom, 病房, bìngfáng, 40
side; edge, 边儿, biānr, 25
simple and crude, 简陋, jiǎnlòu, 305
simple, uncomplicated, 简单, jiǎndān, 55
simple; unadorned, 简朴, jiǎnpǔ, 198
simply must, 非要, fēiyào, 417
simply, really, 简直, jiǎnzhí, 56
simultaneously; in the meantime, 同时, tóngshí, 457
since, 以来, yǐlái, 369
since, 自…以来, zì…yǐlái, 456
since ancient time, 自古, zìgǔ, 111
since one was very young, 从小, cóngxiǎo, 216
since one's childhood, 从小到大, cóngxiǎo dàodà, 235
since, ever since, 自从, zìcóng, 120
since, now that, 既然, jìrán, 25
skirt, 裙子, qún.zi, 98
slaughterhouse, 屠宰场, túzǎichǎng, 355
sleeping pill, 安眠药, ānmiányào, 166
slight, 轻, qīng, 40
slippers, 拖鞋, tuōxié, 342
slogan, 口号, kǒuhào, 432
smart, 聪明, cōng.míng, 215
smooth, successful, 顺利, shùnlì, 8
snake, 蛇, shé, 353
so called, 所谓的, suǒwèi.de, 471
so long as, 只要, zhǐyào, 11
so-called, 所谓, suǒwèi, 98
social status, 地位, dìwèi, 136
social system, 社会制度, shèhuìzhìdù, 99
socialism, 社会主义, shèhuìzhǔyì, 180
society, 社会, shèhuì, 137
sociologist, 社会学家, shèhuìxuéjiā, 368
sole, 鞋底, xiédǐ, 343
sole; the only one, 唯一的, wéiyī.de, 443
solemnly, 郑重, zhèngzhòng, 468
solitary; lonely, 孤独, gūdú, 316
solitary; lonely, 孤零零, gūlínglíng, 318
solution, settlement; to solve, to settle (a problem), 解决, jiějué, 111
some other persons, 他人, tārén, 289
some; certain, 某些, mǒuxiē, 258
sons and daughters; children, 子女, zǐnǚ, 304
sorrow, 悲哀, bēiāi, 293
soup, broth, 汤, tāng, 56
south, 南方, nánfāng, 354
sovereignty, 主权, zhǔquán, 443
speak plausibly and at length, 振振有词, zhènzhènyǒucí, 179
special; particular, 特殊, tèshū, 272
species, 物种, wùzhǒng, 356
specific; concrete, 具体, jùtǐ, 243
speech, 讲话, jiǎnghuà, 428
speed, pace, 速度, sù.dù, 122
spoon, 勺儿, sháor, 56
spotlessly white, 洁白, jiébái, 215
stable; smooth, 平稳, píngwěn, 366

English Index

to bring about; to result in, 导致, dǎozhì, 239
to bring up; to rear, 养育, yǎngyù, 306
to bring; to bring about, 带来, dàilái, 414
to brush, 刷, shuā, 343
to build, 建, jiàn, 305
to burn, 烧, shāo, 86
to burn, to scald; boiling hot, 烫, tàng, 110
to bury, 埋下, máixià, 236
to buy, 购买, gòumǎi, 400
to calculate, 推算, tuīsuàn, 456
to call; to be called, 称, chēng, 289
to care about, 在乎, zài.hū, 152
to carry, 带, dài, 415
to carry on, 发扬, fāyáng, 215
to carry on the name of the family,
    传宗接代, chuánzōngjiēdài, 458
to carry out; to conduct, 进行, jìnxíng, 256
to carry through, 贯彻, guànchè, 243
to cast a vote, 投票, tóupiào, 153
to catch a cold, 感冒, gǎnmào, 55
to catch fire, 失火, shīhuǒ, 86
to cause, 造成, zàochéng, 73
to cause death, 致死, zhìsǐ, 242
to censure; to criticize, 责难, zé'nàn, 431
to censure; to criticize; to find fault with, 指责, zhǐzé, 199
to change, 换, huàn, 72
to change flight, 转机, zhuǎnjī, 8
to change, to transform, 改变, gǎibiàn, 120
to charge, 收钱, shōuqián, 214
to cheap; to dupe, 欺骗, qīpiàn, 239
to check in, 住进, zhùjìn, 343
to choose; to select, 选择, xuǎnzé, 330
to collect; to gather, 收, shōu, 179
to combine; to integrate, 相结合, xiāngjiēhé, 243
to come home from school, 放学, fàngxué, 241
to come into contact with, 接触, jiēchù, 273
to come out; to pay, 出, chū, 41
to compare, 比较, bǐjiào, 112
to compared with, 相比, xiāngbǐ, 429
to compensate, 赔偿, péicháng, 400
to compensate, to pay for, 赔, péi, 110
to complete; to finish, 完成, wánchéng, 456
to condemn, 谴责, qiǎnzé, 442
to conduct, 进行, jìnxíng, 469
to conduct; to carry on, 进行, Jìnxíng, 385
to confess, 承认, chéngrèn, 399
to confirm; to recognize, 确认, quèrèn, 400
to constitute, 构成, gòuchéng, 242
to constitute; to make up, 占, zhàn, 304
to contact, 联系, liánxì, 288
to contaminate; to pollute, 污染, wūrǎn, 215
to continue, 持续, chíxù, 429
to continue, 继续, jìxù, 432
to contract or spread, 传染, chuánrǎn, 343
to control, 管, guǎn, 237
to control, 控制, kòngzhì, 428
to count from the end, 倒数, dàoshǔ, 236
to cover, 覆盖, fùgài, 369
to create, 创造, chuàngzào, 317
to cross, to pass, 过, guò, 40
to cry, 哭, kū, 416
to cultivate land, 种地, zhòngdì, 305
to cut apart; to separate, 分割, fēn'gē, 444
to deal with; to handle, 处理, chǔlǐ, 459
to declare, 声明, shēngmíng, 468

to decrease (only for rates), 负增长, fùzēngzhǎng, 457
to deep fry, 炸, zhá, 353
to defend; to guard, 捍卫, hànwèi, 445
to defend; to safeguard, 维护, wéihù, 243
to delay, 耽误, dān.wù, 41
to deliver (a speech), 发表, fābiǎo, 468
to demand; to request, 要求, yāoqiú, 382
to deny, 否认, fǒurèn, 289
to depend on, 靠, kào, 330
to deploy, 部署, bùshǔ, 469
to deprive of, 剥夺, bōduó, 242
to descend, 下降, xiàjiàng, 196
to describe, 形容, xíngróng, 121
to deserve, to be worth, 值得, zhí.dé, 54
to destroy by burning or melting, 销毁, xiāohuǐ, 470
to develop; to foster, 培养, péiyǎng, 180
to develop; to launch, 开展, kāizhǎn, 317
to die, 死, sǐ, 86
to die; death, 死亡, sǐwáng, 457
to disappear, 不见, bújiàn, 178
to discard, 丢, diū, 73
to discern; to distinguish, 识别, shíbié, 291
to discuss in person, 面议, miànyì, 288
to dislike, to loathe, 讨厌, tǎo.yàn, 72
to dislike; to mind, 嫌, xián, 306
to dislike; to mind; to complain of, 嫌弃, xiánqì, 305
to dispense (lit. spit out), 吐, tǔ, 369
to dispute, to stick to one's guns, 争执, zhēng.zhí, 111
to disregard, 不顾, búgù, 352
to divide up, 分光, fēn'guāng, 305
to divorce, 离婚, líhūn, 198
to do, 干, gàn, 197, 239
to do business, 做生意, zuòshēng.yì, 178
to do embroidery, 绣花, xiùhuā, 238
to do evil things openly and unscrupulously; to have the impudence to do sth., 明目张胆, míng mù zhāng dǎn, 442
to do part time job, 打工, dǎgōng, 276
to do sth by force, 强行, qiángxíng, 401
to do sth. desperately; with all one's might, 拼命, pīnmìng, 199
to do sth. without authorization, 擅自, shànzì, 382
to do; to be engaged in, 搞, gǎo, 216
to dodge; to hide, 躲闪, duǒshǎn, 418
to dress up, 打扮, dǎbàn, 416
to drink, 喝, hē, 56
to drink tea, 喝茶, hēchá, 100
to drop off; to decrease, 下降, xiàjiàng, 457
to drop; to descend, 降, jiàng, 457
to earn, 挣, zhèng, 277
to earn money, 挣钱, zhèngqián, 199
to eliminate through selection or competition, 淘汰, táotài, 55
to embezzle, to practice graft, 贪污, tānwū, 150
to emphasize, 强调, qiángdiào, 152
to enact law; to legislate, 立法, lìfǎ, 430
to encounter, to run into, 碰, pèng, 87
to encourage, 鼓励, gǔlì, 98
to encroach on(other's rights), 侵害, qīnhài, 398
to end, 结束, jiéshù, 212
to endow, to entrust, 赋予, fùyǔ, 385
to endure; to bear, 忍受, rěnshòu, 234
to engage in advanced studies, 进修, jìnxiū, 277
to enhance; to reinforce, 加强, jiāqiáng, 240
to enjoy, 享受, xiǎngshòu, 307

English Index

Y

Z